Financial Management for Water Utilities

Financial Management for Water Utilities

Principles of Finance, Accounting, and Management Controls

Ann T. Bui, Editor

American Water Works Association

Financial Management for Water Utilities: Principles of Finance, Accounting, and Management Controls

Library of Congress Cataloging-in-Publication Data
Financial management for water utilities : principles of finance, accounting, and management controls / Ann T. Bui, editor.
p. cm.
1. Water-supply--United States--Accounting. 2. Water utilities--United States--Accounting. 3. Water utilities--United States--Finance. I. Bui, Ann T. II. American Water Works Association.
HF5686.W3F56 2012
363.6'10681--dc23
2012005593

Hardcover edition ISBN 978-1-58321-859-4
Paperback edition ISBN 978-1-62576-110-1
Electronic edition ISBN 9-781-61300-140-0

AWWA Manager of Editorial Development and Production: Gay Porter De Nileon
Senior Technical Editor/Project Manager: Martha Ripley Gray
Cover Design: Cheryl Armstrong
Production: Sheryl Tongue, Stonehill Graphics

Printed in the United States of America
American Water Works Association
6666 West Quincy Avenue Denver, CO 80235
(303) 794-7711
Printed on recycled paper.

American Water Works Association

6666 West Quincy Avenue
Denver, CO 80235-3098
303.794.7711
www.awwa.org

Contents

PART 4
Accounting Cycle Implementation and Management

PART 5
Financial Management Functions

This page intentionally blank.

Tables

Figures

Preface

Significant changes have taken place in the water utility industry regarding accounting practices and financial management since 1995. The accounting changes mandated by the Governmental Accounting Standards Board (GASB), changing auditing standards with an emphasis on management's responsibilities for internal controls; the increased importance of financial benchmarking; and the complexities and difficulties in optimizing limited resources through capital asset management have increased the importance of sound financial management in the water utility industry.

Financial Management for Water Utilities updates the last edition of *Water Utility Accounting* and incorporates additional information on financial management. This new handbook has been developed as a financial management tool to enhance the ability of professionals in the water industry to build accurate and reliable budget projections, supply better budgeting information, strengthen internal controls, provide sufficient strategic planning information, and incorporate standardized financial measures that will allow managers to compare their operations to the industry's best practices. Information has been included to incorporate general water utility management as well as accounting and financial management functions.

The text focuses on how financial management serves the overall operation of the utility and how the various activities associated with performing the financial management function are conducted. While the book is intended for utility managers as well as financial personnel, portions of the text assume that the reader possesses a basic understanding of financial principles and procedures. It should also be understood that accounting principles and practices change frequently and more recent pronouncements may not be reflected in the text.

This book reflects the pronouncements of several regulatory bodies, including the GASB, the Financial Accounting Standards Board, the Securities and Exchange Commission, and the National Association of Regulatory Utility Commissioners. Since accounting practices for investor-owned utilities are usually prescribed by state regulatory agencies, emphasis has been placed on the practices of government-owned utilities.

Although it was developed utilizing the third edition of the *Water Utility Accounting*, this book has been substantially reorganized, updated, and supplemented with a significant amount of additional information. *Financial Management for Water Utilities* is intended to be a comprehensive financial management tool. The text explores the finance, audit, information systems, performance measurement, and strategic management functions that, together with the accounting function, comprise the major activities generally associated with financial management in water utilities.

It is hoped that this book will add substantially to the resources available to water utility managers and staff.

Ann T. Bui, *Editor*

Acknowledgments

The Finance, Accounting, and Management Controls Committee, appointed by the Management and Leadership Division of the American Water Works Association, prepared and reviewed this edition of *Financial Management for Water Utilities*. Committee members included:

Angela Bricmont, Chief Financial Officer, Denver Water, Denver, Colo.
Derrick Brown, Director of Finance, Greenville Water System, Greenville, S.C.
Ann T. Bui, Director, Black & Veatch Corporation, Los Angeles, Calif.
Mark C. DiPasquale, Senior Civil Engineer, Contestoga-Rovers & Associates/CRA Infrastructure & Engineering Inc., Buffalo, N.Y.
Ed J. Donahue III, President, MFSG LLC, Annapolis, Md.
Amber Halloran, Chief Financial Officer, Louisville Water Company, Louisville, Ky.
Steven C. Hellman, Chief Financial Officer, Aurora Water, Aurora, Colo.
Eric R. Hofeld, CPA, CGMA, Manager of Audits, Portland Water Bureau, Portland, Ore.
Daniel D. Lanning, Director of Consulting, 3rd Generation Engineering Inc.
John M. Mastracchio, CFA, Associate Vice President, Red Oak Consulting, an ARCADIS Group, Albany, N.Y.
Paul L. Matthews, Director of Finance, Tualatin Valley Water District, Portland, Ore.
Robert J. McEvoy, Commissioner, Oyster Bay Water District; Finance Director, Town of Oyster Bay, N.Y.
Gregory P. McLain, CPA, CISA, Gregory P. McLain, Charleston, S.C.
Robert K. Miller, Deputy Director, Sewerage and Water Board of New Orleans.
Theodore Schlette, Vice President, CDM Smith, Philadelphia, Pa.
Larry G. Shaw, CPA, Senior Manager, Peat Marwick Mitchell & Co. (retired)
David K. Shupe, Senior Financial Analyst, HDR Engineering, Austin, Texas
William G. Stannard, President, Raftelis Financial Consultants, Kansas City, Mo.
Mary H. Williams, CPA, Controller, Beaufort-Jasper Water & Sewer Authority, Beaufort, S.C.

Finance, Accounting, and Management Controls Committee would like to extend a special thank you to our technical editor Irene S. Rubin, Professor Emerita, Public Administration Division, Northern Illinois University, for her insightful editing and thorough organizational skills; she took what was a document of many voices and helped turn it into a cohesive book. The committee would also like to thank AWWA Executive Director David LaFrance, Sr. Technical Editor Martha Ripley Gray, Sr. Production Editors Cheryl Armstrong and Sandra Lankenau, and Manager of Editorial

Development and Production Gay Porter De Nileon, as well as compositor Sheryl Tongue of Stonehill Graphics, for their patience and invaluable assistance with this project.

AWWA staff would like to express our gratitude to Eric R. Hofeld, manager of Audits and Special Projects with Portland (Ore.) Water Bureau. His painstaking improvements to art and text, and his efforts to align this book with latest management practices, terminology, and regulations have contributed enormously to its quality.

PART 1

Water Utility Financial Management Overview

This page intentionally blank.

Chapter 1

What Is Financial Management?

Financial management encompasses much more than accounting. Today's financial manager must be a well-rounded strategic business planner. Regulatory compliance, limited resources, competition for funding, and the desire to optimize efficiency have all become major factors in the financial management of water utilities throughout the country.

In the past, the definition of *financial management* was (1) planning for and acquiring resources and (2) planning, monitoring, analyzing, and reporting the use of those resources. The fundamental purpose of financial management was thought to be ensuring that resources would be available when needed and that they would be used effectively and efficiently. Today financial management has taken on a much broader meaning for successful entities. Financial managers for utilities must now see themselves as:

- Business planners, strategically looking at the future financial health of the organization
- Asset managers, allocating scarce resources
- Performance leaders, establishing financial metrics that can be used in a timely manner to adjust efforts to desired outcomes
- Negotiators, ensuring that regulating authorities, commissions, or boards, as well as rate payers, understand the implications of setting rates at different levels
- Economic forecasters, estimating the impact of limited resources and economic changes that may affect the organization

A comprehensive financial plan is essential in ensuring that a utility operates on a self-sustaining basis. Water utilities are businesses, many of which are owned by their communities, their citizens. Utility managers are now required to extend their focus from strictly operations and capital planning to one that encompasses organization, finance, and customer service. Water utility managers must not only demonstrate their ability to operate a self-sustaining business but also respond to the needs of customers.

Financial strength is a prerequisite for meeting short- and long-term obligations. As a consequence every manager in the utilities industry needs to become a financial manager. Regulatory standards put pressure on managers to prevent lapses in operations, which requires more attention to acquiring the most cost-effective capital equipment and maintaining the entire system. The condition of the physical plant, equipment, and delivery systems needs to be routinely monitored and documented. In setting rates, managers need to consider carefully the tradeoffs between affordability to residents and sustainability of effective operations. To keep rates as low as possible while keeping effectiveness high, managers need to formulate and implement policies on capital financing, debt management, reserve levels, and rates, and for private utilities, policies on rates of return on investments. They need to understand and be able to explain the relationship between these policies and service levels.

Functional Responsibilities Included Under Financial Management

Financial management functions are required in every water utility, regardless of size or type of ownership. Typically, these functions include *budgeting and forecasting*, *accounting and reporting*, *financing activities*, *auditing*, *internal controls*, and *financial information systems* (FISs). Custodial and resource management functions, such as facilities maintenance, personnel, and inventory control, may also be included.

A *budget* is a work plan for a specified period of time, usually a year ahead, built up from estimates of the cost of performing each piece of the work. What will it cost to produce a given number of gallons (or cubic feet) of drinking water of a given level of purity over the next year? What equipment, electricity, and personnel costs will be required? In order to make good budget estimates, managers need to look not only at how personnel costs are likely to increase the following year, but also at how the environment might change, such as new developments coming on line that are likely to use more water or water regulations that are likely to reduce summer use for lawns and gardens.

Budgets have three major uses. First, estimates of cost are used in the setting of rates. Second, they ensure that spending will not exceed anticipated revenues. Third, they are guidelines for how revenues need to be allocated internally in order to pay for necessary operating and capital costs in a timely fashion. By comparing anticipated spending in the budget to actual spending during the year as reported in accounting data, managers can see where their estimates were wrong. Sometimes the differences between estimates and actuals can suggest changes that need to be made.

Budgets rely on forecasts, or predictions of what will happen in the future. They require a good sense of prior trends and the factors that drive them. But in looking to the future, managers need to think not only of projecting on the basis of past experience but also of building toward where they want to go or need to go next. To do this well, managers should periodically draw up a *strategic financial plan* that incorporates service goals, evaluates likely future water needs, and estimates the cost of achieving them. Such plans can be critical in rate setting and achieving financial sustainability.

Accounting can be defined as the collecting, analyzing, and classifying of all data relevant to a utility's finances. An accounting system records data on each financial transaction and on the assets, liabilities, and equity levels. These detailed data are aggregated into reports that can be used by decision-makers.

Internal financial reports are used by financial, operational, and administrative managers to ascertain current performance and make timely decisions regarding future financial plans. Internal reports can also provide evidence of compliance or noncompliance with budgets or with other legal or contractual matters.

External financial reporting primarily seeks to achieve both fiscal and operational accountability. Potential users of external financial reports include, but may not be limited to, (1) those to whom the utility is accountable (e.g., customers, local governments, regulatory authority, etc.); (2) those who represent others to whom the utility is accountable (boards, commissions, etc.); and (3) those who lend to the utility or participate in the lending process (investors, creditors, underwriters, rating agencies, insurers, etc.).

The *finance function* manages the flow of funds into and out of the organization and includes borrowing, investing, and cash flow management. Specifically, financial managers consider and evaluate alternative potential funding sources, and may manage the sale of bonds when appropriate. They determine cash flow requirements and manage investments and water bill revenues to assure obligations are paid on time.

Auditing is the systematic review or examination of the assertions or actions of a third party to evaluate conformance to some norm or benchmark and can be either internal or external. External or independent auditors certify the reliability of the financial reports primarily for investors and for the public at large. Internal audits are primarily designed to assist managers in assessing financial controls and operational efficiency. Performance audits may be performed by internal auditors or external consultants, and are often used to determine cost-effectiveness and efficiency in operations.

Management is responsible for assuring that the utility is effective in (1) achieving its objectives, (2) using resources efficiently, (3) complying with all applicable policies, laws, and regulations, and (4) reporting relevant financial and operational data to oversight bodies in a timely manner. These goals are achieved in part by adopting, disseminating, and implementing appropriate financial policies. The importance of fiscal policy cannot be overstated. Where clear policy has not been established and communicated, financial managers may find they need to articulate and suggest policy alternatives to the policymakers.

Management also is required to identify, assess, and minimize potential risks that could prevent the utility from meeting its responsibilities. This is generally accomplished through a system of internal controls, often referred to as the *control environment*. The control environment includes techniques for identifying and monitoring risk, the effective dissemination and implementation of risk control policies and procedures, and ongoing monitoring of the effectiveness of those policies and procedures.

Financial information systems (FISs) also fall under the purview of financial management. These systems can be an important aspect of internal control, but, more importantly, a good financial data management system can generate timely and accurate reports to improve management decision making and reduce staff effort in tasks such as budget preparation, financial reporting, purchasing, cost accounting, and billing. These data also provide some of the information needed for *benchmarking.* Benchmarking can be a useful tool in achieving both affordability and fiscal sustainability. Utility managers can measure the success of their operations compared to their own prior performance and best practices in the industry. To do this, managers need to identify key functions, isolate key indicators of how well those functions are working, and assure a flow of accurate measures on these indicators over time. Benchmarking can help motivate workers because it helps set realistic goals for both managers and employees to work toward.

Benchmarking can answer the following questions for water utilities:

- How does what we are doing now compare to what we have been doing?
- Are we making progress in terms of goals and objectives that we have set?
- How do we compare with other water utilities?
- Are we using the industry's best practices for fiscal sustainability and operational efficiency?

The water industry has become controversial in recent years, as communities agonize about whether to shift from public to private ownership to deal with plant modernization, high capital costs, and rising water rates. Regardless of who owns the physical plant or which sector operates it, the public is increasingly concerned about the availability and cost of pure water. The water industry seems certain to continue in a state of rapid evolution given changes in technology, regulation, environmental concerns, and consumer demand. The challenges are daunting, but there are numerous opportunities to increase efficiency, improve business practices, and assure fiscal accountability and sustainability.

Authoritative Standards for the Functional Responsibilities

The public, the press, bond rating agencies, regulator board members, council members, and employees should be able to pick up any financial report, know what the numbers mean, and be able to evaluate the fiscal condition of the organization. If every organization put its financial reports together in a different way, only insiders familiar with the reports would be able to understand them. *Generally accepted accounting principles* (GAAP) were the accounting profession's answer to this problem. GAAP are a set of minimum standards governing external financial reporting.

Separate boards grew up in the public and private sectors to set additional accounting standards to elaborate on or clarify the basic accounting rules included in GAAP. The Financial Accounting Standards Board (FASB) was established to work out accounting standards for the private sector, while the Governmental Accounting Standards Board (GASB) sets standards for governmental agencies. Both of these boards operate under the auspices of the Financial Accounting Foundation.

While FASB's jurisdiction extends to private-sector businesses as well as nonprofit organizations, GASB is the ultimate authority on GAAP for state and local governments. GASB thus has jurisdiction over all utilities operating within the public sector.

However, it is presumed that all applicable authoritative guidance issued by FASB and its predecessor organizations *prior to December 1, 1989*, will apply to public sector reporting unless such guidance conflicts with or contradicts GASB guidance. Additionally, the public sector may choose to follow *compatible* FASB guidance issued after the cutoff date for *enterprise or business-type* funds only, which applies to most public sector water utilities. FASB pronouncements govern accounting standards for all private water utilities.

While GASB and FASB provide the formal standards for accounting, many other professional associations provide helpful guides and offer standards for various aspects of financial accounting, auditing, and reporting.

The Government Finance Officers Association (GFOA) is the professional association of state/provincial and local finance officers in the United States and Canada, and has served the public finance profession since 1906. GFOA has published documents related to public-sector financial management, and its *Governmental Accounting, Auditing, and Financial Reporting,* while not authoritative, provides detailed guidance on the practical application of generally accepted accounting principles for governments. *Disclosure Guidelines for State and Local Government Securities,* also published by GFOA, provides useful information in the preparation of official statements for issuance of municipal securities. The Certificate of Achievement for Excellence in Financial Reporting (CAFR Program) was established by GFOA in 1945 and is designed to recognize and encourage excellence in financial reporting by state and local governments. Although budget documents are generally not regulated by GAAP, the GFOA established the Distinguished Budget Presentation Award (Budget Awards Program) in 1984 to encourage governments to prepare budget documents of the highest quality to meet the needs of decision-makers and citizens.

The American Institute of Certified Public Accountants (AICPA) has been vitally concerned with developing standards of professional practice for its members. Among its more important publications are *Statements on Auditing Standards,* which are authoritative pronouncements on auditing matters. It has also published *Audits of State and Local Governmental Units,* which provides guidance on audits of governmental units other than the federal government.

The US Government Accountability Office (GAO) has a history of providing standards for audits of recipients of federal financial assistance. It has published *Standards for Audit of Governmental Organizations, Programs, Activities, and Functions*, commonly called the *Yellow Book*, which serves as the manual for compliance with federal requirements.

The National Association of Regulatory Utility Commissioners (NARUC) has published the *Uniform System of Accounts for Class A Water Utilities,* which provides guidance for accounting for regulated utility operations. NARUC has also published the *Manual on Management Audits.* This manual describes how to implement the management recommendations in an audit report.

Industry Guidelines

Founded in 1881, the American Water Works Association (AWWA) is an international nonprofit scientific and educational society. It acts as an advocacy organization to improve the quality and supply of water, and as a source of information for managers. AWWA is the largest organization of water supply professionals in the world, representing treatment plant operators and managers, engineers, scientists, financial experts, consultants, environmentalists, academicians, regulators, administrators, and others who are interested in water supply. AWWA promotes education and training through conferences and seminars, as well as publications. Some of the publications regarding fiscal management include:

- *Principles of Water Rates, Fees, and Charges*, Sixth Edition (M1)
- *2010 AWWA Water and Wastewater Rate Survey*
- *2010 AWWA Water Utility Compensation Survey*
- *Avoiding Rate Shock: Making the Case for Water Rates*
- *Balancing Collection Performance and Service Ratings*
- *Benchmarking Performance Indicators for Water and Wastewater Utilities*
- *Water Conservation-Oriented Rates*
- *Water Infrastructure at a Turning Point: The Road to Sustainable Asset Management*
- *Water Rates, Fees, and the Legal Environment*

Professionals can also seek guidance from many other organizations on standards that are utilized in the industry. The Water Research Foundation (formerly called the *AWWA Research Foundation* or *AwwaRF*) is a member-supported international nonprofit organization that sponsors research to enable water utilities, public health agencies, and other professionals to provide safe and affordable drinking water to consumers. The American Water Resources Association (AWRA) is a multidisciplinary nonprofit professional organization dedicated to the advancement of water resource management, research, and education. The Water Utility Benchmarking Association (WUBA) conducts benchmarking studies to identify best practices within the industry. Not to be overlooked, the most valuable resource within the industry is the interaction with other financial and management professionals. Many organizations, such as AWWA, provide networking opportunities through volunteer committees, conferences, and participation in regional sections.

Book Organization

This book is arranged in five parts. Part 1 provides a general description of the water utility industry and a discussion of the objectives of financial management for water utilities.

Part 2 is an overview that addresses planning and budgeting, the accounting process, and general external and internal reporting of financial information.

Part 3 is devoted to a detailed discussion of the various types of financial reporting including: budgetary reports; a comparison of reports for publicly and privately owned waterworks; rate and regulatory reports; and various management, control, and informational reporting.

Part 4 is concerned with accounting-cycle implementation and management. It includes topics such as cost-of-service rate making, the distinctions between operating and maintenance (O&M) and capital costs and the different treatment of each, the implications of GASB standard 34 for estimating the value of fixed assets, capital improvement planning, and taxes. This section of the book also provides an overview of assets, liabilities, and net assets or equity. The last chapter in part 4 discusses financial ratios and measurements used to determine fiscal sustainability.

Part 5 continues the discussion of how to use financial information for management. Topics covered include financing of capital projects, using internal and external audits and performance audits, and creating appropriate internal controls and a good control environment.

Examples presented throughout the book illustrate financial principles and procedures applicable to water utilities and emphasize sound fiscal and reporting practices for water utilities. Five supplementary appendices are provided on a CD to augment the text discussion, and the volume concludes with a bibliography and a substantive index.

This page intentionally blank.

Chapter 2

Water Utility Industry Description

Almost every business enterprise is concerned with the public interest to some extent and, consequently, is subject to a measure of public regulation. Certain types of enterprises are so greatly concerned with the public interest that they have been subjected to far-reaching regulation by government. Among these enterprises are public utilities.

One of the most important of public utilities is water production. Water utilities *manage the use and reuse of water supplies by treating water and compressing the natural self-purification process of the hydrogeologic cycle into an artificial water cycle that provides sufficient potable water for customers.* Simply put, people need clean drinking water to live. Water also plays a major role in industry and the economy. The increasing scarcity of water, pollution and regulatory concerns, and changing technology all make the fiscal sustainability of water utilities increasingly critical. With its many ramifications, the water utility industry touches almost every phase of national life. One has only to look at China's extensive water pollution or pricing in parts of Latin America that make drinking water unaffordable to realize how important water utilities are.

In the case of business in general, the economic law of supply and demand will act, at least in theory, as an invisible hand to regulate the economy. The demand for a commodity should bring forth the capacity to produce the commodity in the quantities necessary to fulfill the demand. At the same time, the consumer is able to exercise his or her influence over the price of the commodity by choosing among alternative sources of supply. Thus, competition should act as a regulator.

Typically a public utility has a monopoly on the service it provides because duplication of productive facilities is usually considered to be unsound. In the water utility industry, large capital expenditures are required to build pumping stations, treatment plants, and water distribution systems. If duplicate facilities were constructed by competing water utilities, the consumer, in effect, would have to pay for such economic waste through higher prices for water.

Such conditions have resulted in the granting of monopolistic privileges by governmental units to water utilities as well as to other public utilities. When the economic law of supply and demand cannot perform its function, a monopolistic privilege is granted; and federal, state, and local governments regulate public utilities to serve as a substitute for competitors and ensure that the utilities provide a reasonable level of service at a fair price. Such regulation has been exercised by governmental bodies in one of the following two ways: (1) through direct operation of the water utility by an agency of government, such as a water department of the municipal government, a water district, or a water authority; or (2) through public utility commissions or other governmental agencies that regulate the operations of private water utilities. The fundamental purposes of utility regulation have been to establish and control rates and charges to users, to establish and maintain satisfactory levels of services rendered by the utilities, and to ensure the financial stability of utilities. Utility regulation has emphasized protection of consumers.

The legal organization of a water utility may take many different forms, all of which can be categorized either as private or governmental. The most common form of organization of water utilities is as a department of a general purpose local government, either a city or a county. The term "municipally owned" is used in this book to refer to any governmental unit subordinate to a state.

The legal form of organization has little or no effect on most phases of water utility operation. Therefore, unless otherwise indicated, the discussion in this book applies to both private and governmental water utilities. However, the legal form of organization does result in some significant differences in type and extent of regulation, financing, taxes, and organization as described briefly in Table 2-1. The effects of the differences are discussed in subsequent chapters.

Water utilities in North America vary from systems serving large urban areas to very small systems serving only a few connections. In the United States, approximately 22,000 publicly owned and 37,000 private water systems serve about 187 million people. Statistics relating to ownership of US water supply systems ranging from very small to very large are shown in Table 2-2. Publicly owned systems are operated by a great variety of governmental and quasi-governmental authorities including cities, towns, counties, and special-purpose districts.

Typically, a water utility consists of a source of supply, water treatment and storage, transmission and distribution, customer service (metering and billing) operations, and administrative and support services.

Often a water utility is operated in combination with a wastewater utility, in part because they typically have similar financial structures and in part because their functions are complementary. Without a direct way of measuring wastewater, some communities charge for it in proportion to water usage, with the assumption that most of the water will end up in the wastewater system. Moreover, if water operates at a slight profit and wastewater at a slight loss, water can subsidize wastewater, and together they can be financially sustainable. Third, increasingly, wastewater can be treated and reused. Or wastewater may be discharged into bodies of water that are also used for freshwater intake, making the wastewater operation critical to the freshwater processing. For all these reasons, water and wastewater are often combined into one enterprise.

Table 2-1. Important differences in water utilities resulting from type of ownership

Subject	Governmental Water Utility	Private Water Utility
Chart of Accounts	May not be required to adopt the state public service commission's uniform systems of accounts.	Usually required to adopt a uniform system of accounts prescribed by the state public service commission.
Water Rates	Rate schedules are usually not subject to control by state public service commissions. However, in some states, governmental utilities are subject to regulation by state public service commissions on the same basis as private utilities.	Rate schedules are usually subject to the approval of the state public services commission.
Financing	Acquisition, replacement, or expansion of facilities may be financed by existing cash balances, the issuance of bonds to be retired from the income of the utility, contributions from the municipality with the repayment of any resulting bond issue accomplished through taxation or other sources, long-term advances from the municipality, contributions and advances from customers for construction, and contributions from state and federal governments.	Acquisition, replacement, or expansion of facilities may be financed from existing cash balances, the issuance of various types of securities (including preferred stock, common stock, and bonds), contributions and advances from customers for construction, and contributions from state and federal governments.
Taxes	Do not pay income taxes and usually do not have to pay property taxes. In some instances, governmental utilities are required to pay taxes on property (such as source-of-supply facilities) that is located outside their service-area boundaries and within the taxing jurisdiction of other municipalities. Governmental utilities may also be required to render free services to other municipal departments or to make payments to the general fund in lieu of taxes.	Required to pay all forms of taxes. (In a few states, private water utilities are exempt from payment of certain taxes, such as those on property and franchise fees.)
Organization	May be a legal entity in itself, as in the case of a water district or authority; or the utility may be a subdivision of a municipality, as in the case of a water department.	Usually incorporated, although smaller utilities may be either partnerships or individual proprietorships.

Table 2-2. Characteristics of the water supply industry

	System Size by Population						
	Very Small		Small		Medium		
	25 to 100	101 to 500	501 to 1,000	1,001 to 3,300	3,301 to 10,000	10,001 to 25,000	25,001 to 50,000
	Number of Systems						
Ownership Type							
Public	1,987	6,357	3,893	5,716	3,416	1,567	645
Private	17,394	11,653	2,343	2,175	787	207	114
Native American	297	320	74	49	7	1	0
Total	19,678	18,330	6,310	7,940	4,210	1,775	759

	System Size by Population				
	Large			Very Large	
	50,001 to 75,000	75,001 to 100,000	100,001 to 500,000	500,001 to 1,000,000	Over 1,000,000
Ownership Type					
Public	1,567	645	206	90	192
Private	207	114	34	14	41
Native American	1	0	0	0	0
Total	1,775	759	240	104	233

Implications of Ownership

Who owns a water utility makes a difference. Private utilities fall under the aegis of state public service commissions, which create uniform accounting rules and set rates. private utilities have to pay taxes and account for them on financial reports, while publicly owned utilities normally do not.

Governmental Water Utilities

GASB is the ultimate authority on GAAP for state and local governments, including utilities. These utilities are generally accounted for as *enterprise funds*. The use of an enterprise fund is mandated by GAAP when legal requirements or management policy requires that the full cost of services be recovered through customer fees and charges, which is generally the case with a water utility fund of the general government or an established authority.

Enterprise funds, like businesses, recognize revenues and expenses on the accrual basis, which means that revenues (and related receivables) are recorded when costs and/or liabilities are incurred—not when cash is actually paid. Additionally, like businesses, water utilities need to include on their balance sheets all assets and liabilities associated with their operations. Debt is only reported in the enterprise fund if it is directly related to the fund (for instance, a bond issued to construct a water treatment plant) and is expected to be paid for from the fund (i.e., water revenue bond). Where water and wastewater utilities are operated by a local government and separately financed and operated, the water and wastewater utilities may back each other's bonds. Such cross-pledging of repayment can strengthen the attractiveness of the securities to potential investors. In some cases, the utilities are actually operated jointly, and in other cases, some activities common to both utilities are operated jointly, such as equipment maintenance, laboratories, and administrative and financial management. Even where water and wastewater utilities are not operated by the same local government, they generally use the same database for billing.

Private Utilities

Private utilities are water systems where the physical assets are owned by an individual or a group of individuals. Private utilities generally adopt standard industry practices, GAAP, by following similar organizations within the private sector, such as private electric utilities. Private utilities are governed by accounting standards promulgated by the Financial Accounting Standards Board (FASB). Therefore, these utilities are operated as tax-paying corporate entities and typically have franchises granted by local municipalities. The National Association of Water Companies (NAWC) is a national trade association that exclusively represents the private and private water utility industry (see www.nawc.org).

Private utilities that issue securities falling within the provisions of the Securities Act of 1933 and the Securities Exchange Act of 1934 must comply with the reporting requirements of the Securities and Exchange Commission (SEC). Although the SEC relies heavily on accounting principles developed by other organizations, it is nevertheless greatly concerned with the form and content of reports, including financial statements and supporting schedules. It has issued Regulation S-X, titled "Form and Content of Financial Statements," and has published numerous Accounting Series Releases and Staff Accounting Bulletins. Compliance with SEC reporting requirements may require the assistance of expert accounting and legal consultants.

For private utilities, Sarbanes Oxley (SOX) legislation has created new accounting standards for stock exchange–listed companies, requiring disclosure in financial reports of any material weaknesses in financial reporting systems. Companies must not only have their financial statements, internal control systems, and procedures audited, but the chief financial and chief executive officer must each certify that the financial reports are accurate. A significant degree of emphasis is now being placed on management controls by investors, creditors, and the public sector.

Rates and charges for private utilities are generally regulated by state commissions. The National Association of Regulatory Utility Commissioners (NARUC) seeks to advance regulation through the study and discussion of matters concerning public utilities, to promote regulatory conformity, and to promote the common interest of customers with respect to the regulation of these utilities. NARUC is nonprofit and includes members of governmental agencies who are responsible for regulating the activities of telecommunication, energy, and water utilities.

NARUC has recommended a *Uniform System of Accounts* to promote regulatory conformity among its member agencies. The Uniform System of Accounts specifies the accounts in which various expenses are to be recorded and reported. If all the utilities to be regulated classify their accounts the same way, it is much easier for the regulatory agencies to understand their financial condition and operations. The *Uniform System of Accounts for Class A Water Utilities* (published by NARUC) proposes that water utilities' O&M expenses include three digits (600–699), which are further subdivided into the five functional areas: source of supply; water treatment; water transmission and distribution; customer accounts/service; and general and administrative expenses. The majority of private and rate-regulated utilities are required to follow this chart of accounts, which is useful not only for the regulators but also for utility managers because it makes very clear where the costs are. (The suggested system of accounts may be found in appendix A on a CD at the end of this publication.)

Environmental Regulation

Whether public or private, water utilities are subject to environmental laws and regulations that affect operations and finances. Standards for clean water influence the choice, cost, and storage of chemicals used; the monitoring and testing of water purity; filtration or dilution systems for harmful chemicals and biological organisms or radon. Regulatory standards suggest the need to continuously monitor equipment and delivery systems to prevent unwanted inflows of untreated water. They imply backup systems in case of electric or equipment failure, protection against floods of the water plant, and other costs of operations. Failure to meet regulatory standards may result in fines, devastatingly bad public relations, and reduced demand. While compliance can be technically challenging and costly, the goal of regulation is one that is easy to buy into, namely sufficient water supplies and safe drinking water for the nation.

Chapter 3

The Functions of Financial Management

Financial management strives to achieve a clear understanding of the utility's overall financial condition and determine what actions are required to maintain fiscal stability in light of the future fiscal outlook. In order to meet this objective, certain actions are required before management can focus on the typical functional responsibilities of financial management.

In order to maintain balance, ensure that money is available for expenditures when they are needed, and monitor financial well-being, financial managers plan for the upcoming year. They plan spending, they ensure financing, they allocate funds and pay bills, they record expenditures and revenues, and they create reports based on those recorded transactions. Those reports are typically audited to guarantee to external users that the reports represent the true fiscal condition of the utility. They create financial performance measures from accounting reports and a variety of performance data, The goal is the most cost-effective operation possible.

The Financial Management Cycle

A major portion of what financial managers do is oversee the financial management cycle, consisting of planning and analysis, budgeting, accounting and reporting, and auditing. As illustrated in Figure 3-1, significant segments of utility financial management follow a definite pattern and timetable. The cycle of strategic planning, budgeting, recording, reporting, and analysis recurs on a predictable basis, usually annually. Since the strategic plan generally covers a longer period of time, it is updated each year.

Planning and Analysis

Monitoring and analyzing the environment in which the utility operates may be a low-level continuous activity, with noticeable peaks of activity in response to changes in the environment. Forecasts and assumptions regarding events and circumstances exterior to the utility are developed. The broad purposes of the utility are reviewed, explicit objectives set, and alternative strategies to reach those objectives analyzed. Strategic

Figure 3-1. Financial management cycle

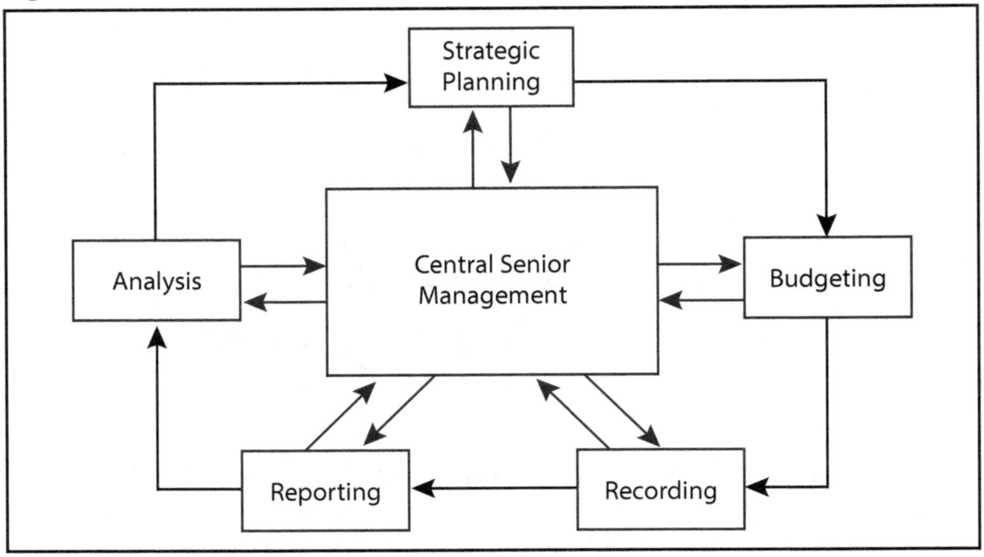

planning may concentrate on the strategies and goals of a selected department or division, or the process may be oriented toward developing overall utility strategies and goals.

Programs translate an externally oriented strategy into an internally focused set of functional plans designed to implement the strategy. A program consists of a set of activities executed in a coordinated and timely fashion in order to achieve a specified goal.

- Budgeting uses the forecasts, strategies, and programs developed in the planning process to produce a plan for a specified time period and states that plan in financial terms. The budget then becomes the roadmap that guides the utility's financial operations.

The transactions of the utility are recorded according to the chart of accounts and summarized as reports, usually covering a fiscal or calendar year. Reports may be classified according to the content and the purpose for which they are issued. Different types of financial reports may be targeted for specific user groups.

Completing the financial management cycle is the audit and analysis process. A formal independent financial audit may be performed annually. Some other types of analysis may be needed on a more or less frequent basis, and periodic major studies, such as operational audits, may be undertaken from time to time.

Budgeting

A budget is a work plan, stated in financial terms, that covers the next time period, usually a year. Water budgets have to start out with a sense of how much water they need to produce of what quality and then calculate what it should cost to produce that amount of water. Cost estimates are built up from the component parts of the operation necessary to produce that level of service—it will cost the utility so much in electricity to produce that water, so much in personnel costs, so much in chemicals and other supplies, so much for system maintenance, and so much for administrative supervision and any necessary expenditures for debt repayment. These estimates for cost come from prior years' expenditures and professional knowledge of pending cost increases or market shifts.

Budgets serve multiple purposes. First, they force managers to think through the goals of production and any expansions or improvements necessary to achieve those goals. Managers need to consider how to fiwnance such expansion or improvements and the timing of such projects. Can some improvements wait, or are they urgent and have to be funded out of the next year's budget? Managers also have to think through any changes in their production processes that might influence costs or the relationship between inputs and outputs. Is there likely to be an expensive labor settlement? Could there be givebacks, what is management asking for, what is it offering, and what is it likely to get? Are electric rates likely to go up next year, and if so, are there ways to cut electricity usage? Will the purchase of some new equipment that uses less electricity reduce operating costs sufficiently to pay for itself within a few years?

Second, budgets aid the coordination process by allocating the appropriate amount of resources to different functions that are dependent on each other. One unit should not get all the staff or new equipment to do its work while others do not. Imagine what would happen if the water production team was able to pump and purify more water due to some innovation, but the delivery team was unable to repair or replace broken pipes, with the result that more water was produced but could not be delivered and billed. A good budget should allocate the right number of dollars and staff to production, delivery, administration, and billing.

Third, budgets can be a way of motivating managers because they represent goals for managers. The budget tells managers what they are expected to do and how much it should cost them to do it so they can work toward those goals. Along the same lines, budgets can be used to help evaluate managers' performance. Do managers overshoot or undershoot the goals built into the budget, do they stretch dollars, innovate, and get to their goals less expensively than anticipated, or the reverse, do they let problems fester until they become expensive to repair, or do they aggravate labor resulting in more tense bargaining and more expensive agreements, overrunning the budget? Do they achieve the goals set into the budget or not, and if not, why not?

Budget Process

Budget processes vary, but often they begin with some kind of guidance from the central office to the department heads, that may include limits on the size of any increases, or suggestions as to what to include or exclude from a request. The budget office may distribute forms on which to make requests, either in hard copy or electronically. These forms typically include step-by-step instructions for building up the budget request. For example, they may ask how many staff each unit has, their current salaries (this figure may be filled in already), and any anticipated increases in salaries or benefits.

Another page might ask about new equipment requests, and ask the operating unit chief to justify the request—that is, explain the estimate of costs, the need, and the budgetary or functional impact. When the budget office or senior managers receive back these forms, they decide what portions of the request to grant, based on the priorities and legal requirements of the entire water enterprise.

When the water production facility is owned and run by the public sector, budgets and rates must be approved by elected officials. Utility managers present and defend their requests in budget hearings. These elected officials may amend the budget request in various ways before approving it, but once they do approve it, the budget has the force of law, setting limits on both rates and spending. In the private sector, budgets tend to be more flexible and can change if necessary during the year, but rates are typically reviewed by a rate regulating agency, which is likely to investigate budget requests carefully before allowing rates to increase. Such commissions are particularly likely to investigate capital requests, as they are aware of the tension between the need to modernize physical plant and water delivery systems on the one hand and the desire to keep rates affordable on the other.

Types of Budgets

Budgets vary in the level of detail and manner of presentation. Spending can be classified in a variety of ways, depending on how one answers the question "Spend how much for what?"

Tables 3-1 through 3-4 show a typical budget format. Some budgets are organized according to administrative units and group expenditures by type, such as training, travel, contractual services, commodities, personnel, and equipment. Some budgets offer detail within each of these categories, listing each piece of equipment to be purchased and breaking down commodities into paper supplies, chemicals, and light bulbs. When a budget is broken down in this way it is called a *line-item* (or object-of-expenditure) *budget* because there is a separate item on each line. Such budgets are useful for control purposes, because it is clear from this format how much each item costs, and managers are not free to spend according to what they think necessary.

By contrast, program or activity budgets are not organized by department or administrative unit but by programs or functions, such as water pumping, meter replacement, main repairs, and billing, and such budgets outline how much is spent on each program or activity. Program or activity budgets tell you how much you spend on each function you perform, and hence can tell you if you are spending a disproportionate amount of money on supervision, or spending an increasing amount of money on maintenance. This format can be helpful in developing policy but does not directly control expenditures. How money is spent within a program is up to the manager, who is responsible for achieving the program's goals in whatever way seems best. Program budgets communicate more clearly with the public, explaining how work is done rather than how much money is spent on each item purchased. It is possible to organize a budget according to programs or activities and then indicate with line items how much each is allowed to spend, curtailing the discretion of the managers.

Table 3-1. Example utility: operating budget summary

For the period July 1, 2007, through June 30, 2011
($000)

	Actual		Amended Budget	Proposed Budget
	FY 07–08	FY 08–09	FY 09–10	FY 10–11
Operating Revenue	94,018	105,969	118,546	128,888
Operating and Maintenance Expense	36,479	39,104	41,861	47,183
Customer Accounting	3,981	4,463	5,199	8,995
Service and General and Administrative Expense	9,595	10,413	12,132	13,492
Total Operating and Maintenance Expense	50,055	53,980	59,192	69,670
Operating Income Before Depreciation	43,963	51,989	59,354	59,218
Depreciation	11,427	11,775	12,206	12,967
Operating Income	32,536	40,214	47,148	46,251
Other Income / (Expense)				
Interest Income	7,437	6,035	5,154	5,480
Interest Expense	(16,782)	(18,007)	(16,879)	(19,622)
Less Capitalized Interest	2,927	4,036	4,842	4,939
Amortization of Debt Issue Cost	(59)	(76)	(140)	(190)
Gain on Sale of Land	0	94	0	0
Loss of Early Extension of Debt	0	(1,496)	0	0
Grant	0	0	1,271	0
Total Other Income / (Expense)	(6,477)	(9,414)	(5,752)	(9,393)
Net Income / (Loss)	26,059	30,800	41,396	36,858

Table 3-2. Example utility: operating revenues

For the period July 1, 2006, through June 30, 2011
($000)

	Actual		Amended Budget	Proposed Budget
	FY 07–08	FY 08–09	FY 09–10	FY 10–11
Retail Revenue	73,563	85,784	97,814	105,449
Wholesale Revenue	16,217	17,236	18,042	20,297
Service Charges	1,265	1,105	810	1,242
Delinquency	1,294	1,295	1,370	1,380
Fire Protection	345	358	360	370
Miscellaneous	1,334	191	150	150
Total Operating Revenue	94,018	105,969	118,546	128,888

Table 3-3. Example utility: operating and maintenance expenses by object

For the period July 1, 2007, through June 30, 2011
($000)

	Actual		Amended Budget	Proposed Budget
	FY 07–08	FY 08–09	FY 09–10	FY 10–11
Personnel				
Source of supply (SOS)	261	261	381	435
Pumping	987	1,062	1,173	1,551
Treatment and Purification (T&P)	8,617	9,575	9,729	11,035
Transmission and Distribution (T&D)	6,832	7,159	7,970	9,227
Total Personnel	16,697	18,057	19,253	22,248
Electrical Service				
Source of Supply (SOS)	2,082	1,670	1,876	1,846
Pumping	837	877	902	951
Treatment and Purification (T&P)	3,191	4,098	4,718	5,051
Transmission and Distribution (T&D)	26	26	28	54
Total Electrical Service	6,136	6,671	7,524	7,902
Supplies				
Source of Supply (SOS)	175	130	228	293
Pumping	267	304	270	317
Treatment and Purification (T&P)	2,014	2,364	2,623	2,505
Transmission and Distribution (T&D)	1,898	1,916	1,935	2,269
Total Supplies	4,354	4,714	5,056	5,384
Vehicle Expense				
Pumping	11	15	47	102
Treatment and Purification (T&P)	363	287	349	307
Transmission and Distribution (T&D)	565	544	667	694
Total Vehicle Expense	939	846	1,063	1,103
Maintenance Expense				
Source of Supply (SOS)	31	16	50	52
Pumping	159	165	226	444
Treatment and Purification (T&P)	407	496	621	834
Transmission and Distribution (T&D)	310	389	350	291
Total Maintenance Expense	907	1,066	1,247	1,621
Other Operating Expenses				
Purchased Water (SOS)	1,508	1,455	1,691	1,908
Geological Survey (SOS)	207	167	167	184
Fuel (T&P)	2,305	1,376	499	606
Natural Gas (T&P)	1,196	1,742	2,940	3,168
Chemicals (T&P)	1,159	1,241	1,064	1,525
Lime (T&P)	89	849	558	714
Security Service (T&P)	210	147	139	144
$CaCO_3$ Removal (T&P)	274	314	199	199
Security Service (T&D)	92	95	114	118
Paving (T&D)	406	364	347	359
Total Other Operating Expenses	7,446	7,750	7,718	8,925
Total Operating and Maintenance Expenses	36,479	39,104	41,861	47,183

Table 3-4. Example utility: operating and maintenance expenses by function

For the period July 1, 2007, through June 30, 2011
($000)

	Actual		Amended Budget	Proposed Budget
	FY 07–08	FY 08–09	FY 09–10	FY 10–11
Personnel	261	261	381	435
Electric service	2,082	1,670	1,876	1,846
Geological survey	207	167	167	184
Purchased water	1,508	1,455	1,691	1,908
Maintenance expense	31	16	50	52
Supplies	176	130	228	293
Total Source of Supply	4,265	3,699	4,393	4,718
Pumping				
Personnel	987	1,062	1,173	1,551
Electric service	837	877	902	951
Supplies	267	304	270	317
Vehicle expense	11	15	47	102
Maintenance expense	159	165	226	444
Total Pumping	2,261	2,423	2,618	3,365
Treatment and Purification				
Personnel	8,617	9,575	9,729	11,035
Electric service	3,191	4,098	4,718	5,051
Supplies	2,014	2,364	2,623	2,505
Vehicle expense	363	287	349	307
Fuel	2,305	1,376	499	606
Security service	210	147	139	144
Chemical	1,159	1,241	1,064	1,525
Natural gas	1,196	1,742	2,940	3,168
Lime	89	849	558	714
$CaCO_3$ removal	274	314	199	199
Maintenance expense	407	496	621	834
Total Treatment & Purification	19,825	22,489	23,439	26,088
Transmission and Distribution				
Personnel	6,832	7,159	7,970	9,227
Electric service	25	26	28	54
Supplies	1,898	1,916	1,935	2,269
Vehicle expense	565	544	667	694
Paving	406	364	347	359
Security service	92	95	114	118
Maintenance expense	310	389	350	291
Total Transmission & Distribution	10,128	10,493	11,411	13,012
Total Direct Operating Expenses	$36,479	$39,104	$41,861	$47,183

Table 3-5. Performance measure examples

Work Load	Efficiency	Effectiveness
Peak day demand gallons or liters treated	Treatment cost per million	Percent of time met peak demand
Number of meters read per meter reader	Average number of meters	Percent accuracy of meter readings per day
Number of paychecks processed	Cost per paycheck	Percent of time paychecks issued on time

Performance measures can be added to program budgets, so both managers and the public can see what the goals of each program are and how well they have been achieved. Three general types of performance measures exist. Work-load measures express the amount of work performed for an activity in a given amount of time. Efficiency measures express output produced compared to the amount of input required to produce it (or inversely, it relates the amount of input to unit of output). Effectiveness measures indicate the extent to which an activity or program meets and fulfills an objective or need or brings about desired results. Examples of each type of performance measure are given in Table 3-5.

Some caution is required in setting up performance measures. While it may be preferable to have some measure, even an imperfect one, to having none at all, measuring the wrong thing can be harmful, as people tend to work to the goal, to improve their performance as measured by whatever indicators you use. If you choose the wrong things to measure, employees may skew their efforts in the wrong direction. The focus should be on a limited number of measures that employees agree are important. One measure commonly used is water losses, that is, the ratio of water pumped to water billed. Water utilities nearly always measure the cleanliness of the water they produce and their compliance with regulations.

Performance measures are useful not only for general managers as advance warnings of problem areas and for program managers as targets and incentives but also for communication with the public. When performance measures are added to the budget format, it is much clearer to the public what it costs to produce what level of service.

Budgets are typically divided into two parts, an operating budget that is primarily concerned with routine annual revenues and expenditures and a capital budget that includes a list of larger, one-time projects or equipment that will be accomplished or purchased during the budget year. A capital improvement plan may cover a number of years and list projects the utility plans to do in the future and large equipment purchases. Large projects may span several years, including preliminary planning, design, site acquisition, and construction. The plan needs to take into account future community growth, changing technology and/or regulation, and repair or upgrade of inadequate existing facilities. The first year of the capital improvement plan provides the basis for the annual capital budget. In municipal government, the approval of the capital improvements program may involve additional hearings and public-review meetings to ensure the program's consistency with adopted comprehensive plans. Funding sources for future capital improvements need to be identified well in advance of the needs for funds.

Revenues

Budgets are not only about spending, but also about revenues, including water rates, fees, grants, and borrowing. Revenues are supposed to equal or exceed expenditures, though in some years retained earnings from prior years may be used to balance the budget. Acquiring adequate financing for day-to-day operations and needed improvements is essential for maintaining the long-term health of a utility. Revenues must be sufficient to provide for proper operation and maintenance, development and perpetuation of the system, and maintenance of the utility's financial integrity. The soundness of the utility's financial condition will be the primary criterion evaluated by rating agencies and will have a significant effect on the cost of debt.

Most governmental water utilities are operated as self-sustaining enterprise funds. According to GASB, enterprise funds are used "to account for operations (a) that are financed and operated in a manner similar to private business enterprises—where the intent of the governing body is that the costs (expenses, including depreciation) of providing goods or services to the general public on a continuing basis be financed or recovered primarily through user charges; or (b) where the governing body has decided that periodic determination of revenues earned, expenses incurred, and/or net income is appropriate for capital maintenance, public policy, management control, accountability, or other purposes." The implication for water utility managers is that they need to set rates and fees at a level sufficient to cover the costs of operations and to pay debt service on all loans. Financial managers in particular need to be able to project the amount of revenue for the budget year.

User charges for services are the primary source of revenue for water utilities. AWWA believes that water utilities should sustain themselves by setting rates that will cover their costs, where those costs are based on sound engineering and economic principles (AWWA 1992). In addition to the basic charges for a given amount of water, a utility can charge for other services it provides, such as the turning-on/turning-off of water services; installation of remote meter-reading devices; meter resetting or testing; inspections; engineering; and tapping onto the water system. Other charges may be set to cover the costs of temporary hydrant permits; new accounts or account transfers; and payment delinquency or returned checks for insufficient funds. These charges should ordinarily be established at full cost.

AWWA Manual Ml, *Principles of Water Rates, Fees, and Charges,* provides guidance on developing rates for water service. The procedures outlined in the manual include (1) determination of the total annual revenue requirements for the period for which the rates are to be effective, (2) allocation of the total annual revenue requirements to basic functional cost components, (3) distribution of the component costs to the various customer classes in accordance with their requirements for service, and

(4) design of water rates that will recover from each class of customer, within practical limits, the cost to serve that class of customer.

Many water utilities are required under their bond covenants or under the bond ordinance that initially paid for their capital plants to set rates and fees high enough to fund not just routine operating costs but also maintenance and equipment replacement. For larger capital costs, a number of alternative financing sources are available, including short- and long-term borrowing, surpluses from prior years (retained earnings), grants, and contributions. In addition, lease financing has become a more important and increasingly used source of funds in recent years. Governmental water utilities may also be subsidized from general funds. AWWA Manual M29, *Fundamentals of Water Utility Capital Financing*, third edition, provides a comprehensive overview of best management financing practices.

Accounting and Reporting

Accounting information is used to answer the following three kinds of questions:

- Score-card questions, for example, "How am I doing?"
- Attention-directing questions, for example, "What problems should I look into?"
- Problem-solving questions, for example, "Of the several ways of doing the job, which is the best?"

While budgeting, forecasting, and financing are all concerned with future activities of the utility, accounting and reporting are concerned with its history. The objective of the accounting function is to classify and summarize the transactions of the utility and to report the summaries in meaningful ways to various interested groups. Information is used to make decisions, and the information needs of various groups are determined by the types of decisions each is required to make.

The following major groups are among the users of water utility information:

- Regulatory authorities
- Taxing authorities
- Stakeholders
  - —Stockholders, in the case of private water utilities
  - —Citizens and legislative-approval officials, in the case of governmental water utilities
  - —Creditors
  - —Customers (rate payers)
  - —Employees
  - —Management

The information needs of any one of the above groups are not mutually exclusive of the needs of others. Some groups of users may need more detail than others; internal users normally require more information and need it more quickly than external users.

Two broad categories of accounting reports are financial and management. Financial reporting conforms with generally accepted accounting principles. Specific statements are usually mandatory and have a historical focus. The most commonly reported accounting period is a fiscal or calendar year. Financial reports are precise and deal with the entire organization.

Management accounting, conversely, has no single unified structure. Reports do not necessarily conform with generally accepted accounting principles. The reporting periods are likely to be shorter than one year and are reported frequently. The focus of management reports is usually on the future and such reports tend to be less precise than financial accounting reports. However, despite the potential for imprecision, management reports provide information that some users demand in a format they understand, and as such are important tools for managers.

Auditing and Analysis

A financial audit is an examination of the water utility's financial statements by a firm of independent public accountants. Through the study and evaluation of the utility's system of internal control, inspection of documents, observation of assets, making appropriate inquiries, and other auditing procedures, the auditors gather the evidence necessary to determine whether or not the financial statements provide a fair and reasonably complete picture of the utility's financial position and its activities during the period being audited. The responsibility for engaging the auditors usually rests with a committee of the utility's board of directors or another governing body of the utility.

A management or operating audit may consist of a systematic and objective review of the entire organization, including its management and operations. A specific segment may be audited independently or internally in relation to specified objectives and relevant standards. The purpose of a management audit is to evaluate performance, identify opportunities for improvement, and develop recommendations for improvement or further action.

Financial audits are performed by outside independent accountants; management audits may be performed by internal staff or outside experts. The techniques of analysis and the objectives of the audit are different. Financial audits are usually performed annually. Management audits are done less frequently. A management audit is more thorough and more time-consuming than routine monitoring of operations.

Cash Management

Besides overseeing the financial cycle, financial managers are responsible for a series of other tasks that contribute to the financial solvency and cost-effectiveness of the water utility operations. One of the most important is cash management.

Ensuring the availability of funds on a day-to-day basis requires management and planning of cash flow. Cash-flow planning assures that sufficient cash is available when it is required and minimizes the necessity (and cost) for short-term borrowing.

Managers generally create a cash budget, that is, a plan for when cash expenditures are likely to be needed. A cash budget may include dates and amounts when money needs to be available to pay employees, creditors, and debt. It may also dictate the timing of purchases of supplies, chemicals, and capital outlays. A cash budget may include dates and amounts when money needs to be available to pay employees, creditors, and debt. It may also dictate the timing of purchases of supplies, chemicals, and capital outlays. Excess cash not immediately needed is normally invested in such a way that some of the investments mature just as cash is needed. If this approach is not sufficient, changing from quarterly to monthly billing may help cash flow (reduction in borrowing needs may more than compensate for increased costs of billing), and some bills may be delayed until cash is available. Many utilities find that a lockbox plan helps cash flow. In such a plan, payments owed to the water utility are put into a (locked) box at a bank; the bank employees regularly empty the box and deposit the checks immediately to the utility's account. Utilities pay the bank for this service.

Measuring Financial Performance

Financial managers need to pay attention to a number of indicators of the financial health of the utility. These are overall performance measures, including annual balance of revenues and expenditures, ratios of capital-to-operating expenditures, adequacy of equipment replacement and contingency funds, and percent of capacity used. Amount of debt and debt service–to–revenue ratios may also be helpful, especially when viewed over time.

Sometimes the size of equipment replacement funds, bond repayment funds, or contingency funds is dictated by bond covenant or fixed by policy. In such cases, it would be a good idea to monitor the actual size of such funds compared with the target. Revenues should be more than sufficient to cover water production costs plus debt service; how much more is often specified. If investors think that the water utility is a risky investment, they may demand a larger margin of safety to make themselves feel secure. Bond rating agencies and those who purchase bonds pay particular attention to such ratios.

Resource Acquisition, Inventory, and Insurance

Financial management staff is often responsible for purchasing and contracting for services, such as painting water towers or hiring a bond adviser. The finance office not only considers the expense of new equipment but is also responsible for examining alternative vendors and comparing products and costs of operation, as well as reliability of equipment. Developing and implementing purchasing and procurement policies are part of what most finance officials do. Once equipment is purchased, the finance office is typically responsible for inventory and may maintain records of service contracts and dates of routine maintenance or repairs. This office may also be responsible for the physical plant maintenance, particularly in smaller utilities. Financial managers are typically responsible for insurance on the equipment, as well as for insuring the entire operation, against losses, damages caused by the utility (say during a repair of a water pipe), theft, and lawsuits.

Internal Control

One of the most important considerations in the design of a water utility accounting system is the provision for internal control. It is inclusive of most of the functions described in this chapter and in further detail in chapter 20. The American Institute of Certified Public Accountants defines an effective system of internal control as enabling "management to deal with rapidly changing economic and competitive environments, shifting customer demands and priorities, and restructuring for future growth. Internal control promotes efficiency, reduces risk of asset loss, and helps ensure the reliability of financial statements and compliance with laws and regulations" (AICPA 2009).

One aspect of internal control is reducing opportunities for theft or fraud and minimizing waste. This responsibility includes identifying places where fraud or theft could conceivably occur and setting up double checks to discourage such activity and catch it if it occurs. What procedures are in place to check deliveries of supplies? Who has access to supplies? Does equipment have to be signed out? How is vehicle fuel authorized? Could an employee fill up the tank of a personal vehicle? How could this be prevented? What policies are in place to inform employees what the lines are? What is permitted and what is prohibited? For example, can employees use department computers or phones for private email or calls, and if so, when and to what extent? Do they need to record each call or use of the photocopy machine (do they have departmental keys)? Can they take laptop computers home with them? It is important to focus on areas where substantial amounts of money are involved, where losses would be considerable and embarrassing or would slow down production.

The goal is not to watch every minor use of the email but to monitor the big ticket items. Personnel having record-keeping responsibilities should not have access to the physical handling of assets. Ideally, there should be a complete separation of the accounting, operating, and custodial functions. For example, the person receiving payments from customers should not have access to the accounts receivable subsidiary ledger. Such procedures will help to eliminate errors in accounting records and prevent fraud by requiring the collusion of at least two persons in any dishonest activity. Two people may be required to authorize the cutting of a check with a similar rationale.

Written instructions should be issued to specify procedures to be followed in carrying out routine functions. Such instructions should include procedures for general operations, authorizations, reviews, and record keeping as a means of providing control over assets, liabilities, revenues, and expenses. The requirement that checks be signed by authorized personnel only after presentation of a voucher prepared from supporting source documents is an example of a routine established to control disbursements. Procedure development will also facilitate temporary and permanent personnel transfers by focusing on positions or functions rather than individuals.

Rotating accounts among receivables clerks is a useful method of preventing dishonesty. The requirements that all employees take vacations to rotate responsibilities among more employees and that key personnel who deal directly with money be bonded (that is, carry insurance that will pay the water utility if they steal any funds) are additional measures for providing against fraud.

Water utility activities should be reviewed periodically to ensure that established procedures are being followed. This may be accomplished through investigations conducted by internal auditors or outsiders, such as certified public accountants.

Simple actions like checking that locks are working, that key ledgers are kept in a safe or locked file cabinet, or that computer files are password protected can help prevent problems.

The extent to which these principles of internal control can be applied will vary with the size of the water utility. For example, a small utility having a limited number of employees may not be able to attain complete separation of duties. However, sufficient separation must always be maintained to ensure adequate control over such key assets as cash, securities, and receivables.

This section has dealt only with the general nature and principles of internal control. The subject of internal control, as applied to specific areas of a water utility's operation, is discussed within each of the appropriate chapters of this book and chapter 20.

PART 2

Financial Accounting Overview

This page intentionally blank.

Chapter 4

Financial Planning and Control

Why plan? Why not just do an annual budget and be done with it? That would be a bit like walking down the sidewalk looking at your feet: you would never know if the pavement were broken ahead of you and you were heading for a fall. Periodically, you have to look up to see where you are going. If you do not have a clear view of your destination, you can never get there. The essence of management is figuring out where you need to go, how to get there, and then actually taking the steps that get you there. The effective management of any entity, government or private, requires accurate planning and the ability to govern or control the execution of those plans.

Financial planning is a subset of planning more broadly. While generally managers may focus on issues such as personnel needs or relationships with regulatory agencies or elected officials, financial planning has a more limited focus: financial planning establishes long- and short-term goals and objectives that deal with the ability of the enterprise to pay its bills, balance its budget, and serve its customer base over time. Some of these goals may be explicitly financial, such as targets for reserve funds, while others are more general but have major financial implications, such as expansion of a facility to serve a larger population. This planning process is a necessary step that must be followed regardless of the level of autonomy experienced by the entity. Even entities that are under larger departments or are controlled by other bodies need to establish appropriate goals and objectives for their own operations.

The financial planning process has three components: (1) a strategic plan, (2) an annual operating plan, and (3) an annual capital or construction plan. Once strategic plans have been developed, annual operating plans as well as annual capital and/or construction plans can be derived using the general guidelines established by the strategic plans. Since the business environment is a dynamic one, monitoring the environment is an ongoing effort. The entity stops only long enough to take a "picture" of the requirements necessary to meet short-term goals and objectives during the following year. This "picture" is the annual operating, capital, and/or construction budget.

No matter how good the plan, it is of no use unless it is implemented. The strategic plan must be turned into capital and operating budgets, which in turn must be carried out. One measure by which financial performance is judged is the difference between actual and planned results. Implementation needs to be monitored, major variations analyzed, and appropriate actions carried out. There may be good reasons why major projects are delayed or budgets are being overspent or underspent, but such variances may also be an early warning that something is amiss and needs to be fixed. The level of concern and accountability for variances from planned activities is a matter for top management to determine.

Implementation of financial plans is easier if they are laid out logically and the tasks of each manager under the plan clearly stated. The goals must be plainly stated and easily understood, and the steps to achieve those goals linked transparently to the goals. Each of the steps must be feasible within the staffing and budget limits set forth. If line managers have been involved in the formation of the goals and objectives, the results are more likely to be both achievable and achieved. Managers will not buy into a plan they feel they cannot accomplish. Properly organized and prepared budget documents are essential to the success of any financial plan.

Financial Planning Process

Strategic Plan

The strategic plan for an entity defines goals and objectives that are long-range in nature. Strategic plans often start with and evolve around the basic mission statement of the entity. A typical mission statement for a water utility might be to provide the highest-quality water in a cost-effective manner. Given this basic mission statement, the task becomes one of identifying secondary goals and objectives that make the attainment of the mission possible. Factors that influence these secondary goals and objectives need to be considered. An analysis of the environment in which the entity operates is essential. Any long-range plan would necessarily have an impact on or be impacted by long-range plans of other related entities or governing bodies, so part of the planning process should be consultation with other related entities. For example, if a city has a plan to reach a particular population level by a certain year and has plans for housing subdivisions that will come on line 5 or 10 years hence, those plans need to be figured into the utility's strategic plan. Often the long-range plans of a utility are coordinated by central planning departments.

Long-range plans have to be flexible. If they are too general, they provide too little guidance for annual plans; if they are too specific, they have to be changed all the time, resulting in too frequent changes to the annual plans. The middle ground is to revisit the long-range plan at intervals, updating it, modifying it as necessary, and then using the updated plan to guide the shorter-term plans as needed. It is the responsibility of top level management to monitor the environment and determine if any changes are required in the mission statement or long-range goals and objectives. Line managers report regularly on their implementation of the short-term plans, while top managers observe and react to variations from the plans.

Annual Operating Plan

Refinement and expansion of the strategic plan in the short term result in the annual operating plan. The annual operating plan is most often described as the "annual budget." It is called an "annual budget" because it typically covers a year (though it can be amended during that time), but it may take much longer than a year to estimate revenues, plan and approve the budget, implement it, and evaluate the results.

Annual operating plans consist of two primary sections, an estimation of expected revenues and an estimation of expected expenses. In a budget, generally speaking, revenues are expected to equal or exceed expenditures. In water utilities, both revenues and expenditures are largely driven by demand. Water billing revenue depends on the number of gallons of water customers use, and expenditures depend on the cost per gallon of water produced. Projecting demand and knowing how much it costs to produce each gallon of treated water are therefore critical to putting together the annual operating plan.

Revenue projections are to a large extent influenced by factors that are external to the organization. The political environment may set limits or control the timing of rate and fee increases; the physical environment in the form of weather has an even greater impact on revenues by influencing the demand for water. The economic environment may also have an impact, as new developments come on line with increasing numbers of users, or recessions force bankruptcies, closed businesses, and abandoned homes. Financial managers can sometimes influence revenue at the margins by careful investment of cash on hand. Top level managers can try to make the best possible case for rate increases when these are considered necessary.

The number of users and demand for water also influence expenditures, as does the cost of energy, goods, and services, all of which may increase regardless of the efforts of management. Managers may be able to influence the cost of labor by limiting wage and benefit increases, and may be able to exert some control over spending by selecting equipment that is reliable and uses less electricity, and by controlling the timing of expansions or other capital projects. Hiring capable staff can reduce the number of staff needed and so help control costs. Changes in physical plant and technology can affect costs, as can labor negotiations.

The estimation of revenues during the proposed budget period is normally the first step in the budgeting process. Projection of revenues is done separately for each source of revenue. Operating revenues are separated from nonoperating revenues. There are two reasons for separating revenues by source. First, it is much easier to estimate separately revenue sources that have different drivers; second, operating revenues are used to calculate coverage ratios, the formal or informal requirements of investors that the utility's net revenue (operating revenues minus operating expenditures) be more than enough revenue to cover debt service. Revenue from bonds or other borrowing is also listed separately, and naturally does not get included in the calculation of coverage ratios.

The operating revenues are dependent on the rates charged to customers and amount of water sold, while other revenue responds to different factors, such as new

Table 4-1. Statement of revenues and their disposition

	Amended Budget FY 09–10	Proposed Budget FY 10–11
Operating Revenues		
Metered Water Sales	$57,696,549	$59,432,333
Grants	3,109,752	3,720,457
Fire Protection	1,153,931	1,468,647
Penalties and Miscellaneous	2,875,471	2,981,750
Total Operating Revenues	64,835,703	67,603,187
Nonoperating Revenues		
Interest Earned and Miscellaneous	8,103,729	6,979,000
Total Revenues	$72,939,432	$74,582,187
Disposition of Revenues		
Operation and Maintenance	34,549,905	35,495,745
Operating Reserve Requirement	320,000	380,000
Revenue Bond Debt Requirements	17,239,090	16,682,456
Interest Costs	6,007,500	6,614,167
Retirement of Bonds Reserve Funds Provision	1,671,214	1,663,966
Capital Requirements		
Capital Outlay	1,080,630	1,274,805
Equipment Additions	242,400	216,150
Other Requirements on Debt Service–Annexed Systems	1,322,991	1,219,997
Revenues Available for Construction and Contingencies	10,505,702	11,034,901
Total Disposition of Revenues	$72,939,432	$74,582,187

construction or interest rates on investments. Estimated revenues from the sale of water and any other operating revenues are normally listed first, and then revenue from other sources, such as fees, permits, interest, transfers from other funds, and appropriations from the fund balance (Table 4-1).

The second section of the annual operating plan shows how these revenues are distributed across categories of expenditures. By showing how much money is earmarked for each separate purpose, managers can assure themselves of legal compliance during the budgeted period. Details of annual operating expenses can be determined either by a "top-down" or a "bottom-up" information gathering process.

The "bottom-up" approach involves individual profit centers in the budgeting process. Each center is required to provide estimated expenditures for the coming period. It becomes the task of the budget department to collate and organize the information provided by the individual centers. A simple test for reasonability is the only control exercised by the budget department in the early phases of the "bottom-up" budget compilation. It is the job of each successive level of managerial control to keep estimated expenditures within the scope of the parameters established by the strategic plan.

"Top-down" budgeting takes the opposite approach. Top management decides the level of expenditures allowable. These expenditure levels are then divided among the lower levels of control as management perceives the need to do so. The task of the budget department in "top-down" budgeting is to follow the directives of top management and prepare the actual planning guide for each subordinate department.

Regardless of the method of budget planning, it is important that the adopted budget be flexible. The business environment is dynamic and changes often occur that result in a change in plans. Quarterly amendments to annual operating plans are common. Needed budgetary amendments are usually discovered through the monitoring process. A series of reports detailing actual expense variance from the budget provides the key to monitoring the budgetary health of the organization (see Table 4-2).

Annual Capital or Construction Plan

As with the case of the annual operating plan, the annual capital or construction plan is a refinement and expansion of the strategic plan. Through the implementation of specific projects, management can continue to move toward the final goals and objectives of the organization. Programs that are designed to meet those goals should be identified and prioritized. As pointed out earlier, it is important that the construction budget be flexible because the priority of specific projects tends to be dynamic as well. Having established, identified, and prioritized projects, the next step is to identify possible financing alternatives for each one. Examples of possible funding sources include sales-generated revenues; receipts derived from the issuance of debt; monies made available from local, state, or federal programs; contributions from developers or nontypical sources, such as funds from successful litigations. Since the prioritizing of specific projects plays such an important part in the construction budget, top management needs to be involved at each step of the budget preparation process.

Financial Control Process

In order to effectively manage and control expenditures, it is necessary to monitor utility performance relative to its budget during the year. Overexpenditures (actual expenditures exceeding budgeted expenditures) need to be identified as quickly as possible in order to apply corrective measures before major variances occur. Underexpenditures (budgeted expenditures exceeding actual expenditures) can either indicate that some portions of the short-term plan are not being performed or that expenditure estimates were overstated. The former requires management attention to determine how shortages will be funded or if program revisions are necessary; the latter may indicate a possible source of additional revenue that could be applied to other projects experiencing underexpenditures. Early action also must be taken when variances in revenues are identified, particularly if revenues are falling short of predictions.

Warnings of significant departures from expectations can be in the form of dollars or percentages of variations or both. A large percent variance on a small number is

Table 4-2. Amendments to the 2010–2011 annual operating budget

	Proposed Budget FY 10–11	Changes to Date		Amended Budget FY 10–11
		No. 1	No. 2	
Revenues				
Operating Revenues				
Metered Water Sales	$59,432,333	2,650,000	300,000	$62,382,333
Grants	3,720,457			3,720,457
Fire Protection Penalties	1,468,647	53,000	6,000	1,527,647
Penalties and Miscellaneous	2,981,750			2,981,750
Total Operating Revenues	67,603,187	2,703,000	306,000	70,612,187
Nonoperating Revenues				
Interest Earned and Miscellaneous	6,979,000	11,475		7,091,838
Total Revenues	$74,582,187	$2,714,475	$306,000	$77,704,025
Disposition of Revenues				
Operation and Maintenance	$35,495,745		180,000	$35,675,745
Operating Reserve Requirement	380,000		1,800	381,800
Revenue Bond Debt Requirements				
Interest Costs	16,682,456			16,682,456
Retirement of Bonds	6,614,167			6,614,167
Reserve funds Provision	1,663,966			1,663,966
Capital Requirements				
Capital Outlay	1,274,805		345,000	1,619,805
Equipment Additions	216,150		85,000	301,150
Other Requirements				
Debt Service on Annexed Systems	702,792		582,075	1,284,867
Debt Service on Purchased Systems	478,555			478,555
Debt Service on Equipment Purchases	38,650			38,650
Revenues Available for Construction and Contingencies	11,034,901	2,714,475	(786,512)	12,962,864
Total Disposition of Revenues	$74,582,187	2,714,475	407,363	$77,704,025

often not meaningful, because it may only involve a few dollars (going from two dollars to four dollars is a 100 percent increase). Conversely, a small percentage increase on a large number may involve many dollars. Hence you may want to look at both the dollar differences from expectations and the percentage of variation.

In order to work as an early warning system, budget variance reports should be compiled at regular intervals, such as monthly or quarterly, and presented at the first opportunity following the completion of the chosen interval (Table 4-3). While computer programs can provide alerts on a daily basis, too many alerts for items too small

Table 4-3. Sample budget variance sheet

Current Period Allotment	Current Period Activity	Variance Over/ (Under)	Classification	Annual Allotment	Amended Budget	Year-to-Date Expense	Variance Over/ (Under)	Percent Variance
$14,090	13,973	($116)	Administrative Salary/Wages	$183,180	88,065	85,958	($2,106)	(2.39)
14,090	13,973	(116)	**Personnel Services**	183,180	88,065	85,958	(2,106)	(2.39)
0	0	0	Operating Expense	50	20	18	(1)	(7.50)
0	0	0	Maintenance Expense	3,910	3,910	3,257	(653)	(16.70)
0	0	0	Membership/Subscription	240	200	40	(159)	(79.60)
0	0	0	Data Processing Services	0	0	0	0	0.00
0	0	0	Teleprocessing Charges	0	0	0	0	0.00
0	0	0	**Contractual Services**	4,200	4,130	3,316	(813)	(19.70)
330	111	(268)	Operating Materials	4,600	2,280	1,845	(434)	(19.07)
330	111	(268)	**Materials and Supplies**	4,600	2,280	1,845	(434)	(19.07)
0	1,748	1,748	Bank Charges	7,160	4,050	3,992	(57)	(1.42)
670	645	(24)	Insurance	8,040	4,020	3,874	(145)	(3.62)
1,490	1,476	(13)	Retirement	19,390	9,690	9,492	(197)	(2.03)
2,160	3,870	1,710	**Other Charges**	34,590	17,760	17,359	(400)	(2.25)
16,630	17,955	1,325	**Operating Requirements Before Transfers**	226,570	112,235	108,479	(3,755)	(3.35)
(420)	(471)	(51)	Transfers to Other Funds	(5,660)	(2,820)	(2,830)	(10)	0.36
(420)	(471)	(51)	**Interfund Transfers**	(5,660)	(2,820)	(2,830)	(10)	0.36
$16,210	17,483	$1,273	**Total Operating Requirements**	$220,910	109,415	105,649	($3,765)	(3.44)

to pay attention to are likely to be numbing and make it too easy to ignore major differences when they occur.

Presentation of Annual Financing Plans

The presentation of the actual budget document is important. When properly presented, the budget document conveys the data in a clear, concise, and readable format. A solution to the problem of providing only the required information to a specific category of reader lies in using a comprehensive approach to the presentation of the data. Detailed line items for each profit center should be addressed in the body of the report. Each level of supervision should have its own summary. As the budget is compiled, each successive summary is rolled into the next higher supervisory level. In this manner it is possible to address every item of control and responsibility.

A comprehensive budget provides much more detail than most managers need and is unlikely to communicate to the press, the public, or boards, commissions, and investors or rating agencies. Most users want and need summary information. Because of this, it is necessary to provide a narrative overview of the budget. This overview should explain the major environmental impacts on the organization (such as mergers with other facilities), expansions of physical plant, or new developments coming on line. Major increases in electricity rates might also be worth mentioning. In addition, the summary should list projected revenues and expenditures, and predicted changes in fund balances. The summary might also include a few key financial indicators, such as coverage ratios for debt repayment, comparisons of water pumped to water billed, and fund balances. New initiatives such as green targets or switching core technologies for purification can be described briefly. Expenditures by function can be presented at the aggregate level. Anyone who needs more detail can look at the rest of the document.

For those unfamiliar with the organization, it can be helpful to include somewhere in the document (at the beginning or at the end) a description of the structure of the organization. This can be accomplished by including an organizational chart and a listing of account codes and their descriptions in the appendix of the report. A brief glossary of key terms is sometimes included as well.

Summary

Financial planning is a process by which the top management of a utility can first define its long-range goals and objectives and then implement those plans through a short-term annual plan. The financial planning process is composed of three major elements: (1) the strategic plan, (2) the annual operating plan, and (3) the annual capital or construction plan. The short-term plans—the capital and operating budgets—need to be clearly laid out, with a useful executive summary for those who do not need more detail. Managers supervise the implementation of these plans, monitoring the differences between the plans and what is actually occurring, and taking appropriate action when necessary. Budgets need to be flexible, to cope with a dynamic environment, and hence may be amended during the year.

Chapter 5

Accounting

Accurate, complete, and timely recording and reporting of financial transactions are key objectives of the accounting function. This information has many uses, including external financial and regulatory reporting and internal management reporting. This chapter explains what should be recorded and reported and what the information means. Some of the differences and similarities between accounting for private and publicly owned water utilities are described as well.

Accounting Functions

Accounting also performs a number of other functions, including supporting other units of the organization, helping to safeguard physical resources, providing information to internal and external users, and maintaining internal control. As described in the previous chapter, accounting helps managers implement the budget, by showing any discrepancies between what was planned and approved and what is currently happening. The accounting function facilitates financial control.

Support for Managers

Accounting collects data on transactions and activities and summarizes it at various levels of aggregation for managers to use. For example, Accounting can tell managers how much they spent on personnel in the prior year or whether insurance costs are rising, or how much revenue was collected in fees in the prior year. Such data are essential in pointing out problem areas that need management attention and are fundamental to putting together the budget for the next year. Accounting can also create useful ratios to monitor, such as the ratio of personnel costs to total operating costs, or capital to operating costs. It can help measure performance, such as the cost to process 1,000 gal (3,785.4 L) of water, or progress toward goals, such as a reduction in kilowatt hours required to process that 1,000 gal of water.

Timely and accurate recording and reporting of transactions by Accounting can also inform managers how they are doing with respect to the budget, whether they are over or under and by how much. As described in the previous chapter, this information becomes an early warning system to alert managers of potential problems that need immediate attention. Accounting provides managers information on how much—how much spending has gone on, how much spending capacity remains, how much production has occurred, how much leakage there is, how much overtime has been paid, how much supplies are on hand—in real time, as it occurs.

Accountability for the Utility's Physical Resources

The safeguarding of the utility's physical resources is one of the objectives of accounting function. At the simplest level, the accounting system can record hours of use by piece of equipment, as well as associated repair records and costs for each vehicle, pump, or other piece of equipment. These data may suggest when equipment needs to be replaced for maximum efficiency. At a slightly more sophisticated level, accounting data can provide the cost per hour to operate equipment and tell managers whether these costs are going up, are stable, or declining. These data allow for comparison between models of equipment or brands and permit life-cycle cost estimates, greatly facilitating purchasing in the future. Did the new motor last as long as they claimed? Did the new pump reduce electricity usage as promised? How much did it cost over its life span?

When equipment, furniture, or rolling stock is purchased, the accounting system should capture the data necessary to create and maintain an inventory of such assets. These data include at a minimum what was ordered, when it was delivered, and how much it cost. Accounting maintains the asset inventory and, with periodic counts, can determine whether any assets are missing and their dollar implications. Sales and abandonment of fixed assets can also be recorded.

Provide Information to Internal and External Users

In addition to providing detailed data to different units of the utility describing how much money they have spent or how much they have produced, the accounting function can also provide more aggregated data in the form of reports to a variety of users, inside and outside the organization.

In addition to the budget, general purpose financial statements, and other reports prepared for external users, an example of internal operating information that Accounting can provide is metered water sales. An accounting report might begin with aggregate sales to customers, and then break down the data by customer classes (such as commercial, residential, and industrial users), amount of water used, meter size, or location in different parts of the community. The report could include variation by time of year or even time of day, and include comparisons with prior years, underscoring trends. Armed with such data, managers can ask questions such as what is the elasticity of water usage when rates go up; that is, what happens to usage when water becomes more expensive? How does this behavior differ by user class? It is difficult to budget without some grasp of the future impact of rate increases, and accounting data provides this information.

Maintain the System of Internal Control

Establishing and maintaining an effective system of internal controls is the responsibility of everyone in the organization. However, some control functions are the exclusive responsibility of Accounting. By recording and storing all financial transactions and comparing sets of records that should match, accounting helps assure that every dollar of revenue and expenditure is tracked and that there are no major mistakes or thefts. Procedures such as reconciliations of customer deposits, accounts receivable, and bank statements provide important internal controls for utilities. How much is owed us, how much did we collect, did the money get into the correct accounts? The bank says we have more money than our records indicate we have, what is going on here? Where is the error?

Policies and procedures are the basic guidelines and instructions to the staff for the processing and recording of transactions. Standard operating procedures allow a consistent method of handling transactions occurring under different circumstances or processed by different individuals. Consistency in reporting also allows for comparison between reporting periods and expedites management analysis and decisions.

The accounting system records financial and other statistical data and formulates reports for managers and outsider users such as regulatory agencies. To be meaningful, detailed data needs to be sorted and summarized systematically and consistently throughout the organization. An effective system of internal control facilitates this process.

Designing the Accounting System

If you were going to design an accounting system from scratch, you would probably work backward, from the intended users and their information needs, to the reports that would be required to fulfill those needs, to the accounts necessary for those reports and those functions, and from there to the detailed transaction data that would need to be collected. Then you would have to decide when and how the raw data would be recorded. Much of this work of design has been done for utilities by professional societies and regulators; managers can use an off-the-shelf model, adjusting it for their own needs.

A Chart of Accounts

At the core of the accounting system is a flow of data (see Figure 5-1), recording financial and operating information. Before any of that data can be recorded, utilities need to adopt or set up a chart of accounts. These accounts are the filing system of the accounting recording function. Each bit of financial and operating data goes into the equivalent of a labeled file. These labels should clearly describe and capture all of the different categories of asset, liability, equity/fund balance/reserve, revenue, and expenditure transactions of the utility. They are selected to provide useful managerial information and to respond to the requirements of regulatory and oversight boards. Once

Figure 5-1. Flow of accounting information

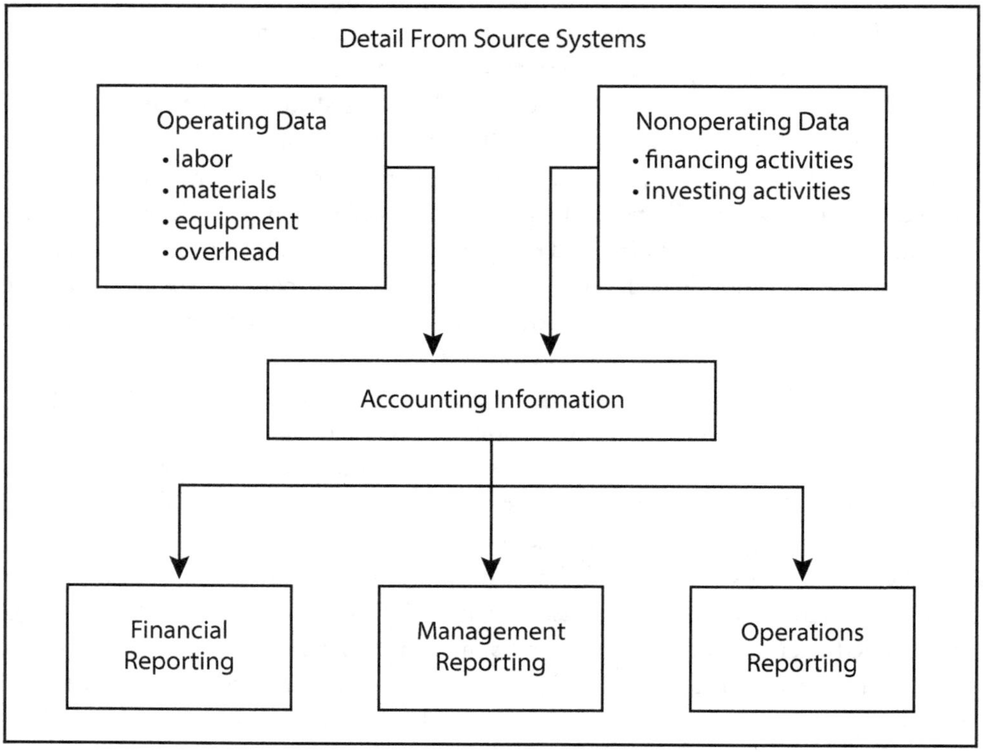

financial information is sorted into these files, it is easily retrievable for needed reports. How inclusive, that is how broad or narrow each category should be, depends on the need. For example, it usually is not necessary to have a separate label for each item of office supplies, unless for some reason you need to track paper usage. One account number for all office supplies should suffice. But for personnel, managers might want more details, such as wages, overtime, health insurance, pension contributions, workers' compensation, and part-time or temporary help. Such a breakdown can help managers track changes over time, for example if the amount of overtime is increasing. Everyone in the organization needs to use the same chart of accounts.

Recommended Chart of Accounts

A chart of accounts should be designed to facilitate record keeping and report preparation and to provide for control and accountability. The chart of accounts must provide for the accumulation of data in sufficient detail and in such a manner as to facilitate the preparation of reports to meet the needs of all interested groups. In designing the chart of accounts, it is important to balance the desirability of increased information with the cost of obtaining it.

Minimum requirements concerning the chart of accounts to be kept by an private water utility are usually prescribed by the appropriate utility regulatory agency of the state in which the utility operates. Some states also require governmental water utilities to follow a prescribed uniform chart of accounts. In fact, the need for accounting information by state utility commissions to aid in fulfilling their regulatory obligations is so important that the general design of accounting charts used by regulated water utilities is usually based on commission requirements. This basic design must be adjusted, as appropriate, so that the information requirements of other interested groups are also met.

The basic chart of accounts set forth in this chapter, and the detailed listing of accounts given in appendix A (see CD), is predicated on the recommendations of the National Association of Regulatory Utility Commissioners (NARUC) and is representative of charts required by most state utility regulatory agencies. Since the NARUC chart is designed for private water utilities, it must be modified slightly to meet the needs of governmental operations, which are discussed later in the chapter and in the appendix, based on recommendations of the Governmental Accounting Standards Board (GASB).

The NARUC-published chart ("system") of accounts for each class of water utilities consists of the following: (1) general instructions and definitions, (2) instructions concerning utility plant and operating expense, (3) a prescribed list of accounts, (4) a definition of each account and instructions concerning the types of transactions to be recorded in each account, and (5) the general sequence for balance sheet and income statement items. NARUC also issues, periodically, interpretations of the *Uniform System of Accounts for Class A Water Utilities.* Appendix A of the accompanying CD includes the complete Uniform System of Accounts for Class A Water Utilities and related interpretations as of 1996. Readers are encouraged to contact NARUC for any changes or updates.

In this section, the logic of the NARUC chart is explained. Figure 5-2 is a graphic presentation of the interrelationships of the groups of accounts provided in the recommended system. This figure, as well as the detailed listing of accounts given in appendix A, reflects the coding scheme employed by NARUC, adjusted to accommodate governmental water utilities. Accounts are assigned code numbers to facilitate identification and to allow for proper consolidation or combination of accounts when preparing and presenting reports to regulatory agencies or other interested groups. The account numbers are shown in parentheses in Figure 5-2.

The accounts in Figure 5-2 are divided into three major sections: the first consists of summary balance-sheet accounts (the accounts that are used to prepare the balance-sheet report), and the second consists of summary income and expense accounts. A third section, comprised of the retained earnings accounts, forms the connecting link between income accounts and balance-sheet accounts.

Balance-Sheet Accounts

The balance sheet or statement of net assets is one of the financial statements used to report the assets, liabilities, and net worth or fund balance of a utility at a single point in time. The name 'balance sheet' derives from the basic accounting equation: assets = liabilities + owner's equity. For public utilities, fund balance replaces the term owner's equity.

Figure 5-2. A chart of accounts for water utilities

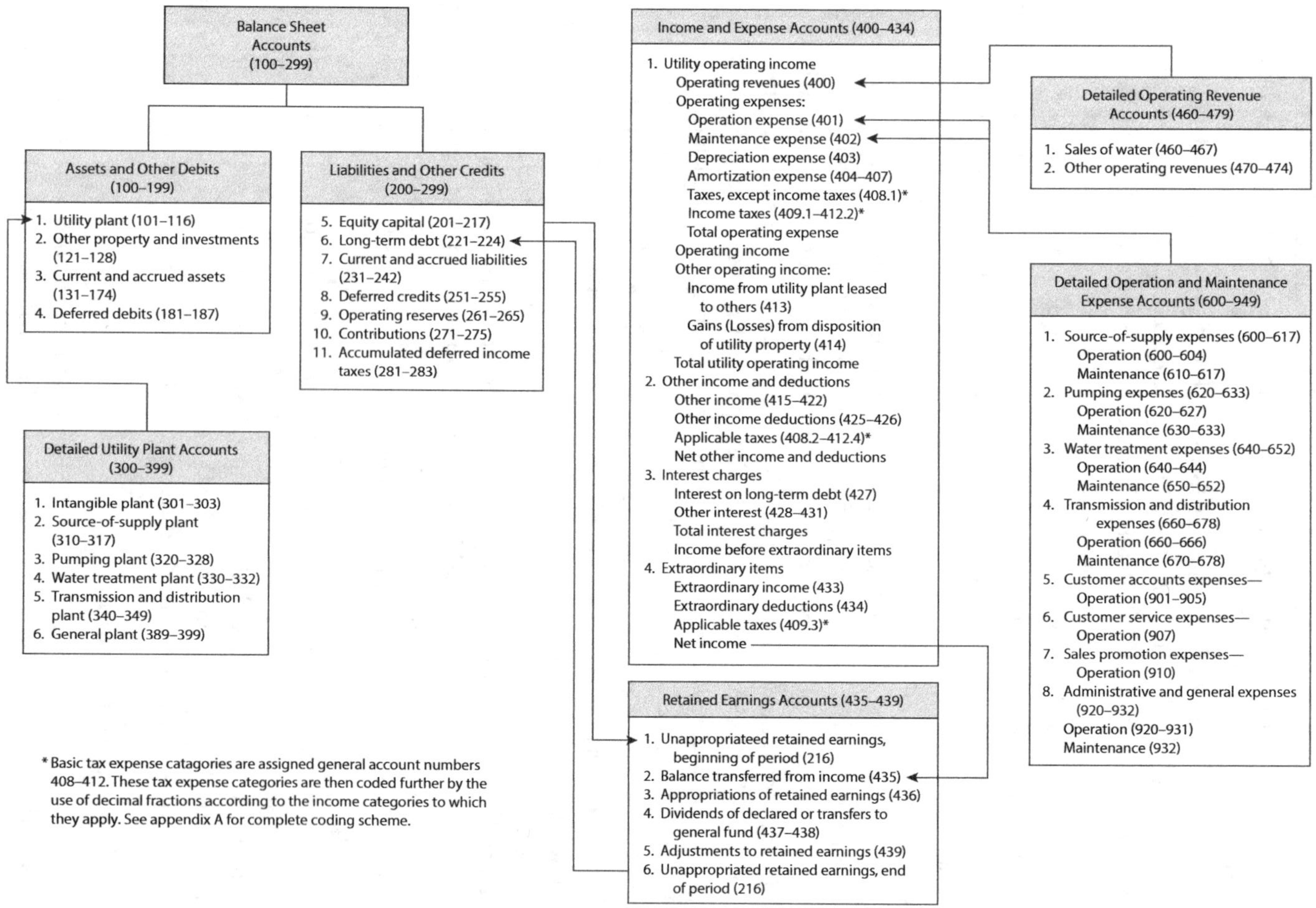

* Basic tax expense catagories are assigned general account numbers 408–412. These tax expense categories are then coded further by the use of decimal fractions according to the income categories to which they apply. See appendix A for complete coding scheme.

Summary Balance-Sheet Accounts

These are grouped within the following 2 categories: (1) "asset and other debits" (accounts numbered 100–199) and (2) "liabilities and other credits" (200–299). These 2 broad categories are further divided into 11 groups of summary accounts, as shown in Figure 5-2. Many of the individual summary balance-sheet accounts are supported by subsidiary accounts or records that provide additional details as to specific components of the summary or controlling accounts. One particular group of summary balance-sheet accounts, "utility plant" (101–116), is supported by 6 functional groups of detailed subsidiary utility plant accounts (300–399) under the NARUC system. This detailed structure is necessary because of the importance of plant facilities information to regulatory bodies for determining the appropriate rate base and to appropriately record depreciation. Detailed utility plant information also facilitates effective management control of plant assets.

Income and Expense Accounts

The summary income and expense accounts shown in Figure 5-2 are grouped into the following four categories: (1) utility operating income, (2) other income and deductions, (3) interest charges, and (4) extraordinary items. Operating income is the income derived from the normal operations of the water utility during a stated period of time. Operating income is computed by subtracting operating expenses (401–412.2), which include all expenses applicable to the furnishing of water utility services, from operating revenues (400), which summarize the revenues derived from normal operations of the water utility. In situations where the utility has income derived from the leasing of the utility plant to others (413) or gains or losses from the disposition of utility property (414), the adjustment for these items must be considered in determining total utility operating income.

Operating income is closely associated with the concept of "above and below the line," which reflects the regulatory point of view of public service commissions. A regulated water utility is entitled to operating revenues sufficient to cover operating expenses and to provide for a fair or reasonable return. From the viewpoint of a public service commission, the return (or operating income) to a water utility is the amount in dollars that remains after operating expenses have been subtracted from operating revenues. Revenues and expenses recognized in the determination of operating income are considered to be *above-the-line* items. *Below-the-line* items, although included as adjustments of operating income in arriving at the net income of the water utility, are not considered as operating items in calculations of rates and the determination of a fair or reasonable return. See chapter 16, Rate and Regulatory Reports, for more discussion of the below-the-line concept.

Expenses are above-the-line if they are reasonable in amount and of such a nature as to be considered chargeable against customers for services rendered. Income gained from activities of a nonutility nature (415–422), together with nonutility income deductions (425–426) and related income taxes (408.2–412.4), are considered to be below-the-line. Interest charges (427–431), while considered in determining the allowable rate of return, are not classified as operating expenses and, therefore, are below-the-line. Finally, extraordinary items (433–434) and net of related income taxes (409.3), considered by regulatory authorities to be of doubtful propriety as operating items, are also classified as below-the-line.

Water utility management does not always agree with state commission rulings concerning the treatment of a particular income statement item as an above-the-line or below-the-line item. Different state commissions also differ in their attitudes toward treating particular items as above-the-line or below-the-line.

As shown in Figure 5-2, the summary account titled "operating revenues" (400) and two summary accounts for operating expenses, "operation expense" (401) and "maintenance expense" (402), are supported by detailed revenue and expense accounts.* The detailed operating revenue accounts are grouped into two categories, and the detailed operation and maintenance accounts are grouped into eight functional categories.

The "other income" accounts (415–422) include income of the utility that does not result from its normal business of supplying potable water. Examples of such income include charges for installing meters owned by customers or revenues from the sale of water appliances (415); cost of merchandise sold and materials used for jobbing work (416); income derived from operations that are nonutility in nature but nevertheless constitute a distinct activity of the utility, such as providing sewage disposal service (417); and interest and dividend income (419).

The "other income deductions" accounts (425–426) include miscellaneous amortization charges not included in the expenses used to compute utility operating income (425) and miscellaneous income deductions (426). Examples of the latter account include charitable donations, expenditures for the purpose of influencing public opinion with regard to the election or appointment of public officials, and losses on write-downs or sales of securities.

Interest charges (427–431), also deductions from income, include interest on both long-term and short-term debt; the amortization of debt discount, debt premium, and debt-issue expenses; interest on debt to associated companies; and all other interest expense. Extraordinary items (433–434) include atypical, infrequently recurring gains and losses that would significantly distort the income of the current year if such items were reported as operating revenues or expenses.

Retained Earnings Accounts

The net income of the water utility, the income minus the above described deductions, is transferred to an account titled "balance transferred from income" (435) in the retained earnings category. The purpose of the retained earnings category is to explain changes in a water utility's retained earnings balance over a particular time period.

* Note the difference in the terms "operating expenses" and "operation expense." The term "operating expenses" has a broader meaning in that it includes depreciation, amortization, and taxes, as well as the charges to the operation and maintenance accounts.

Such changes may be caused by increases or decreases in income, in expenditures, by use of retained earnings during the year, or in the case of private water utilities, dividend declarations, and other accounting adjustments related to prior periods.

Accounting for Managerial Information

An accounting system is designed not only for external reports such as the balance sheet but also to serve the needs of managers. The central idea of management accounting is that managers should be provided with sufficient, timely, relevant information so that the entity may be managed efficiently and effectively.

For planning and control purposes, management is interested in cost information, such as labor, fuel, and rent. Effective cost control requires that definite responsibility for costs be established. A manager should be held responsible only for those costs that he or she can control. Therefore, the system of accounts must allow for identification and presentation of costs incurred by each responsibility segment (organization unit) of the water utility organization. Cost data and related operating statistics enable utility management to set standards of performance and to prepare realistic operating plans (budgets). Comparison of actual costs and operating statistics with planned costs and performance standards, by responsibility segment, enables management to control cost and performance and to improve future planning.

In addition to providing information to facilitate planning and controlling current activities of the water utility, a good system of accounts should be designed to facilitate the evaluation of proposed alternatives to current technology and current activities. Proposed alternatives often involve capital expenditures. Information needed for capital expenditure decisions is discussed in chapter 12.

Limitations of the Recommended System of Accounts

Any system of accounts, including that suggested in this chapter, is based on a set of assumptions as to the organizational structure and operating activities of a water utility. If a given utility varies in organizational plan or in operating activities from the assumptions underlying the suggested system, then the details of the system should be adapted to fit the actual conditions. The essential features of the suggested system should be retained by all water utilities because the system is based on accounting principles advocated by NARUC and GASB. Use of the essential features of the suggested system of accounts will promote uniform reporting by water utilities, which is a prerequisite to effective regulatory control. In addition, uniform reporting allows financial reports to be more easily understood and permits comparisons between individual utilities and comparisons to industry standards.

When to Record Transactions: Accrual Versus Cash Accounting

The discussion to this point has been about where (in what accounts) to record detailed financial transactions so the information is readily available for a variety of reports that address the needs of users. A second consideration is when to record each transaction. There are two basic alternatives, cash and accrual.

Under the cash basis, revenues are recognized and recorded when cash is received, and expenses are charged when cash is disbursed. Under the accrual basis, revenues are recorded in the period in which service is given, although payments may be received in a prior or subsequent period. Expenses are recorded in the period in which the benefits are received, although payments may be made in a prior or subsequent period. (Systems may also be partly accrual and partly cash. Such systems are described as modified accrual or modified cash systems.) Using full accrual accounting helps financial managers match costs against the revenues generated by these costs. Businesses and business type activities such as utilities normally rely on accrual accounting.

How to Record: Double-Entry Bookkeeping

To ensure accuracy, most accounting systems record data twice: each item of expenditure appears as a plus in one column and as a minus in a second column. One way to think about it is to consider every expenditure as a reduction of an available balance, and therefore a negative number: you subtract it. But you also want a total of expenditures, so put them in a separate column and add them up, in which case the expenditures are positive numbers. The two columns should be equal: all of the items subtracted should equal all the items added up. The two sets of figures are reconciled or compared at regular intervals. This is a way of double checking the numbers, like adding up and adding down a column to make sure you get the same number twice and have not made a mistake.

Public Sector Water Utilities

Much of the forgoing discussion on setting up an accounting system applies both to private and to publicly owned facilities. Every organization needs a chart of accounts, and managers need information for internal control and efficiency regardless of sector; both sectors use full accrual accounting for utilities (though cities often use modified accrual for their own books); and nearly every enterprise beyond the smallest and simplest ones use double-entry bookkeeping. And although the content of the balance sheets may be different—they have different purposes and different users—the basic idea and structure of the balance sheet remains the same. Nevertheless, there are some major differences in accounting for governmental water enterprises.

Self-Sufficiency

Private sector organizations normally have to cover costs plus make a profit in order to succeed and attract investors to pay for needed capital maintenance and improvements. Rates are determined by public regulatory agencies based on industrywide standards of fair return on capital. In publicly owned water utilities, the utility may be completely self-funding or it may be subsidized in various ways by the government of which it is a part. To the extent that it is completely self-funding, it pays for operations and capital improvements and repays bonds entirely from water sales. The goal is not to make a profit, though surpluses in some years can be carried over to the next few years, in order to stabilize rates. The first few years after a rate increase may create some surplus, which is used up the following few years, and then another rate increase would be required. Rates are not set by a regulatory board but by the elected officials, and generally they are set to cover costs. While private utilities have to pay taxes, government organizations do not, but some jurisdictions require that water rates be set sufficiently high that the utility can pay the government the equivalent of taxes. Some cities are dependent on their water funds for cash flow, borrowing and paying back internally rather than from outside sources; others may borrow from water fund surpluses or even claim water fund surpluses without repayment, to balance municipal budgets. Bond covenants may restrict such transfers, requiring water revenues to be used for water utility purposes.

Fund Structure

One of the major differences between the public and private sectors is the fund structure of public organizations, and the treatment of a water utility as a fund, divided into a set of accounts. Funds are self-balancing sets of accounts, set up to catch, hold, and account for earmarked revenues. There may be transfers between funds, for purposes that need to be specified and permitted by law.

A governmental water utility should be accounted for as a separate enterprise fund. GASB states that the purpose of an enterprise fund is

> to account for operations that are financed and operated in a manner similar to private business enterprises—(a) where the intent of the governing body is that the costs (expenses, including depreciation of providing goods or services) to the general public on a continuing basis be financed or recovered primarily through user charges; or (b) where the governing body has determined that periodic determination of revenues earned, expenses incurred, and or net income is appropriate for capital maintenance, public policy, management control, accountability or other purposes.

Because publicly owned water utilities are treated as separate enterprise funds, transfers into and out of the fund need to be carefully recorded and, ideally, explained.

Interfund Transactions

Publicly owned enterprises are part of local governments and related in a variety of ways to that government and to other funds. At the same time, they are expected to be self-funding, to cover their own costs, or nearly all their costs, from revenues from sale of water. As a result, water utilities need to pay attention to transfers into and out of the water fund.

The purchasing office for a city or county may take advantage of economies of scale and purchase vehicles and/or commodities for the water department. The city or county finance office may provide billing services for water and wastewater, and may provide snow plowing for the utility in the snow belt. A city may borrow money for the water department, because it can borrow less expensively than the water utility.

The water utility needs to not only pay for the goods and services it buys through the centralized purchasing office, but should also pay for the overhead, a prorated portion of the costs of employing billing clerks, or purchasing agents.

As the water fund pays for such services or repays debt, there would be a transfer out from the water fund to the general fund. On the one hand, some cities require utilities to pay a fee to the general fund in lieu of taxes, as if they were a privately owned company. This, too, will result in a transfer out of the water fund. On the other hand, the water fund may perform services for other city or county departments, such as providing water for the Fire Department or Public Works. (That water may show up in the difference between water produced and water metered and billed.) The general government may subsidize the water fund, for whatever reason, so that water rates do not reflect the full costs of production. The result would be a transfer into the water fund.

With regard to all of these interfund relationships, it is most important to recognize a strict adherence to individual fund entities; therefore, the system of accounts must be designed to record the interfund transactions resulting from the relationships between municipal funds.

Restricted Assets

Though both private and publicly owned utilities may have restricted assets, governmental water utilities are likely to have more restrictions. To meet these restrictions, money is segregated into special accounts for stated purposes, such as for bond repayment, for equipment replacement, and for reserve accounts. Customer deposits may also be placed in a restricted account. These are not funds, technically speaking, as they do not have their own revenue sources; they are not self-balancing. They are technically restricted asset accounts, but they are often called "restricted funds."

To meet the requirements imposed by the restrictions, the appropriate liquid assets are segregated within the utility enterprise fund. The segregated assets may include assets restricted for debt service (for both general obligation bonds and revenue bonds), assets restricted for replacement of utility plant, and assets derived from customer deposits. Although the restricted assets bear some resemblance to funds, they are offset by corresponding liabilities or restrictions of retained earnings. Since restricted assets are not completely independent self-balancing entities, they are not funds, as that term is defined in government accounting. Although these segregated assets are commonly referred to as "funds" (for example "sinking funds" and "construction funds"), GASB has recommended that, in order to avoid confusion, the portions of a water utility's assets restricted for a particular purpose be referred to as "restricted asset accounts."

The recommended system of accounts differentiates between operating reserves and the restriction of retained earnings (called "appropriated retained earnings"). Additions to operating reserve accounts are made by charges to operating expenses; the reserve accounts represent provisions for estimated liabilities or contingent losses. By contrast, appropriations of retained earnings arise directly from charges to the unappropriated retained earnings.

The operating reserves category includes accounts called "property insurance reserve" (261), "injuries and damages reserve" (262), "pensions and benefits reserve" (263), and "miscellaneous operating reserves" (265). The appropriated retained earnings (215) account includes restrictions of retained earnings for bond debt service, constructions, replacement, and similar purposes. Restricted assets are discussed in detail in chapter 15. Operating reserves and appropriations of retained earnings are discussed in chapter 17.

Capital Recovery Fees

Publicly owned water utilities sometimes are required by state or local laws to charge fees for the cost of expansion of the system to new users. Such fees help the utility cover its own capital costs as it expands. These fees are sometimes called *capital recovery fees*, or *impact fees*. When such fees are charged, the revenue from them and the expenditures made to extend the service should be carefully accounted for, because the fees are supposed to be proportional to the costs actually generated by the development. In reality, fees may be averages of costs to extend or expand water services rather than actual costs, but in order to stand up in court if the fees are challenged, the utility must be able to show "nexus," that is, the connection between the costs generated by the development and the fee charged.

Organizing the Office

The systems and procedures of utility accounting have been summarized in this chapter, but to make any of this work requires trained personnel. The personnel of an accounting division or department usually include the following types of staff and associated training:

- Professional staff have a university degree in accounting and relevant experience for the position.
- Paraprofessional staff usually have a combination of some formal studies and experience enabling them to perform certain tasks with minimum supervision.
- Clerical staff usually have little formal studies but have been trained in the procedures of the function. This group usually requires more supervision.

The systems available to an accounting division or department are very important as these are the tools accountants work with to process the information received. Accounting and finance systems were among the first to be transferred to computerized environments at the beginning of the age of computers. The first programs were quite simple, compiling only the basic data for generation of ledgers and transaction reports. Today, however, the most sophisticated packages are fully integrated systems, including everything from fleet management to project tracking. Accounting staff must at the least be familiar with data entry systems, some of which may be automated, such as computerized meter reading. Professional staff also need to be familiar with the computerized programs they use to maintain data and generate reports and what such programs can and cannot do. The basics of an accounting system should integrate the data flow from one function to the next with minimum duplication of data files or data entry. Whether computerized or not, the system tracks the same basic data.

Chapter 6

Reporting of Accounting Information

Criteria for Good Reports

Accounting reports are the end product of the accounting cycle. The reports convey information about the financial condition and results of operations of the water utility to managers, creditors, regulatory agencies, customers, investors, developers, public interest groups, and the news media. Though the reports may be tailored to one or another user, five principles of reporting should be adhered to across the board: accuracy, materiality, consistency, timely information, and accessibility.

First, the financial and managerial information presented in each report should be accurate. Nothing major should be omitted; the calculations should be done properly and checked. Transactions should be recorded in the appropriate accounts, production and costs attributed to the organizational units that generated them. An accounting report that is not accurate may be worse than useless; it may be harmful, or even illegal, if distorts information given to a regulatory agency or to potential lenders or investors. When it comes to performance measurement, however, since performance can be difficult to measure, the advice is generally to measure the right thing approximately, or as best you can, rather than the wrong thing exactly.

The second criterion for good accounting reports is materiality. *Materiality* means focusing on what is important, either in terms of the amount of money involved or the possible consequences. Good reporting should not distract the reader with minor or technical accounting issues or treat them in the same way as more important issues that will form the basis for key decisions or that respond to authoritative requests for information. The need to pay attention to the big issues should be a consideration in the development of any system of accounting and reporting.

The third criterion for good reports is to provide consistent information. The principle of consistency requires like treatment of like transactions from one accounting period to the next. Financial information presented on a consistent basis fosters meaningful financial analyses. Changes in accounting principles or estimates may result in the need to restate or reclassify prior-year data in order to promote the consistency principle. Similarly, if you measure performance differently from quarter to quarter, managerial information will be uninterpretable. If the analysis involves discount rates, the same discount rates should be used throughout; if information is given in real dollars, corrected for inflation, then that analysis should be consistently used throughout the report. Switching between real and nominal dollars for different parts of an analysis is likely to be confusing to readers, unless there is a very good and explicitly discussed reason for doing so.

Fourth, accounting reports must be timely. For any information to be useful in the decision-making process, it must be provided in a relevant time frame. In order to report information by the time it is needed or required, the information demands of the intended users must be anticipated and a system designed to provide the needed information routinely. The design of the information system should also facilitate the presentation of data needed occasionally but not routinely. No matter how insightful a report is or how well done, it if is late, it is useless.

Fifth and finally, the format and content of financial and managerial reports must consider the requirements of the readers and users of the report. They need to communicate. Data should be arranged in a logical and readily understandable manner. Accessibility is vital. The wording of the report should be concise and convey the precise meaning intended. Technical terms should be kept to a minimum. If the readers are not trained in accounting, explanations of technical terms can be included in a glossary. Summaries that address the key issues of the targeted users can be placed at the beginning. Tables and graphics must match the text and provide evidence for conclusions. As much or as little detail should be shown as the intended reader is expected to need.

Reports for Different Users and Purposes

Accounting reports fall into two broad categories: external and internal reporting. External reports are usually financial in nature and focus on the financial condition of the enterprise, the revenues, expenditures, retained earnings, amount of debt outstanding, the size of contingency funds, and trends in key indicators. Internal reports for management usually focus more narrowly on performance data, such as the number of gallons of water produced and sold, cost per gallon processed, the number of leaks in the system, staffing levels, implications of collective bargaining, changes in the costs of electricity, and breakdowns in equipment. Managers need information for decision making, such as whether to expand a plant and when, decisions that may require information from outside, not just from the water utility.

Management Accounting and Reporting

The central idea of management accounting is that managers should be provided with sufficient timely information so that the water utility can be managed efficiently and effectively. If this central idea is accepted, then the following corollary ideas follow:

- The focus of management accounting is on the future. The past is of importance only as a guide to the future.

- All important information relevant to a decision should be provided at the time it is needed. Implicit in this statement are the ideas that:
    1. Information as to legal, political, and social conditions, as well as economic and business conditions (and expected changes in these conditions), is often more important than internal information. Much of the external information must be derived from professional judgment guided by experience. Therefore, although the expected effects of external forces often must be expressed numerically, the reliability of the numbers may vary.
    2. Internal information relating to employee attitudes and behavior must be considered, as well as accounting and statistical information related to the production of water, distribution of water, and other activities' outcomes of the water utility. Defensiveness about mistakes, rudeness to customers, and distortion of performance measures for fear of reprimand or punishment are all related to the performance of the organization. Willingness to innovate or experiment with new equipment or techniques, excitement or resentment of new technology, and need for training are issues managers need to understand and address.
    3. No more time or money should be spent in obtaining an item of information than the item is expected to be worth. Estimates may be adequate for many managerial purposes.
    4. All information systems should be integrated. It is inefficient for accountants, statisticians, economists, and operating executives to maintain overlapping systems for deriving information. Some data should be routinely collected and some sampled at intervals as part of a plan to serve individual users and get them the reports they need when they need them.

For accounting to fulfill its role in assisting management planning and controlling, a number of basic concepts of management accounting should be employed in the design of a water utility accounting system. Table 6-1 presents a concise statement of the basic concepts of management accounting. These concepts are described in the following paragraphs.

Collection of Cost and Revenue Data by Responsibility Center

The first basic concept of management accounting is that costs and revenues must be measured routinely for each responsibility segment of the water utility. Financial data are collected and reported for the entire enterprise, but managerial information has to drill down to the units actually doing each part of the work. Upper level management needs to know how each unit is performing, how much work it is doing, and whether it is reaching its goals. A failure in any unit can compromise the entire operation. Pumping may be fine, but if treatment is off, say too much or too little chlorine or a failure of rust dispersant, water may smell strange, look odd, or be impure. Pure water may be produced, but if there is leakage in the pipes or a major failure in metering, water

Table 6-1. The basic concepts of management accounting for water utilities

Basic Concepts	Example of Techniques Used to Apply the Basic Concepts
1. Historical costs and revenues should be collected routinely for each responsibility center.	Responsibility accounting.
2. Historical cost and revenue data for each responsibility center must be related to the factors that caused the behavior of past data, so that the manager of each center may prepare realistic future plans.	Budgets or profit plans that consider all important items of cost and revenue.
3. Standards of performance are established for each activity and communicated to the managers so that the managers know how they are being judged. Formal cost standards are established when the expected benefit exceeds the cost of establishing the formal standards.	Standard or estimated costs, return on investment, or other measure of performance.
4. Alternatives to present operations are evaluated before management makes a decision or takes action.	Return on investment.
5. Actual performance is compared with budgeted or standard performance, and variances are investigated to determine necessary management control action.	Periodic reports flowing from responsibility accounting and work measurement programs, and special reports.
6. Adequate internal control is established over resources, including physical control, insurance coverage, accounting, and statistical controls.	Control accounts and subsidiary ledgers, perpetual inventory systems, locked storerooms, night watchman, etc.
7. Internal and external audits are used to make sure that management plans and policies are being followed and that the internal control system and information system are functioning as they are supposed to.	Generally accepted auditing standards and procedures.

produced may not be metered and billed. Upper level managers need to know how a major meter replacement and modernization program is progressing.

Lower level managers can only be responsible for the units they supervise and so must have relevant information on their own units. Overtime may not be increasing overall in the utility but might increase rapidly in the unit that repairs main breaks because of the age of the water pipes. Such a situation requires managerial attention.

Specific goals for the upcoming year may require units within the organization to undertake specific tasks, such as replacing aging equipment or connecting new subdivisions to the water utility. These goals may influence costs, staffing levels, and performance measures of the affected work units.

Relating Causes and Costs

In order to aid water utility managers in preparing realistic plans, the management accounting or management information system must provide information that relates past cost, revenue, and performance data to all conditions that caused the past data to behave as it did. Such conditions are both external to the water utility and each responsibility segment, as well as internal to each responsibility segment. Thus if water pumping, sales, and revenue go up during a drought as people water their lawns and gardens, information collection and reporting need to include the cause as well as the effect. There is a major difference when projecting future water demands whether the increase in water use was related to weather or to an increase in population or the startup of a new high-water-using industrial plant.

Effective planning by water utility management, however, does not simply involve the forecasting of causative conditions and the subsequent computation of cost and revenue figures on the same basis as in past periods. Effective planning by water utility management involves a determination of whether the relationships that existed in the past are likely to continue to exist in the period for which plans are being prepared. For example, the cost of electricity might in the past been a major driver of expenditures, but with new low energy equipment, the relative contribution of energy costs to overall operating costs might be much less than in the past. New techniques for repairing broken mains may require more training or fewer staff or different equipment, thus changing the dynamics of cost projections. It is possible that some steps in water production and delivery might be eliminated and new ones added. Thus, in projecting future costs, the first question to be asked by each water utility manager in charge of a responsibility segment should be, have the cost drivers changed? And second, should we consider a change that might influence the future costs or outcome measures?

Performance Measurement

Each responsibility unit should have some standards that measure key elements of its performance, and the organization as a whole should have summary measures of accomplishment. For the organization as a whole, the measure is likely to refer to standards of purity that are routinely measured and recorded, such as particulate matter, grains of hardness, color and smell, bacterial load, radium, and the like. The cost per 1,000 gal of producing water of a given quality is an overall measure of performance of the utility. The entire organization contributes to this measure of performance. Individual units may have more narrowly targeted goals, such as respond to 80 percent of complaints within 24 hours or respond to 80 percent of calls for water connections within 1 week. Some targets may involve quantity, such as targets for the number of times equipment is tested or the number of times maintenance is performed. Others measure quality and outcomes. It is important to measure only key indicators, those that are most important and that employees agree are important standards. It is critical that managers only be held accountable for measures over which they have control; if the number of gallons sold depends not only on leakage rates, over which managers exert some control, but also on the weather and population increases or decreases, managers should not be held accountable for the number of gallons sold. Rather they should be held accountable for reaching given targets for reducing leakage.

Data should be collected regularly on these performance measures, and at intervals, reports should be compiled showing the performance targets and the actual results. These reports can be very useful in locating trouble spots, when failures to reach targets suggest something was wrong. Possibilities include: costs that were misestimated, so that budget was inadequate to carry out the number of tasks assigned; or the tasks were completed in a different way because of lack of equipment to do it right, or inability to modernize the operation, or inadequate training of staff, who did not know how to use the equipment so that projected costs savings did not occur. Suppliers could have been late or have provided the wrong materials. Floods or other storm conditions may have affected operating conditions and caused equipment failures. Each missed target suggests a different strategy for the future.

Evaluation of Alternatives

The process of planning the future operations of each activity or responsibility segment of a water utility may disclose a number of alternatives to present operations. A system needs to be established so that the alternatives are objectively and impartially evaluated before management commits the resources of the utility.

Managers have the responsibility to consider alternatives that may be more cost-effective than present practice, and costing out these alternatives is a function of the finance office. Much of the information used in projecting future costs, savings, and benefits is derived from accounting data. For example, a new water tower may cost more initially than a well alone but may save on electricity because water can be pumped and stored during the night when electricity rates are lower. Cost comparisons between the well alone and the well and tower together require an estimate of the capital costs of construction and maintenance of the tower and the anticipated savings in electricity, and comparing those costs to the costs of a simple well. Such an analysis relies on data maintained by the accounting system, tweaked and updated to include current prices and prices likely to be in place for the foreseeable future.

Many managerial decisions revolve around whether particular jobs should be performed in house or be contracted out. Such decisions may depend on the skills and availability of staff but also depend on costs. If the task has been performed in house in the past, historical data should reveal how much it costs to provide the service in house; if not, accounting data can build estimates of how much the service would cost in house, by adding up the costs of labor, equipment, and materials. Decisions about whether to contract out or perform particular services in house depend on comparing estimates of the cost of provision of that service in house with the costs that contractors bid.

Control of Resources

If the operations and changes in the operations have been planned and controlled as outlined previously, then it would appear that management has done its best to preserve and enhance the capability of the water utility to make a profit or to be self-sustaining, to furnish quality water service, and to attain any other goals set for it. Clearly, preservation of the capability of a water utility to achieve the goals set for it by its owners or their representatives requires more than merely safeguarding the resources used by the water utility. However, the resources must be safeguarded or there is considerable possibility that they will not remain available to the utility.

The sixth concept of management accounting for water utilities is that, in order to safeguard the resources of the water utility, the management control system must provide for internal control in the broadest sense: accounting control, physical control, adequate and appropriate insurance coverage, and statistical control. Thus managers may require equipment inventories to be updated, equipment to be inspected periodically, and reports made on the condition of equipment. They may require an annual review of insurance costs and losses experienced, with a suggestions on alternatives and costs.

Evaluation

The evaluation process provides critical information for managers. This information may be provided by performance and compliance audits, performed internally or externally.

Compliance audits ask, to what extent has the utility complied with laws, regulations, and mandates? Where has it failed or almost failed, or where is it likely to fall down in the future? How important is it to comply with this rule or ordinance or law, what are the consequences of ignoring it, or delaying compliance? How long would it take to bring the utility into compliance if it is found, for example, that there is too much radium in the water? What alternatives are available for solution of this problem, and how much would they cost? Managers would then have to plan where the money should come from.

Water utilities have to comply not only with regulations specifying the level of cleanliness of the water they produce and sell, but also with contract provisions, with regulators or state laws describing accounting standards, and in the case of public-sector utilities with ordinances and with state laws on bidding procedures.

Performance audits ask how well the organization is performing its assigned tasks. Have capital projects been completed on time and under or at budget? Have goals for plant modernization or expansion or reducing environmental impact been met? Has the utility responded quickly to requests for the return of deposits and generally served the public with courtesy and effectiveness? The system for monitoring performance should itself be periodically monitored. Are the right measures being used so that effort is directed to accomplishing the key targets of the organization, not drained from one purpose so that managers will look good on some other measure? Are the data being reported honestly and accurately? When performance measurement is linked to the evaluation of staff and to merit bonuses, there is great temptation to fudge the data. Similarly, if reporting is onerous, if the data appear to be unused in decision making, or if employees do not see the utility of the data, they may fail to collect it or may make it up, while they concentrate on what they consider to be more important tasks of production. An evaluation system cannot be better than the data it is based on, so periodic review of the quality of this data is necessary.

Internal audits must also be made to ensure that plans and policies of the owners and managers of the water utility are being followed and that necessary changes and exceptions are brought to the attention of appropriate managers. A management accounting system for a water utility should have periodic independent or external audits to ensure that the system is functioning as it is supposed to.

Summary of Management Accounting

A management accounting system for a water utility should provide utility management with sufficient timely information to facilitate planning and control. This information should be in the form of easily readable reports. Such reports are often projections of alternatives, based on existing and historical data, combined with expert opinion on what is likely to happen next. The costing out of alternatives gives managers a way of continually evaluating current practices and improving cost-effectiveness. Management reports also deal with the gaps between planned objectives and actual accomplishments for each functional unit in the utility. Such reports help motivate managers to achieve the targets set and demonstrate the trouble spots where managers may need to pay more attention, find out what is going amiss, and work out solutions. These solutions may require reallocation of resources. Management reports also focus on evaluation, how well is the utility doing compared to the plans and goals it has to achieve, and how well is it complying with laws and regulations. Such evaluations help managers stay on track and alert them to when new plans are needed to get back on track when for whatever reasons, plans have not worked as expected.

Accounting Reporting for Financial Condition and Control

Financial trends and ratios are key indicators of a utility's financial strength, stability, credit worthiness, and growth capabilities. Financial-trend and ratio analysis provides valuable information for management in planning for the future growth and development of the enterprise. Because such ratios are widely used, they enable managers to compare their own utility with industrywide averages or standards. Deviations from the industry trends may but do not always indicate problems, as such deviations may result from a unique feature or element of the individual utility's operations or a temporary condition brought on by unforeseen occurrences.

Indicators of Financial Condition

Following are some commonly used indicators assessing the financial condition of a water utility. They can be computed from the balance sheet.

- *Working capital* is computed by subtracting current liabilities from current assets. This is a key indicator of a utility's ability to meet its short-term obligations from available business-cycle resources.
- *Current ratio* is computed by dividing current assets by current liabilities. The current ratio is a measure of short-term solvency because it indicates the extent to which the claims of short-term creditors are covered by assets that

are expected to be converted to cash in a period roughly corresponding to the maturity of the claims.

- *Net funded debt* is computed by dividing total assets less balances in debt-service funds and reserve funds by net debt.

Following are a selected number of trends and ratios commonly used in assessing the operating or income statement components of a water utility:

- *Net revenues* are gross revenues minus operation and maintenance expenses. This amount represents the amount of funds generated by the utility that are available to support debt service and also fund capital and construction requirements.
- *Operating ratio* is computed by dividing maintenance and operation expense by operating revenues.
- *Net take down* is computed by dividing net revenues by interest requirements for the year.
- *Debt-service coverage* is computed by dividing net revenues by principal and interest requirements for the year. This ratio may also be based on average annual or maximum annual debt-service requirements stipulated by debt-maturity schedules. The selection of average annual or maximum annual debt-service requirements is normally specified in the governing bond order.
- *Debt-service safety margin* is computed by dividing net revenues less principal and interest requirements for the year by gross revenues.

Managers can select a set of measures and use them to examine trends over time. Ideally they will be working with a set of financial policies that will include goals for the key indicators. Managers work to assure that those goals are met on a continuing basis. Trends that are in a negative direction suggest that managers need to examine what the reasons are, and if necessary, take appropriate steps to reverse direction.

Guidelines for Financial Accounting Reports

Financial indicators such as those listed above are not only used by managers to assure the fiscal health of the utility; they are also used by outsiders, such as regulators, bond-rating agencies, and the investing public, along with the basic financial reports that underlie them. As a result, guidelines for reporting financial information have been developed in order to promote consistency and comparability of data disclosed. All utilities should have ready access to these guidelines in order to assure that complete, consistent, and comparable financial reports are produced.

However, implementing a uniform industrywide standard for reporting is problematic because the water industry has some utilities that are investor owned and some that are government owned. GASB is empowered to review and promulgate accounting and reporting standards for state and local government entities. FASB is empowered to promulgate accounting standards for entities other than state and local government organizations. To the extent that their reporting standards differ, the desire for an industrywide standard may not be met.

Guidance on resolving this jurisdictional conflict is addressed in *The Structure for Establishing Governmental Accounting Standards: Report of the Committee to Review Structure for Governmental Accounting Standards*, issued by the Financial Accounting Foundation and Governmental Accounting Standards Advisory Council and dated Jan. 26, 1989. The general principle is that utilities should keep on doing things the way they have been doing if those standards have been working for them. Most of the industry has operated under FASB rules and therefore should continue to do so. For governmentally owned utilities, their special needs for reporting may be added to the basic model as GASB sees fit.

In short, the public interest would be best served by having the FASB responsible for the standards applicable to the separately issued general purpose financial statements of water utilities, and the GASB responsible to promulgate, only for those entities that are governmental, requirements to present such additional information as the GASB determines is necessary in the interest of public accountability.

Standards developed by GASB and FASB are issued as "statements" of the respective bodies and are numbered consecutively as issued. The format of the statements typically consists of:

1. Introduction and background information
2. Standard of accounting and reporting, as it relates specifically to the situation being addressed
3. Effective date
4. Appendices, often including examples of disclosure and basis of conclusions (majority and minority opinions) reached regarding the standard promulgated

Both GASB and FASB offer subscription services, or statements can be ordered separately. Statements are also published in monthly editions of the *Journal of Accountancy*.

Part 3

Financial Reports

This page intentionally blank.

Chapter 7

Budgeting

Budgets are plans to accomplish a certain amount of work for an estimated cost. For public utilities, once budgets are adopted by the governing body, they become legally enforceable constraints on where (or on what) and how much the utility can spend. They include all the resources necessary to reach the annual goals of the organization, including personnel, supplies, equipment, and contractual services. However, like most plans, they can be derailed by unforeseen circumstances. Employees get sick or retire, equipment breaks down, bonds may not be issued timely, rate and other revenues may fall short due to weather or rate increases. As a result, managers need to keep a close watch on what is actually being spent from month to month or quarter to quarter, and on a yearly basis. Comparisons between budget estimates and actuals through the year give managers an early warning of problems, allowing adjustments to be made in a timely fashion. Budget reports compare actual results against the plan detailed in the budget.*

Information Content

Budgets vary in terms of the emphasis, organization, and inclusiveness of the information provided. The three major categories are traditional budgets, program budgets, and performance budgets. Each category is described in more detail in the sections to follow.

Traditional Budgets

The traditional budget, and related budget reports, follows the administrative structure of the organization, that is, a sum of money is allocated to each unit of the organization. A manager is in charge of the unit and implements the budget in that unit. The budget is not usually a lump sum but broken down by categories—so much for personnel, so much for equipment, so much for supplies, so much for training, so much for transportation. Managers are responsible for seeing not only that the budget is properly

* Utility revenues require estimation as well and are often included within the budget umbrella. However, revenues are beyond the scope of this discussion.

and efficiently spent to achieve the organization's goals but also that spending does not exceed the total in any one of these categories.

For management and control purposes, these categories are often broken down further. For example, personnel costs might have separate totals for regular wages, overtime, part-time or temporary employees, health insurance, workers' compensation, and for pension contribution. How detailed these breakdowns need to be depends on the use to which they will be put. Whatever the desired level of detail, the accounting system should normally match the budget so that actual spending on each of these items can be tracked in real time and compared to the budget. Because each of these items appears on a separate line in the budget, this format of budget presentation has been called a *line-item budget.*

Since traditional budgets follow the structure of the organization, they can be applied to every level of the organization. Starting from the organization as a whole, they can go down to the smallest unit of the organization that is considered important enough to have its own budget.

Program Budgets

Traditional budgets tell you how much you are spending and on what, but do not tell you how efficiently or effectively you are working. To meet this need, more modern budgets often include a program and performance orientation. Program budgets may be merged with older style line-item budgets or layered on top of them or may be substituted for them. Instead of allocating money to an administrative unit, program budgets allocate money to functions and programs. One department or administrative unit may have several programs that it is responsible for, and several different administrative units may share responsibility for any given program. Programs thus do not necessarily follow organizational lines.

This perspective requires a different way of looking at the organization. What programs does a typical water utility have? Programs might, for example, cover pumping or water production, processing or purifying, testing and compliance, delivery, meter reading and billing, among others. One can think of administration as a program, though managers may in fact work for several programs, in which case their time should be allocated out among those programs. In addition to these basic programs, there may be special ones, such as a meter modernization program, or a system expansion or improvement program. As long as managers can define the purpose of the program and attribute costs to its accomplishment, the program can be included in the budget.

In the budget, each program lists its goals and objectives, how much work or how much output it plans to achieve for the dollars in the budget. Program budgets are designed to answer the question of how much work or how much output is expected to be achieved for the dollars allocated to the program. Program budgets often show details on the various cost categories of the program such as personnel, equipment, energy, supplies, and so forth. Program budget reports are then designed to show actual amounts spent by cost category and program accomplishments to date compared to budgeted costs and goals. This information is useful for managers of the separate programs, and can be combined by upper level managers to answer questions such as how much did it cost us to produce 1,000 gal of water at USEPA standards of cleanliness compared to what we thought it would cost, how close were we, and if we were off substantially, what was the reason?

Performance Budgets

Some of the measures in performance budgets are workload or quantity measures. How many gallons are we treating, how many hours does it take to do that job, how long does it take to repair a water main. These are important and useful measures of "throughput," that is, process, what we do; and they help establish costs, but they do not address how well the work is done and hence cannot be used to measure effectiveness. To do that requires measures of outcomes, how we know we are doing a good job. These measures may be more elusive and take some time to develop. They need to be measures that employees as well as supervisors agree on. Some will be obvious, such as the measures of water cleanliness and compliance with regulations; some may deal with customer feedback or the speed of responding to complaints or requests for service. Water leakage may be another indicator of system quality. Breakdowns in equipment may suggest inadequate maintenance; downtime for equipment or rolling stock may also suggest inadequate maintenance, lack of repair parts, or poor inventory.

There should be quality measures for each major program in the utility, and goals should be set for each one, and costs estimated for reaching those goals. Within the resources allocated, what is a reasonable goal for us to work toward? Budget reports can then report how well managers are doing in making progress toward those quality goals. It is also possible then to examine cost data holding constant for quality. For the same level of quality, are our costs going up or down? Did a budget cut in one area result in a decline in quality in another?

Frequency of Reporting

Budget reports are prepared annually at a minimum. Annual preparation generally coincides with Comprehensive Annual Financial Report (CAFR) requirements and minimum statutory reporting requirements. Annual reports summarize the past year's activities and are of greatest value to elected officials, investors, and citizens who are interested in a recap of recent past performance including evaluating annual trends. Unfortunately, the publication of annual budget reports can often take up to six months past year-end closing because of end-of-year accounting activities including an outside third party audit, and as such are not sufficiently timely to enhance ongoing internal utility management decision making. However, budget reports can also be prepared on an interim basis, typically monthly or quarterly for the benefit of internal management decision making. Since interim reporting is not typically required by statute, it must add economic value to be rationally pursued. To say it another way, the perceived value of interim budget reporting should easily exceed its cost.

Table 7-1. Example budget report by account detail

Portland, Oregon—Water Bureau **FY 20XX–XX** **Bureau Budget Report by Account Detail**		**Accounting Period: 8** **Period End: 02/06/20XX** **% Year to date: 60.5%** **% Year remaining: 39.5%**	
Account—Description	**Annual Revised Budget**	**Year-to-Date Expenditures**	**Percentage of Budget Expended**
511000 Full-Time Employees	$35,591,961	$21,372,675	60.0%
512000 Part-Time/Limited Term	$813,407	$672,177	82.6%
514000 Overtime	$1,163,000	$734,464	63.2%
515000 Premium Pay	$142,000	$152,535	107.4%
517000 Benefits	$14,611,167	$8,953,301	61.3%
Total Personal Services	$52,321,535	$31,885,152	60.9%
521000 Professional Services	$9,568,980	$1,877,435	19.6%
522000 Utilities	$3,351,500	$1,632,957	48.7%
523000 Equipment Rental	$67,000	$102,275	152.6%
524000 Repair & Maintenance	$844,501	$415,058	49.1%
529000 Miscellaneous Services	$1,260,500	$465,098	36.9%
532000 Operating Supplies	$6,907,242	$4,670,119	67.6%
535000 Clothing	$113,100	$78,968	69.8%
539000 Other Commodities	$23,800	$14,406	60.5%
541000 Education	$546,048	$201,157	36.8%
542000 Local Travel	$11,100	$3,441	31.0%
543000 Out-of-Town Travel	$174,075	$78,261	45.0%
544000 Space Rental	$18,400	$14,098	76.6%
545000 Interest	$0	$0	0.0%
548000 Facilities Operating Lease	$50,000	$25,784	51.6%
549000 Miscellaneous*	$2,709,969	$1,998,571	73.7%

(Continued next page)

General Budget Development

Budgets can be developed for any level of planned use of resources (spending) throughout a utility but should only be developed at that level where they are useful in making management decisions or required by statute. Generally, formal statutory budget requirements are at a fairly high organization level that rarely includes specifically defined accomplishments.

The formal budget development process, structure, and document for a public utility are often set out by local budget law at a fairly summarized level. In those cases where a utility is part of a larger public entity, the utility may only be required to "fit in" with the general government structure. As noted previously, this highly summarized level of budget reporting and development provides some general knowledge

Table 7-1. Example budget report by account detail (continued)

Portland, Oregon—Water Bureau			**Accounting Period: 8**
FY 20XX–XX			**Period End: 02/06/20XX**
			% Year to date: 60.5%
Bureau Budget Report by Account Detail			**% Year remaining: 39.5%**
Account—Description	**Annual Revised Budget**	**Year-to-Date Expenditures**	**Percentage of Budget Expended**
Total External Materials & Svcs	$25,646,215	$11,577,628	45.1%
551000 Fleet Services	$2,614,336	$1,712,086	65.5%
552000 Printing/Distribution	$1,329,457	$615,364	46.3%
553000 Facilities Services	$2,319,921	$1,643,636	70.8%
555000 Technology Services	$5,810,737	$3,471,433	59.7%
556000 Insurance	$1,152,241	$672,140	58.3%
559000 Other Inter Fund Services	$8,829,860	$3,635,562	41.2%
573000 Major Equipment Cash Transfer	$17,000	$17,000	100.0%
576000 Minor Equipment Cash Transfer	$0	$0	0.0%
Total Internal Materials & Svcs	$22,073,552	$11,767,221	53.3%
Total Materials & Services	$47,719,767	$23,344,849	48.9%
561000 Land	$250,000	$8,950	3.6%
562000 Buildings	$0	$137,386	0.0%
563000 Improvements	$0	$18,450	0.0%
564000 Capital Equipment	$5,695,000	$1,656,924	29.1%
567000 Infrastructure	$19,624,653	$4,053,434	20.7%
Total Capital Outlay	$25,569,653	$5,875,144	23.0%
Water Bureau Total	$125,610,955	$61,105,145	48.6%

*Account 549000 (Misc) includes budget and expenditures of $1,720,000 for the water growth impact reimbursement

Source: Portland Water Bureau

to the public and elected officials, but is not in sufficient detail for utility managers to gain insight and enhance their day-to-day internal management decision making. Where utilities operate as a single-purpose entity, the formal budget may be framed by regulatory agency requirements or investors' needs. In either case, managers may need more information from the budget than is formally required by external actors. They are free to add as much additional information as they require for decision making and monitoring. Often and strongly recommended, the summarized formal budget is initially developed in much greater detail using more specifically defined and distinct cost centers that can be accountable to a single organization or program manager or both. At this detailed but manageable level, budget reporting can be a useful tool in meeting the objectives of the utility and provides reliable information for ongoing decision making (Table 7-1).

Elements of Budget Reporting

Budget reporting requires not only a budget plan that is sufficiently detailed and provides the appropriate goals for the organization but also ongoing data on what is actually happening on those measures. Meaningful actual results require care and effort to ensure that the relevant data are accurate, sufficient, consistent, and timely. Failing any of these criteria can render budget reporting useless at best and misleading at worst. Managers need to know how the data are prepared, what is included or excluded, and whether the reports are exact counts that are verifiable.

Organizational Reporting

As noted previously, a traditional budget is organized by work unit and line-item. The account/line-item refers to the cost inputs or resources required to accomplish the utility's objectives. These cost types are usually broken into personal services, materials purchases, external and internal services, and capital investments. The manager of each work group–based cost center is responsible for budget implementation and accountability reporting. The accounting system should match the organizational structure on the one hand and the line-items on the other, so that information on line-items by work unit can be provided at whatever intervals seem most useful (Table 7-2).

Organizational reporting is of greatest value for determining how much of a budget has been expended and is especially useful in determining if sufficient monies are budgeted to carry out the mission of any organizational work unit. If the rate of spending is too high compared to last year and there are no obvious reasons (such as a flood or lightning strike that takes out equipment), managers need to figure out what is going on and take appropriate action.

For many overhead/support organizations and operational work groups, there is a one-to-one relationship between the organization/work group and its purpose. In this simple case, performance measures can be added to the line-item budget for each work unit. If one work unit has two or more programs entirely under its control, performance measures can be developed for each of them. Programs that are shared between units, however, cannot be easily measured, as one unit may not have responsibility for the outcomes and should not be held accountable for outcomes it does not control. Organizational budget reporting may include both the Operating and the Capital Improvement (CIP) budget elements, but more typically, large capital projects such as plant expansions are budgeted and reported at the level of the organization as a whole rather than at the work unit level. Only capital items that are limited to the use of a particular work group would normally appear as a line-item in that work unit's budget, such as backhoes or front-end loaders for the unit responsible for repairing main breaks, or pumps for the water production unit.

Accounting for large projects is done separately from routine recording of operating expenditures, as it may involve hours of use on particular equipment or vehicles, labor from several different work groups, and outside contractors. Each major project will typically have its own budget, including personnel costs, contractual services, equipment costs, and materials. It can be monitored at regular intervals, in the same

Table 7-2. Example budget report by district

Portland, Oregon—Water Bureau
FY 20XX–XX

Accounting Period: 8
Period End: 02/06/20XX

Organization (Org) 40 - North District Budget Report by Account

% Year to date: 60.5%
% Year remaining: 39.5%

		Org 40 - North District				
Account Detail	**Account Description**	**Annual Revised Budget**	**Year-to-Date Expenditures**	**% of Budget Expended**	**Plan FTE (Full-Time Equivalent)**	**Actual FTE (Full-Time Equivalent)**
511000	Full-Time	$848,532	$543,260	64%	17.9	18.0
514000	Overtime	$82,700	$71,425	86%	0.9	1.5
515000	Premium Pay	$0	$14,003	N/A		
517000	Benefits	$427,928	$246,543	58%		
	Total Personal Services	$1,359,160	$875,231	64%		
523000	Equipment Rental	$8,500	$596	7%		
532000	Operating Supplies	$0	$13,455	N/A		
535000	Clothes/Uniforms	$4,200	$2,788	66%		
	Total External Materials and Services	$12,700	$16,839	133%		
551000	Fleet Services	$168,000	$125,435	75%		
555140	Telecomm Services	$1,100	$1,791	163%		
555152	Long Distance	$0	$3	N/A		
555153	Cell Phones	$3,750	$3,441	92%		
	Total Internal Materials and Services	$172,850	$130,670	76%		
	Total Capital Outlay (none)	$0	$0	0%		
ORG 40 - North District TOTAL		$1,544,710	$1,022,740	66%	18.8	19.5

Source: Portland Water Bureau

way as work unit reporting, to make sure that the initial estimates of costs were correct, and to give managers time to fix any problems that emerge by rebudgeting or reassigning staff and equipment to meet budget and time deadlines.

Individual work units involved in carrying out capital projects should receive budgets for their share of the work, and should list the work they are doing and their goals for completion in any performance reporting they do (Table 7-3).

Program Budget Reporting

Program budgeting is either an addition to or an alternative to organizational budgeting. One dimension of budget reporting targets the purpose of programs, activities, and projects.* By adding purpose to the equation, what a work group intends to accomplish can be explicitly budgeted and monitored and tells managers how well (efficiently) work is carried out.

Program budgeting can also be a useful component of the utility's annual cost-of-service study. A program budget with performance measures can tell managers not only what a program costs but also what the program was intended to accomplish compared to what it has in fact accomplished. By focusing on individual programs, the budget report allows managers to monitor key components of the costs utility customers pay.

If several programs span two or more organizational units, it will be difficult to add program elements to a budget structured by organizational units and line-items. The organization may need to go to a full program budget in lieu of an organizational format. Instead of initially being organized by administrative units, the budget is initially organized by programs, which may overlap departments or span two or more units. Within each program, the goals and performance targets are described, as well as the resources needed to reach those targets.

For the purpose of seeing how expensive particular programs are, the components of a program that span two or more organizational units may need to be added together. The problem of who will then administer the budget for that program has two possible solutions. One is to appoint an administrator to oversee the cross-unit program and see that the budget is implemented and performance measures are reported accurately and in a timely way. The second is to move the components of a program so that they are all in the same organizational unit.

The accounting system, which is typically geared to departments rather than programs, may need to be tweaked in order to present the actual data on expenditures by program. For example, if a department manages two programs inside it, a traditional budget may give the summary figures for personnel for the whole department, without regard to the programs. With the addition of a single extra code, however, the accounting system should be able to distinguish between personnel for, say, water pumping and

* Project budgets may reside within an umbrella program, subprogram, or activity and may not have specific budget dollars assigned as they may be immaterial and/or too difficult to estimate individually.

Table 7-3. Example budget report by major account and budget type

Portland, Oregon—Water Bureau | **Accounting Period: 8**
FY 20XX-XX | **Period End: 02/06/20XX**

Bureau Budget Report by Major Account and Budget Type | **% Year to date: 60.5%**
% Year remaining: 39.5%

	Operating Budget			Capital Improvement Budget			Total Budget		
Account Summary	**Annual Revised Budget**	**Year-to-Date Expenditures**	**% of Budget Expended**	**Annual Revised Budget**	**Year-to-Date Expenditures**	**% of Budget Expended**	**Annual Revised Budget**	**Year-to-Date Expenditures**	**% of Budget Expended**
% Year to date: 60.5%									
Personal Services	$38,402,481	$24,550,681	64%	$13,919,054	$7,334,476	53%	$52,321,535	$31,885,158	61%
External Materials and Services	$13,661,757	$6,966,682	51%	$11,984,458	$4,610,958	38%	$25,646,215	$11,577,640	45%
Internal Materials and Services	$16,794,467	$9,169,633	55%	$5,279,085	$2,597,619	49%	$22,073,552	$11,767,253	53%
Total Material and Services	$30,456,224	$16,136,315	53%	$17,263,543	$7,208,577	42%	$47,719,767	$23,344,893	49%
Capital Outlay	$0	$7,350	N/A	$25,569,653	$5,867,794	23%	$25,569,653	$5,875,144	23%
Water Bureau Total	$68,858,705	$40,694,346	59%	$56,752,250	$20,410,847	36%	$125,610,955	$61,105,195	49%

Source: Portland Water Bureau

Table 7-4. Example budget report by subprogram

Portland, Oregon—Water Bureau
FY 20XX-XX
Organization (Org) 40—North District Budget Report by Subprogram

Accounting Period: 8
Period End: 02/06/20XX
% Year to date: 60.5%
% Year remaining: 39.5%

	Expenditures									
Subprogram	**Total Personal Services**	**Total Internal Materials and Services**	**Total External Materials and Services**	**Fleet**	**Total Expenditures**	**Total Annual Budget**	**% of Budget Expended**	**% of Total Expenditures**	**Budgeted Full-Time Equivalent**	**Actual Full-Time Equivalent**
Services—New and Replacement	$304,794	$13,551		$51,599	$369,944	$773,381	48%	36%	8.95	6.99
Mains Repair and Maintenance	$106,410			$15,627	$122,037	$396,349	31%	12%	4.58	2.12
Services—Repair and Maintenance	$100,636			$11,510	$112,146	$172,388	65%	11%	1.82	2.21
General Field Support	$71,126	$3,288	$5,235	$3,321	$82,970	$28,623	290%	8%	1.13	1.84
Reimburseables—Engineering	$54,525			$8,695	$63,220	$0	N/A	6%	0.00	1.22
PDOT Adjustments	$48,490			$6,749	$55,239	$0	N/A	5%	0.00	0.93
Distribution Mains Program	$43,066			$8,112	$51,178	$0	N/A	5%	0.00	0.96
Large Meters Replacement	$21,253			$4,125	$25,378	$0	N/A	2%	0.00	0.47
Organization Development	$19,071			$618	$19,689	$0	N/A	2%	0.00	0.43
BES Adjustments	$15,411			$2,577	$17,988	$0	N/A	2%	0.00	0.31
Hydrants Replacement	$13,716			$1,685	$15,401	$0	N/A	2%	0.00	0.29
Employee Investment	$12,368				$12,368	$46,854	26%	1%	0.62	0.26
Reimburseables—Maintenance and Construction	$10,179			$1,632	$11,811	$85,414	14%	1%	0.93	0.23
All Others (<$10,000 in Expenditures to date)	$54,185			$9,185	$63,370	$41,701	152%	6%	0.77	1.24
Org 40 Total	$875,230	$16,839	$5,235	$125,435	$1,022,739	$1,544,710	66%	100%	18.80	19.50

Source: Portland Water Bureau

personnel for water purification. If the utility goes to the program format completely, the accounting system substitutes programs for departments or organizational administrative units. Those portions of a program attributable to a particular unit should be tagged and easily identifiable, allowing information to be returned by department or unit, and also by program, as needed for different reports.

Regardless of whether a performance component has been added to a traditional line-item budget or has been substituted for the traditional budget (Table 7-4), the program itself is now a distinct budget reporting element for measuring utility performance. The utility's budget reporting programs can be easily summarized and aggregated from the first line program manager up to the total utility budget. The performance measures may be different at each level of the organization, as what the lower-level managers need to know, control, and report may be different from what top managers need to know, control, and report. The targets may be quite different and may occasionally clash. Said another way, is it more important for a utility to meet its ongoing system needs or manage its annual resources? Traditionally, staff have tended to follow their resource/work group manager directives, but utility customers might prefer the program perspective since it targets system and customer needs. One possible resolution is to make program managers responsible for the *effective implementation* of their programs, and resource managers responsible for the *efficient deployment and execution* of resources in support of those programs. Regardless, neither should be ignored, and an honest evaluation of a utility's preference and primary perspective is likely to be a valuable exercise for all concerned (Table 7-5).

Nonfinancial Output Measures

Fully developed program budget reporting also includes output/performance measures. These performance measures are developed along with each program budget's spending estimates. Program performance measures should be consistent with the utility's overall mission and be useful in evaluating the overall success of each individual program. In some cases, more than one program performance measure is necessary, but the number should be limited and focus attention on the most important goals and objectives (Figure 7-1).

At a minimum, performance measures address the effectiveness of a program—typically as number of units or some operational condition expressed as a percentage. Since performance measures require some element of information beyond dollars, a separate information system beyond the general ledger is required to accurately track productivity data. It is not unusual when first developing performance measures that the best measure will require an entirely different perspective—likely a customer perspective. For example, main breaks results in customer outages and the desire is to target an acceptable level of those outages on an annual basis. So, in addition to focusing on the number of main breaks, the number of services without water will also need to be tracked.

To address efficiency, the cost of the program or some other input such as hours worked needs to be divided by the performance output. Hourly data are often preferred

Table 7-5. Example subprogram report by organizations

Portland, Oregon—Water Bureau	**Accounting Period: 8**
FY 20XX-XX	**Period End: 02/06/20XX**
Subprogram Budget Report by Orgs	**% Year to date: 60.5%**
	% Year remaining: 39.5%
Program: Distribution	**Performance Measures:**
Water Program:Distribution Mains	**1. Fix minor leak within 48 hours of utility locate**
Subprogram: Mains Repair and Maintenance	**2. Fix major leak within 24 hours of utility locate**
	3. Onsite assessment of leaks within 8 hours if no damage reported,
Org owner—South District (33)	**2 hours if damage is reported**

		Expenditures								
	Org	**Total Personal Services**	**Total Internal Materials and Services**	**Total External Materials and Services**	**Fleet**	**Total Expenditures**	**Total Budget**	**% of Budget Expended**	**Budgeted Full-Time Equivalent**	**Actual Full-Time Equivalent**
33	South District	$76,528	$28,684		$12,836	$118,052	$343,859	34%	1.62	2.38
31	Maintenance I/A			$60,580		$60,580	$270,250	22%	0.00	0.00
40	North District	$59,262			$8,300	$67,566	$396,349	17%	4.58	2.12
59	Apprentice	$25,068			$5,021	$30,092	$29,886	101%	0.61	1.01
44	Gates/Hydrants	$17,481			$2,962	$20,445		N/A	0.00	0.57
53	CIP Construction	$15,396			$3,549	$18,947		N/A	0.00	0.63
52	Mains Construction	$14,787			$3,449	$18,237		N/A	0.00	0.47
39	Distribution Maintenance	$10,430			$1,487	$11,920	$11,205	106%	0.14	0.38
37	Large Meters	$5,510			$645	$6,157		N/A	0.00	0.20
46	Carpenter Shop	$4,020			$1,612	$5,633		N/A	0.00	0.12
47	Stores/CMMS/Fleet	$3,703			$1,222	$4,928	$9,898	50%	0.12	0.10
51	Grounds/Painters	$279				$279		N/A	0.00	0.01
63	Operating Engineers	$462			$39	$504		N/A	0.00	0.04
Total		$232,926	$28,684	$60,580	$41,122	$363,340	$1,061,447	34%	7.07	8.03

Source: Portland Water Bureau

Figure 7-1. Example of budget program description

Budget Program—Distribution

Water Program—Distribution Mains

Purpose:

- Transport water to customers from terminal reservoirs through mains to local storage, and then through mains to customer services and hydrants.

Effectiveness Measure(s):

- Less than 5 percent of customers shall experience a cumulative outage of water for more than 8 hours in a year.
- Planned outages, causing disruption of service, shall be limited to 8 hours.
- Emergency outages are limited to 24 hours, except for mains exceeding 16 in. in diameter, for which emergency outages are limited to 48 hours.

Program Inventory:

- 2,100 mi of distribution main

Work:

- Maintenance, repair, replacement, and installation of distribution system mains (pipes). (Note, main replacement and installation projects often include valves, regulators, hydrants, and/or services associated with that construction.) Main flushing work is also included here although this work may benefit water quality compliance.

Bureau Lead/Contact: Charles Smith

to dollar information as that data get directly at what is ultimately managed—expected crew hours per job to do the work. If more than one performance measure is in play, then efficiency measures become problematic if the combined costs/hours cannot be distinctly applied to each measure. For example, when tracking all service installations including new and replacements within the same program, unless costs/hours are tracked separately for new services and renewed services, a useful efficiency measure can only be calculated for total service installations. Efficiency also takes on a different form when evaluating operational effectiveness expressed as a percentage, such as a performance measure that requires meeting federal water quality standards 100 percent of the time. In this case, it becomes a question of optimizing dollars spent to meet this productivity measure rather than maximizing output for a given dollars spent (Table 7-6).

Relevance, Accuracy, and Timing of Interim Budget Reporting

As noted earlier, budget reports can be prepared on an interim basis, typically monthly or quarterly for the benefit of internal management and day-to-day decision making. For the perceived value of this information to easily exceed its cost it must be relevant, accurate, and timely.

Table 7-6. Example budget by program

Portland, Oregon—Water Bureau	**Accounting Period: 8**
FY 2007–08	**Period End: 02/06/2008**
Bureau Budget Report by Water Program	**% Year to date: 60.5%**
	% Year remaining: 39.5%

Program/Water Program	Annual Revised Budget	Year-to-Date Expenditures	% of Budget Expended	Budgeted Full-Time Equivalent	Actual Full-Time Equivalent
Supply					
Bull Run Watershed	$3,547,298	$1,315,072	37%	18.5	19.7
Groundwater	$5,041,482	$1,593,869	32%	8.3	8.5
Supply Totals	$8,588,780	$2,908,941	34%	26.8	28.2
Transmission and Terminal Storage					
Terminal Reservoirs	$6,247,636	$2,449,951	39%	8.7	13.1
Conduits/Transmission Mains	$5,302,229	$1,468,930	28%	9.1	10.7
Transmission and Terminal Storage Totals	$11,549,865	$3,918,881	34%	17.8	23.8
Distribution					
Pump Stations/Tanks	$6,748,854	$3,048,461	45%	29.0	29.0
Distribution Mains	$17,544,505	$7,350,930	42%	90.6	74.4
Services	$5,206,840	$3,247,787	62%	35.5	30.8
Meters	$3,997,731	$2,205,717	55%	28.1	28.3
Hydrants	$1,384,388	$713,608	52%	14.2	16.2
Valves/Gates/Regulators	$1,574,924	$657,089	42%	13.2	9.3
Field Support	$8,211,212	$5,072,960	62%	56.4	48.8
Distribution Totals	$44,668,454	$22,296,552	50%	267.0	236.8
Regulatory Compliance					
Regulatory Compliance	$7,125,901	$2,954,755	41%	38.8	34.8
Regulatory Compliance Totals	$7,125,901	$2,954,755	41%	38.8	34.8
Customer Service					
Customer Service	$15,931,769	$7,966,471	50%	123.6	125.7
Conservation/Sustainability	$988,369	$374,817	38%	6.0	5.0
Security/Emergency Management	$2,644,011	$1,820,987	69%	25.4	35.5
Fountains	$935,874	$307,842	33%	2.7	3.5
Grounds/Parks	$1,666,480	$675,886	41%	12.2	8.8
Customer Service Totals	$22,166,503	$11,146,003	50%	169.9	178.5
Support					
Bureau Support	$13,371,529	$9,266,778	69%	65.2	60.3
Employee Investment	$5,165,965	$2,402,980	47%	53.6	45.7
Data Management	$2,779,221	$1,662,180	60%	25.0	28.8
Planning	$3,327,819	$1,334,488	40%	22.0	18.8
Facilities	$6,866,918	$3,213,613	47%	3.5	8.0
Support Totals	$31,511,452	$17,880,039	57%	169.3	161.6
Water Bureau Total	$125,610,955	$61,105,171	49%	689.6	663.7

Source: Portland Water Bureau

Relevant means that the report provides information that is useful for decision making. If lower-level managers determine that the information is not useful, they may ignore it or, at best, respond merely to comply but give no consideration to what a report could be telling them. The result may be wasteful at the least and harmful at worst.

Accurate means the information is correct and can be relied on. Sloppy and inconsistent accounting data may misrepresent trends or hide problems that need to be addressed.

Timely means the information is from the current period and is provided early enough for managers to make midcourse corrections if needed. Information that is reported after a fiscal period is useful to external users.

This leads to a need to give strong consideration to balancing the accuracy and timeliness of any interim budget reporting process. If data reporting is kept to a minimum, just what is needed for decision making, it is much easier to provide accurate reports that are also timely. Also, performance reporting that relies on data that the organization already records and hence require no additional work eases the performance reporting task.

This page intentionally blank.

Chapter 8

Financial Statement Reports

The purpose of financial reporting is to convey information about the water utility. The information presented in financial reports serves as an important foundation on which are based decisions by regulatory authorities, taxing authorities, owners, creditors, customers, employees, management, and other groups interested in the affairs of a water utility. The information needs of each group are discussed in chapter 6.

The end products of the accounting system used by the water utility are the financial reports presented to interested groups in an effort to satisfy the information requirements of each. Although the data accumulated by the accounting system are not the only sources of information available to those interested in the affairs of the water utility, they do represent a significant portion of such information. Therefore, it is important that the financial reports generated by the accounting system present information relevant to the specific needs and problems of the interested groups in a form readily understood by the intended readers.

Guidelines for Reporting: Financial Statement Standards

To be useful, financial reporting should strive to meet the needs of all stakeholders. Some readers may require separate reports but the reports and disclosures should, if possible and practicable, follow generally accepted accounting principles (GAAP) and consider the following where applicable:

- Compliance with reporting requirements of the Securities and Exchange Commission (SEC)
- Information needs of regulatory commissions
- Disclosures required or of interest to creditors and lenders
- Demonstration of compliance with legal requirements and expectations of governmental bodies and agencies
- Compliance with the requirements and recommendations of standard-setting bodies

It should be noted that GAAP as well as standards for external financial reporting are undergoing continual change by the various standard-setting bodies—principally the FASB and SEC for private and/or publicly traded water utilities, and the GASB for governmental water utilities. As a result, report examples herein may become dated over time.

The format and content of certain reports to public service commissions, to the Securities and Exchange Commission, and to taxing authorities are usually designed by these particular groups. When this is the case, the water utility merely furnishes information in the manner prescribed. In preparing reports for which the format and content are not specified by law, the utility is free to apply general principles of report preparation. Briefly, these principles may be stated as follows:

1. The requirements of the readers for whom the report is intended should dictate the nature of the data presented and the manner of presentation.
2. The data reported should be arranged in a logical and readily understandable manner.
3. The wording of the report should convey to the reader the precise meaning intended.
4. The information should be reported at the time it is needed.
5. The time and effort expended in obtaining the information reported should not exceed the value of the information.

The first of these principles is the most important. Reports are compiled in order to convey a message. For the message to be read and understood, preparers of the report must understand the uses that the intended readers may be expected to make of it. The second and third principles amplify the first: like items should be grouped; as much or as little detail should be shown as the intended readers are expected to need; and the significance and relative importance of the various groups of data should be brought out through the use of subtotals, totals, various typographic styles, and other devices. The third principle suggests that technical terminology should be used in a report only if the intended readers have a technical background. Where annual financial reports are prepared for external readers, it is a common assumption is that such readers have a basic knowledge of accounting and GAAP.

The fourth of the general principles of report preparation is concerned with timeliness. In order to report information by the time it is needed or required, the information demands of the intended users must be foreseen and a system designed to provide the needed information routinely. The design of the information system should also facilitate the presentation of data needed occasionally but not routinely. Complete accuracy is often less important than timeliness; estimates are adequate for many purposes as long as they are so labeled. Where annual financial reports are prepared for external readers, it is a common assumption is that such readers have a basic knowledge of accounting and GAAP.

The fifth principle is a corollary of the fourth. Some of the information desired by water utility managers, or by individuals or groups outside the management team, would cost more to obtain than the information would be worth. The fifth principle also places a lid of reasonableness on the other four; however, it should not be used as an excuse for failure to be diligent and creative in attempting to meet the needs of those who have a valid claim for information about the water utility and its activities.

The preparation of reports involves the accumulation, sorting, and summarization of detailed financial and statistical data generated by the accounting system. Report preparation is costly, and procedures that minimize its expense should be employed. The procedures instituted are, to a certain extent, dictated by the size of the water utility organization. In some cases, manual preparation may be the most economical. For large systems, the use of electronic data processing equipment will be feasible. In other cases, a combination of these data processing systems may be the most efficient and economical. The application of various combinations should be studied before a decision is reached concerning the most appropriate method for report preparation.

Reports of Private Water Utilities

Reports to External Users

While there are a variety of external users of private water utility financial reports, this section is primarily devoted to reporting to stockholders. Subsequent sections of this chapter will discuss other forms of external reporting.

Stockholders or prospective stockholders of an private water utility usually are not involved in the day-to-day operations of the entity and thus do not have a complete knowledge of the utility's activities. To a considerable extent, stockholders depend on reports rendered by the water utility as their principal source of information. In examining the reports of an private water utility, a stockholder is most interested in the earnings and dividend record, financial position, and growth (in revenues, profits, and assets) during recent years. Information concerning these aspects and other information of interest permit the stockholder to estimate the future financial success of a utility and to estimate the risk and return associated with ownership of this stock.

In preparing reports to stockholders of private water utilities, there generally are some restraints, either legal or conventional, within which water utility management must operate. For example, the form and content of a report (prospectus) including financial information to potential stockholders concerning a new securities issue is dictated by SEC under the Securities Act of 1933 if the private water utility issuing the securities falls within SEC jurisdiction. After securities have been issued, SEC under the Securities Exchange Act of 1934 specifies the frequency, form, and content of reports filed directly with SEC by publicly held corporations, including the annual (10-K) and interim (10-Q) reports. Although adherence to SEC reporting regulations is not generally required in reports not filed with SEC, SEC has had a substantial influence on the content of external financial reports issued to stockholders.

Annual financial reports to stockholders are subject to audit by an independent certified public accountant who is charged with issuing an opinion concerning whether or not the financial statements and accompanying footnotes present fairly, in conformity with GAAP, the operating results, financial position, and cash flows of the water utility. The three principal accounting and financial reporting standards underlying corporate financial reporting have been the Committee on Accounting Procedure (CAP) of the American Institute of Certified Public Accountants (AICPA) from 1939 to 1959, the Accounting Principles Board (APB) of AICPA from 1959 to 1973, and presently the

Financial Accounting Standards Board (FASB). Unless superseded by a more recent standard, pronouncements of all three accounting organizations remain in effect today. Although the pronouncements of these authoritative accounting organizations are not legally binding, as SEC reporting requirements are, members of AICPA are required to disclose all material departures from authoritative accounting pronouncements in the companies' published financial statements to stockholders.

GAAP for Private Utilities

Uniform systems of accounts prescribed by state public service commissions to control the accounting practices of water utilities customarily serve as the foundation for rendering financial reports to the SEC and to stockholders, as well as to the state public service commissions. The uniform system of accounts basically follows GAAP promulgated by organizations such as APB and FASB. Nevertheless, there commonly exist certain differences between accounting requirements of state public service commissions and GAAP applicable to nonregulated enterprises. The differences, which can have a significant effect on financial statement measurements, result mainly from the regulatory emphasis on achieving rate-making objectives.

The influence of rate regulation on accounting practices of private utilities has been recognized by accounting rulemaking organizations. In 1982, FASB issued its Statement of Financial Accounting Standards (SFAS) No. 71, *Accounting for the Effects of Certain Types of Regulation.* This statement recognized that:

- Regulation of an enterprise's prices (hereinafter referred to as "rates") is sometimes based on the enterprise's costs. Regulators use a variety of mechanisms to estimate a regulated enterprise's allowable costs, and they allow the enterprise to charge rates that are intended to produce revenue approximately equal to those allowable costs. Specific costs that are allowable for rate-making purposes result in revenue approximately equal to the costs.
- In most cases, allowable costs are used as a means of estimating costs of the period during which the rates will be in effect, and there is no intent to permit recovery of specific prior costs. The process is a way of setting prices—the results of the process are reported in general-purpose financial statements in accordance with the same accounting principles that are used by unregulated enterprises.
- Regulators sometimes include costs in allowable costs in a period other than the period in which the costs would be charged to expense by an unregulated enterprise. That procedure can create assets (future cash inflows that will result from the rate-making process), reduce assets (reductions of future cash inflows that will result from the rate-making process), or create liabilities (future cash outflows that will result from the rate-making process) for the regulated enterprise. For general-purpose financial reporting, an incurred cost for which a regulator permits recovery in a future period is accounted for like an incurred cost that is reimbursable under a cost-reimbursement-type contract.

- Accounting requirements that are not directly related to the economic effects of rate actions may be imposed on regulated businesses by orders of regulatory authorities and occasionally by court decisions or statutes. This does not necessarily mean that those accounting requirements conform to generally accepted accounting principles. For example, a regulatory authority may order an enterprise to capitalize and amortize a cost that would be charged to income currently by an unregulated enterprise. Unless capitalization of such cost is appropriate under this Statement, generally accepted accounting principles require the regulated enterprise to charge the cost to income currently.

Under SFAS 71, an enterprise may capitalize all or part of an incurred cost that would otherwise be charged to expense if both of the following criteria are met:

- It is probable that future revenue in an amount at least equal to the capitalized cost will result from inclusion of that cost in allowable costs for rate-making purposes.
- Based on available evidence, the future revenue will be provided to permit recovery of the previously incurred cost rather than to provide for expected levels of similar future costs. If the revenue will be provided through an automatic rate-adjustment clause, this criterion requires that the regulator's intent clearly be to permit recovery of the previously incurred cost.

Rate actions of a regulator can also reduce or eliminate the value of an asset. If a regulator excludes all or part of a cost from allowable costs and it is not probable that the cost will be included as an allowable cost in a future period, the cost cannot be expected to result in future revenue through the rate-making process. Accordingly, the carrying amount of any related asset shall be reduced to the extent that the asset has been impaired. Whether or not the asset has been impaired shall be judged the same as for enterprises in general.

Rate actions of a regulator can also impose a liability on a regulated enterprise. Such liabilities are usually obligations to the enterprise's customers. The following are the usual ways in which liabilities can be imposed and the resulting accounting:

- A regulator may require refunds to customers. Refunds are recognized as liabilities and as reductions of revenue or as expenses of the regulated enterprise.
- A regulator can provide current rates intended to recover costs that are expected to be incurred in the future with the understanding that if those costs are not incurred, future rates will be reduced by corresponding amounts. If current rates are intended to recover such costs and the regulator requires the enterprise to remain accountable for any amounts charged pursuant to such rates, those amounts are recognized as liabilities and taken to income only when the associated costs are incurred.
- A regulator can require that a gain or other reduction of net allowable costs be given to customers over future periods. That would be accomplished, for rate-making purposes, by amortizing the gain or other reduction of net

allowable costs over those future periods and reducing rates to reduce revenues in approximately the amount of the amortization.

At present, important areas of conflict between water utility regulatory accounting and accounting for nonregulated enterprises under the provisions of SFAS 71 include accounting for extraordinary gains and losses through early extinguishment of debt, accounting for income tax expense, accounting for leases, accounting for pension and other postemployment retirement expenses, and accounting for the cost of funds used during construction. These issues, and others, are discussed later in this book.

Annual Reports

An annual financial report is one of the principal sources of information to stockholders concerning the operations of an private water utility. An annual report is primarily an account of management's stewardship. The primary financial statements included in an annual report are the balance sheet, income statement, statement of retained earnings, statement of cash flows, and five-year summary of operations accompanied by management's discussion and analysis. A portion of the report is also devoted to explaining the activities of the water utility and to highlighting future plans and prospects. Appendix B (on CD) contains an excerpt from a sample private water utility's annual report.

Content

As previously noted, the form and content of this annual reporting is dictated by the standards of the SEC. This reporting may be satisfied in one annual filing (Form 10-K) or in two fillings (an annual report to stockholders and a Form 10-K that incorporates information contained in the annual report to stockholders). The structure and content of annual financial reports to stockholders typically include the following:

Highlights of the financial and operating results of the year. The summary of current financial results may be compared with that of the previous year.

Letter to stockholders by the president or board chairman, or both. The letter generally includes a brief statement concerning the year's activities and the plans and prospects of the utility.

Detailed narrative review of the activities of the water utility. This review may include brief discussions concerning revenues, operating expenses, pumpage and production, new construction, new franchise areas, subsidiary operations, water rates and service, stockholder relations, employee relations, customer and public relations, marketing programs, relations with public utility commissions, new financing, and plans for the following year and beyond. The discussions may be supplemented by graphs, charts, maps, and pictorial representations where applicable.

The informal explanation and review of operations is prepared at the discretion of management. Additional information to be included is specified by the SEC in its Regulation S-K, which requires public companies to include in both the 10-K annual report to the SEC and in the annual report to stockholders (1) a summary of operations for the last five years and (2) management discussion and analysis of financial condition and results of operations, including unusual variations, for the most recent three years. Although the exact content and format of management's narrative explanation of changes in operating results will vary somewhat among companies, the essential purpose of the year-by-year narrative explanation is to analyze major reasons for changes in the company's liquidity, capital resources, and operating results over the most recent three-year period.

A brief description of the business and properties, as well as legal proceedings, security ownership, and management remuneration, are disclosures required by the SEC in the Form 10-K filing, along with the following financial statements:

Financial statements. Financial statements in comparative form, supplemented by explanatory notes and supporting schedules and accompanied by the report of an independent public accountant, provide the basic data concerning the financial position and results of operations of the water utility.

Balance sheet. The balance sheet shows (1) the assets of the water utility and (2) the creditor and stockholder interests in the assets on a specified date.

Income statement. The income statement shows the operating revenue and expenses of the water utility along with other revenue and expense items. Computations for earnings per share for common stockholders are also shown.

Retained earnings statement. The statement of retained earnings shows the beginning balance in retained earnings, the transfer of income, deductions for dividend declarations, other adjustments, and the ending retained earnings balance. In some cases, the income statement and the retained earnings statements may be combined into a single statement. In other cases, it may include changes in other equity components.

Statement of cash flows. The statement of cash flows shows the cash flows for the year from operating, investing, or financing activities. Two formats may be used in the preparation of this statement for the operating activities. The formats include reporting actual cash receipts and payments (the direct method) or a reconciliation of net income to these cash flows using changes in other working capital components (an indirect method).

Explanatory notes. The amount and type of information required both by SEC and GAAP have expanded significantly over the decades. In order to better understand the nature and content of this material, the following comments highlight selected notes found in water utility reporting:

Accounting policies. In 1972, the Accounting Principles Board (APB) issued Opinion No. 22, Disclosure of Accounting Policies, which recommends that companies disclose in the annual report the identification and description of all significant accounting principles and methods that involve selection from among alternatives and/or those that are common to a given industry. This information is generally shown in the first note to the financial statements.

Assets subject to lien. Assets mortgaged, pledged, or otherwise subject to lien, and the approximate amounts thereof, are to be designated and the obligations collateralized briefly identified in accordance with SEC Regulation S-X.

RESTRICTIONS THAT LIMIT THE PAYMENT OF DIVIDENDS BY THE COMPANY. Regulation S-X requires disclosure of the most significant restrictions on the payment of dividends by the company, indicating dividends' sources, dividends' pertinent provisions, and the amount of retained earnings or net income restricted or free of restrictions.

SIGNIFICANT CHANGES IN BONDS, MORTGAGES, AND SIMILAR DEBT. Any significant change in the authorized or issued amounts of bonds, mortgages, and similar debt since the date of the latest balance sheet are disclosed in the notes. Debt disclosures include annual maturity and sinking fund requirements, letter-of-credit arrangements, and a summary of short-term debt activity.

INCOME TAX EXPENSE. APB Opinion No. 11, SFAS 96, and Regulation S-X include note disclosure requirements for income tax expense. This includes:

- The components of income (loss) before income tax expense (benefit) as either domestic or foreign.
- The components of income tax expense, including (1) taxes currently payable and (2) the net tax effects, as applicable, of timing differences (indicate separately the amount of the estimated tax effect of each of the various types of timing differences, such as depreciation).
- A reconciliation between the amount of reported total income tax expense (benefit) and the amount computed by multiplying the income (loss) before tax by the applicable statutory federal income tax rate, showing the estimated dollar amount of each of the underlying causes for the difference. This reconciliation may be presented in percentages rather than in dollar amounts.

LEASED ASSETS AND LEASE COMMITMENTS. SFAS 13 and Regulation S-X both call for lease disclosures. Among other items, lessees must disclose total rental expense associated with leased assets, minimum rental commitments for future periods, and the rate-making treatment of the leases.

PENSION AND POSTRETIREMENT BENEFITS. SFAS 87 and 106 include disclosure requirements related to these benefits. These disclosures include the components of benefit cost, funded status of the plan, and significant actuarial assumptions used in the determination of the funded status.

SEGMENT INFORMATION. SFAS 14 requires industry and geographic segment reporting. This includes summarized income statement and balance-sheet information.

COMMITMENTS AND CONTINGENCIES. SFAS 5 requires note disclosure of significant commitments and contingencies affecting the company. This may include construction commitments as well as legal and regulatory proceedings.

Report of independent public accountant. Independent auditors attest to the fairness of the financial statement presentation in conformity with generally accepted accounting principles. Note that the financial statements remain the responsibility of management and not of the independent auditor.

Interim Reports

Another primary financial report issued to stockholders that attempts to disclose the stewardship function of corporate management is the interim report. Unlike annual reports, which are audited by independent public accountants, interim reports are generally unaudited, and the type and amount of data presented in them have, for the most part, been left to the discretion of management. As a result, a wide variety of interim reporting formats has existed, and the information presented has ranged from a minimum of publication of quarterly sales and earnings figures as required by most stock exchanges to comprehensive reports containing a complete set of comparative financial statements and explanatory notes.

In May 1973, APB issued Opinion No. 28 on interim financial reporting. The opinion (1) attempts to clarify the application of generally accepted accounting principles as they apply to interim periods and (2) sets forth the minimum disclosure requirements for interim reports of publicly owned companies. In addition to disclosing summarized revenues and net earnings, companies are encouraged to publish balance-sheet and cash flow data on an interim basis.

SEC has also influenced the type and amount of information disclosed in quarterly reports to shareholders. This includes quarterly filings on Form 10-Q of summarized financial information, along with updates to the annual reporting for known or anticipated changes.

Reports of Governmental Water Utilities

Reports to External Users

The primary users of financial reports for governmental water utilities are the citizens within the utility's service territory and current and potential bondholders and other lenders. This section deals with reports to citizens, customers, and the elected officials responsible for overseeing the water utility. Reports of special interest to lenders are discussed later in the chapter.

The form and content of reports to citizens, customers, and elected officials are not dictated by law or regulation to the same extent as reports to stockholders of private water utilities. Generally, in the case of reports to the public, there are no specific legal requirements for reporting. The information to be included in the reports, the form of the reports, and the frequency of the reports are largely dictated by conventional reporting practices. However, this does not mean that citizens are any less entitled to a full disclosure of the operating results and activities of a governmental water utility than are stockholders of private utilities. The Government Accounting Standards Board (GASB) has stated

> Timely and properly presented financial reports are essential to managers, legislative officials, creditors, financial analysts, the general public and others having need for government financial information.

The extent of reporting to citizens is primarily at the discretion of water utility management or the elected officials who oversee them. Distribution of detailed and comprehensive reports to citizens is not deemed necessary by the managers of some governmental water utilities. Other managers believe that communication of selected information is useful for maintaining and promoting the goodwill of the general public and for keeping citizens adequately informed of the operations of the water utility. Increased public interest in and concern for the activities and operating results of governmental entities in recent years have caused local governments to disclose more information to citizens.

In 2010, GASB issued the Suggested Guidelines for Voluntary Reporting, *SEA Performance Information*. These guidelines for voluntary compliance for performance reporting apply to state and local governments, and therefore affect publicly owned water utilities as well. If a water utility has used performance measures in the budget, it is relatively easy to report its measurements of service and accomplishments in annual reports. GASB has been encouraging public-sector organizations to do so.

GAAP for Governmental Water Utilities

Financial reporting and accounting standards for governmental water utilities are similar to private utilities. Established in 1985, GASB is the recognized authoritative standard-setting body for governmental units. Prior to GASB, the National Council on Governmental Accounting (NCGA) set standards for government.

When formed, GASB dealt with the issue of which accounting principles governmental water utilities should use. Since the activities of governmental water utilities were similar to those of private utilities, it only made sense that the reporting standards be similar. The structural agreement establishing GASB recognizes that separately issued financial statements of utilities in the public sector, prepared in accordance with GAAP, should be guided by the standards of FASB unless GASB has issued a pronouncement applicable to utilities. As previously mentioned, GASB Statement No. 20 also provides interim guidance.

Conflicts can arise between the two standard-setting bodies. Government in structure is unique and often requires different standards to meet its users' needs. Specific conflicts will be discussed later in this section.

Nature of Fund Accounting and Reporting

Because a governmental water utility endeavors to be a self-supporting activity of a governmental unit, financed primarily by charges to consumers, the water utility should be accounted for as a separate enterprise fund. The significant attribute of an enterprise activity is that the accounting for it must make it possible to determine if the unit operated at a profit or loss. In this regard, a governmental water utility is comparable to an private water utility.

Generally, the governmental water utility should use the same system of accounts as an private water utility. Minor variations in the NARUC *Uniform System of Accounts for Class A Water Utilities* (see appendix A) to accommodate the particular needs of a governmental unit, such as interfund transactions and restricted assets, are included in the modified system of NARUC accounts.

The reports rendered by a governmental water utility to citizens may include annual financial statements audited by an independent public accountant and interim financial statements. An annual financial report to citizens may include a statement of net assets; statement of income, expenses, and changes in fund net assets; a statement of revenue and expense compared to budget; and a statement of cash flows.

Annual Reports

Annual financial reports to citizens of governmental water utilities are generally subject to some variation, both in content and format. In a majority of areas, a close parallel can be drawn between the content of the annual reports of governmental water utilities and the content of the annual report of an private water utility. The GASB standards state that "every government should prepare and publish, as a matter of public record, a comprehensive annual financial report (CAFR)." If the government is a component of a larger government (i.e., a city-owned water utility), this report would be a component unit financial report (CUFR). Appendix C (on CD) contains excerpts from the annual report of a governmental water utility.

Content

The CAFR or CUFR generally contain three distinct sections: introductory, financial, and budgetary. These sections may be supplemented by certain specialized sections as the need arises.

Introductory section of a CAFR or CUFR. It is intended to familiarize the reader with the organizational structure of the utility, the nature and scope of the services it provides, and a summary of the utility's financial activities and the factors that influence these activities. Some of the introductory material is subjective in nature, in contrast to the relatively objective information reported in the financial and statistical sections. The introductory section also includes future-oriented information, such as economic forecasts and discussions of future initiatives. Because of the subjective and predictive nature of the introductory section, it is ordinarily excluded from the scope of the independent auditor's examination.

Financial section. This includes the utility's financial statements. As in the case of an private water utility, financial statements, supported by notes and schedules and accompanied by the report of an independent public accountant, provide basic information concerning the financial position and operating results of the governmental water utility. Differences in financial presentations between private and governmental water utilities result primarily from (1) particular governmental or fund accounting requirements for governmental water utilities and (2) the greater dependency on creditor financing by governmental water utilities. The second difference may be reflected by the inclusion of special tables or schedules in the annual report to provide information concerning long-term debt (including amounts outstanding), annual debt service requirements, and annual debt service coverage. Governmental financial statements typically report on a single year and do not usually present prior year numbers for comparison purposes.

Statement of net assets. The statement of net assets for a governmental water utility shows assets, liabilities, and equity. They may be listed in order from current to fixed items, consistent with that recommended by GASB, or presented on a basis more in keeping with that generally used by private water utilities. The GASB has also required that assets and liabilities be classified as either restricted or unrestricted depending on the type of obligation and nature of the restriction.

Statement of income, expenses, and changes in net assets. A statement of revenues, expenses, and changes in fund net assets is required to be included in the annual report to citizens. Changes in revenue invested in the water system (analogous to a retained earnings statement) are also included as part of this presentation. The GASB has recently issued Statement No. 54, which changes and restructures the net asset section of this statement.

Statement of cash flows. This statement is similar to the cash flow statement used by private utilities to classify cash flows by operating, investing, or financial activities. GASB, in its Statement No. 9, divides the financing component into two activities: capital and noncapital.

Summary of debt service requirements and coverage. Special tables or schedules that provide information concerning long-term debt balances outstanding, annual debt service requirements, and annual debt service coverage may also be included in annual reports of governmental water utilities. This information serves to provide additional data on debt service and is supplemental to the financial statements.

Explanatory notes. Explanatory notes for governmental water utilities contain much the same types of disclosure as the private water utility notes previously discussed. Because of their governmental nature, governmental water utilities also disclose the legal aspects of their structure and compliance with legal provisions. This includes disclosures on the legally adopted annual operating budget and the utility's compliance or noncompliance with the provisions of the budget.

Statistical and budgetary sections of the CAFR or CUFR. This reporting is no different than with private water utilities; however, these sections are not usually subject to audit and covered by the auditor's opinion.

Statistical data. This is usually the last section of the CAFR or CUFR and contains comprehensive statistical data for the utility. It is intended to provide CAFR or CUFR users with a broader understanding of the utility and the trends in its financial affairs than is possible from the financial statements and supporting schedules included in the financial section alone. Most of the data included in the statistical section cover a period up to ten years. Thus the statistical section might provide a chart showing ten years of income data, or ten years of quantity of water produced. This section of the CAFR or CUFR might include information on peak usage and list the largest water users in the community. Another distinguishing feature is that some of the data—physical, economic, and social in nature—are derived from sources outside the formal accounting maintained by the utility. Thus, population trends, water consumption trends, the composition of the community in terms of industrial, commercial and residential usages, in short anything that might impact future water demands or supply, may be included in this section. If the utility is reporting on its performance accomplishments, those measures may appear in this section of the report.

Budgetary section. This may or may not be included in a separate section and contains comparisons of budgeted revenues and expenditures to actual revenues and expenditures. If the budget and actual numbers are prepared on a different basis of accounting (cash or modified accrual) from the GAAP basis used for the basic financial statements, then GASB requires a reconciliation between the two accounting bases for the ending fund balance.

Interim Reports

Formalized interim reporting by governmental water utilities is not required, so few utilities prepare interim reports. When prepared, their format may or may not be similar to the annual reporting format, only at a summarized level. This could include (1) a letter from the general manager disclosing highlights and a comparison of operating results of the previous year, (2) a comparative "balance sheet" showing assets and equities as of the end of the quarter and at the end of the previous fiscal year, (3) a comparative statement of revenues and expenses for the quarter and for the same quarter of the prior year, and (4) various other statistics that might prove of interest to readers.

Other Financial Statement Reporting

Creditors, customers, employees, and other groups interested in the activities and operating results of a water utility seek information relative to their special interests. Such information may be obtained from general-purpose reports, such as the annual reports to stockholders and citizens discussed earlier, or in special-purpose reports prepared for specific purposes or specific interested groups or persons.

Reporting to Creditors: General

Present and prospective creditors are interested in a water utility's financial condition, the results of its operations, and other information that can be used to evaluate the risk involved in lending funds to the utility. Loans obtained from commercial banks, although varying in length of maturity, are in the broad category of short-term credit. Bonds generally are in the category of long-term credit. Therefore, information included in reports for commercial bankers is relevant to other short-term credit grantors, and information included in reports for bondholders or their representatives is relevant to other long-term creditors.

Reports to Commercial Bankers

Reports to bankers must answer such questions as Why does the utility need money? How much is required? Will the loan be repaid? How? The particular reporting requirements (specific financial statements and extent of detail) accompanying the extension of credit to a water utility by a bank typically depends on the size and term of the loan. Other factors, such as the size of the water utility and the quality of management, also affect reporting requirements. The request for a small loan usually does not require as much information as a request for a large loan, since bankers assume less risk in accepting a small loan. In granting short-term loans, bankers are primarily interested in reports that emphasize the manner in which the proposed loan is to be repaid. If it is to be repaid from cash generated from operations, a projection of earnings, together with a cash flow forecast showing estimated sources and uses of cash and the estimated future cash balance available for repaying the loan, should be made available to the bank. If the loan is to be repaid by issuing long-term debt, bankers generally will be interested in the effect of the added burden of noncurrent indebtedness on the capital structure of the utility and in the ability of the utility to market proposed long-term issues successfully. Bankers also are interested in the income statement as an indication of the earning power or potential of the utility.

In addition to financial statements, the report accompanying a request for a short-term loan or a line of credit typically includes supplementary information related to other aspects of the water utility, including the following:

- Contingent liabilities
- Assets pledged as collateral
- Insurance carried
- Names and addresses of officers and directors
- Statement by board of directors or other policy-making group indicating that the proposed loan is authorized or approved by them

As the size or term of the requested loan increases, commercial bankers desire additional, more detailed financial statements. In such cases, audited financial statements and supporting schedules similar to those found in the published annual report ordinarily serve the needs of commercial bankers. The financial statements and supporting schedules that accompany a request for an extended-term loan customarily include the following:

- Balance sheet
- Statement of income
- Statement of changes in retained earnings
- Statement of cash flows
- Notes to financial statements
- Independent public accountant's report

The preceding discussion has been limited primarily to historical financial statements. However, it should be emphasized that because commercial bankers are concerned with whether or not the water utility will be able to repay the loan at maturity, the future is of great interest. Therefore, requests by water utilities for bank loans should be supported by projections expressed in terms of forecasts and budgets. Specifically, such requests for loans should be accompanied by the following:

- Statement of estimated revenue and expense for the forecast period
- Statement of estimated cash flow for the forecast period indicating source and application of cash
- Statement of financial position at the end of the forecast period

Once a loan is obtained or a line of credit is established, a utility will be required to render to the bank periodic financial reports, reports regarding the fulfillment of protective covenants, and reports concerning any material changes affecting the water utility. The sophistication of a utility's financial reporting system and the size and term of the loan are some factors that may influence a bank's request for additional information during the period when loans are outstanding.

Protective covenants contained in loan agreements impose restrictions on the financial activities of the water utility. Protective covenant clauses in loan agreements may include provisions that (1) limit the issuance of additional debt instruments until the loan is repaid, (2) limit payment of dividends (in the case of private water utilities), or (3) limit payments to the general fund (in the case of governmental water utilities). Water utility management must understand the provisions contained in the loan agreement so that the utility will adhere to the restrictions and obligations imposed on it.

Reports to Bondholders

Another major class of creditors to whom reports must be rendered is comprised of present and prospective bondholders or their representatives. The prospectus or bond-offering document is the major report rendered by the water utility to prospective bondholders. In the case of bonds already issued, periodic reports by water utilities are usually required by bondholders or trustees acting as agents for bondholders.

In the case of an private water utility under the jurisdiction of SEC, a public bond offering and the prospectus relating to the sale of the bonds must comply with requirements of that regulatory agency. Bonds of an private water utility generally are issued under an indenture that defines the rights and privileges of the bondholders and the duties and obligations of the utility. Among other items, the indenture will specify the principal and interest payments to be made by the issuing utility to the bondholders, identify pledged assets, state call provisions, provide details as to the levels of working capital that the issuing utility must maintain, and specify the annual and interim reports that must be rendered to bondholders or their trustees. Restrictions or protective covenants contained in the indenture, such as liquidity requirements and maximum cash dividend distributions, are included to indicate the protection afforded the bondholders.

A bond issue of an private water utility generally is covered by an indenture; however, some governmental water utility bonds, such as general obligation bonds, are usually not issued under the terms of a trust indenture. In cases where bonds issued by a governmental water utility are not covered by an indenture, the rights and obligations of the governmental water utility typically are defined by statutes and ordinances. In addition to providing details as to various terms and restrictions, such ordinances generally specify the audited financial reports that periodically must be made available to bondholders.

Content of Bond Offering

The contents of a prospectus or official statement relating to the sale of water utility bonds typically include the following information:

- History and nature of the water utility's operations
- Purpose of the bond issue and expected use of the proceeds
- Description of the bond issue, including details concerning interest rates, interest payment dates, maturity schedule, redemption provisions, security, and priority
- Authority for the issuance of the bonds (in the case of governmental water utilities) and provisions of the bond ordinance or indenture
- Description of the management and operating personnel of the utility, including names, addresses, background, and experience of members of the board of trustees or board of directors of the utility, executive officers, and key operating personnel
- Important terms of franchises under which the utility operates
- Details of bonded debt, other long-term debt, short-term debt, and capital stock (in the case of private water utilities)
- Details of the utility plant and other property, including cost, accumulated depreciation, age, and location of major units of property
- Audited financial statements, including comparative balance sheets, income statements, retained earnings statements, statements of cash flows, and a complete set of explanatory notes
- Projected debt service requirements for interest and principal
- Other forecasted and historical financial and statistical data reflecting operations of the water utility for a number of comparative years

Regardless of whether bonds are issued by a governmental or an private water utility, prospective bondholders will be greatly concerned with the total amount of bond indebtedness, the annual fixed requirements for interest and principal payments on bonds, and the relationship between earnings of the utility and fixed interest charges. Therefore, some of the most important information in a notice of bond sale or a prospectus will be shown in tables of interest coverage and bond indebtedness.

Periodic Reports to Bondholders

Once bonds are issued, periodic reports to bondholders or their representatives may be required under the terms of the bond ordinance or indenture. The reports rendered by a water utility to bondholders or their trustees include both annual financial statements, audited by an independent public accountant, and interim financial statements. In general, the periodic reports provided to bondholders or their trustees for private and governmental water utilities will parallel the annual and interim reports issued to stockholders and citizens, which were discussed earlier in this chapter.

Information other than financial statements is generally included in reports to holders of debt instruments issued by water utilities. In each case, the trust indenture or other agreement between the water utility and the security holder must be considered in determining what information, at a minimum, must be included in creditor reports. The information may include detailed financial and statistical data concerning the utility plant and other property, operating revenues and expenses, and other aspects of the water utility's activities. In addition, information relating to the fulfillment of protective covenants may also be required.

In the case of loan agreements, protective covenants included in a trust indenture or ordinance are quite detailed and complex, imposing restrictions on the financial activities of the water utility as well as providing increased security to the creditors. Protective covenants contained in a trust indenture or other agreement between the water utility and the security holders may include provisions that (1) limit the issuance of additional debt instruments, (2) limit the payment of dividends (in the case of private water utilities) or payments to the general fund (in the case of governmental water utilities), (3) limit the sale of mortgaged plant assets and stipulate that money received from sale of such property be substituted as security, (4) require that specified amounts be expended annually for maintenance, replacement, and improvement of mortgaged property (this requirement frequently may be met, in part, by certifying that plant additions shall not serve as the basis for issuing additional bonds), and (5) require the segregation of assets for the purpose of retiring bonds. It is important that water utility management understand the provisions contained in trust indentures or other agreements between the water utility and security holders to ensure that the restrictions and obligations imposed on the utility are respected. Thorough understanding of the provisions will enable management to certify in reports to bondholders or their representatives that the provisions of indentures or other agreements are being fulfilled.

Reporting to Customers and Employees

The extent of reporting to customers and employees is primarily at the discretion of the water utility. Private and governmental water utilities may wish to design a single annual report to be published and distributed to stockholders (in true case of private water utilities), citizens, creditors, customers, and employees. A single comprehensive report to all interested groups may be adequate in situations where stockholders, citizens, creditors, customers, and employees form a homogeneous group whose information needs and interests are similar. In cases where the needs and interests are divergent, specialized reports directed to particular groups may be most effective. As a practical alternative, a published annual report may be issued to all interested groups, supplemented by specialized reports to meet the particular needs of customers and employees.

Reports to Customers

Information for customers typically includes reasons for rate increases and facts relating to the quality of water, as well as planned improvements in the system. Such information may be included in customer bills or be mailed separately. Additionally, some utilities supply each customer with a rate schedule and a set of rules and regulations governing the relationship between customer and water utility.

The general public, which is the source of present and potential customers, is interested in much of the same information as are customers. In addition to information supplied to customers, reports to the general public may include some financial data, such as taxes and contributions paid by the water utility to finance publicly supported activities (for example, municipal government operations). In the case of governmental water utilities, the general public may require reports concerning the efficiency of the utility's operations (in terms of meeting budgeted costs), the degree to which the utility is self-supporting, and the extent, if any, to which the taxpayer is supporting the operations and capital construction activities of the water utility. Media for distributing information to the general public include direct mail and notices or advertisements in the financial and other sections of the public press.

Reports to customers and the general public must be presented in an understandable manner. Generally, detailed financial information should be omitted and pertinent information should be expressed in terms of basic relationships and trends, using graphs and charts as aids. Such reports should use wording that is familiar and understandable to customers and the general public.

Reports to Employees

Employee earning reports, such as federal wage and tax statements (Form W-2), must be furnished to employees in accordance with applicable regulations. For private utilities, specified information concerning pension plans must be furnished to employees in accordance with provisions of the Employee Retirement Income Security Act of 1974 (ERISA). Beyond required earnings and pension information, the nature of reports submitted to employees is determined primarily by water utility management. As in the case of reports to customers, reports to employees should present this message in a clear and understandable manner.

In addition to general information, employee reports often emphasize information pertaining to wages, pension plans, fringe benefits, and other data of particular concern to employees. For example, labor costs (wages, pension plan costs, and other fringe benefits) may be expressed as a percentage of revenues of operating expenses. Labor costs and other employee benefits also may be compared with similar elements in other water utilities or in other industries. Employee reports also may emphasize employee productivity and efficiency. For example, operating costs per unit of processed water and the extent of customer complaints may be compared for a number of years. Information expressed in terms of investment, profit, taxes, and labor costs per employee also may be included in employee reports.

Where possible, information expressed in terms of pie charts, bar graphs, and other graphic representations should be used to emphasize various relationships and trends to employees. The financial and statistical data furnished to employees should be supplemented with a narrative report that explains the data, indicates future plans and outlook for the utility, outlines job opportunities, and explains any changes in wage, pension, welfare, and other employee benefits and policies.

Chapter 9

Rate and Regulatory Reports

Governmental water utilities in the United States are generally not subject to the types of rate and regulatory reporting of their private counterparts. In most cases, governmental water utilities are regulated by a city council, a county board, the board of a commission or authority, or some similar body. As a result, rate and regulatory reporting for governmental water utilities is widely variable both as to its extent and content. Therefore, this chapter presents rate regulation essentially from the viewpoint of a private water utility.

State agencies generally establish the rate and regulatory reporting requirements for private utilities subject to their jurisdiction. The stage agencies are generally known as public utility commissions, public service commissions, or some similar name. While some differences exist in the regulatory process from state to state, a fair degree of similarity and commonality from state to state is found with regard to private utilities. One reason for this similarity is the influence of a nonprofit entity called the *National Association of Regulatory Utility Commissioners* (NARUC), which creates a framework of consistency that enables the various states to oversee private utilities that operate across state lines or that share common expenses (e.g., the various operating utilities that are owned by a common holding company).

The rate-making process represents an important aspect of the operations of a public utility. Essentially, the state public utility commission fills the same role as the city council by providing a mechanism to assure accountability for an approved monopoly. It is the rate regulatory process that determines the utility's ability to charge customers for services rendered and to earn what is judged to be a fair return on assets invested for utility operations. The ultimate outcome of the rate-making process is the tariff sheet, which indicates the rates that can be charged to a customer based on the type of customer and types and quantities of service provided.

Rate-making can be a long political process. The utility designs a "rate case" that presents its proposed rate structure based on historical or projected financial and operational results. The case is presented to the appropriate regulatory body for its review, consideration, and approval. The case is reviewed by the regulator and its staff, plus interested third parties, such as large customers or consumer interest groups (commonly referred to as *intervenors*). Hearings are held on the merits of the utility requests and an order is issued by the regulator. This chapter expands on this process and discusses the theories behind the determination of the utility rate design.

Goals

The rate-making process is generally designed to accomplish three goals. The first is to protect the consumer. Because a water utility is usually a monopoly in a given service territory, there is limited, if any, competition that can serve to control prices. The regulator acts as this control and designs rates that are as low as possible considering the next two goals and still ensure reliable service to the utility's customers. The rate-making process includes a review of expenditures to ensure prudent management operating decisions and efficient operations. It provides a forum for customers to review management decisions and plans, and it challenges the utility to provide reliable service at a specified level for the lowest cost possible.

The second goal is to protect the financial integrity of the utility. The rate-making process ensures that the utility is reimbursed for prudent expenditures related to providing services to its customers so that rates achieve equity among customer classes. This includes recovery of period costs, plus depreciation and amortization of long-lived assets. Although a regulator's goal is to keep prices low, the regulator must also ensure that the utility has sufficient resources available to provide the necessary services.

The third goal of the rate-making process is to provide the opportunity for shareholders of the utility to earn a fair rate of return on their investment. The process results in the computation of a rate of return to be earned on assets invested in utility operations. This return is designed to recover debt and equity costs, including a return on common equity. It should be noted that the rate-making process is designed to provide the opportunity to earn a fair return. It does not guarantee that return. The utility must operate in an efficient and effective manner in order to achieve its desired return.

Rate Process

The rates that the utility may charge for its services are generally established through a formal proceeding. The amount of revenues that the utility ultimately earns is a product of its rates multiplied by the volume sold. The rates are designed to recover the utility's cost of service (operation and maintenance expense, depreciation, taxes, and other general utility costs) for each customer class, plus a fair return on the invested assets. When volumes sold and actual expenses incurred vary significantly from expectations, the utility's actual return will be higher or lower than projected. When this variance is material, the utility will enter into new proceedings by filing a rate case with its regulators. The rate case process can take 18 months or more and includes planning, preparation, testimony, hearings, rebuttal, and, ultimately, an order. It involves an accumulation of data from all sources within the utility and many external sources.

The rate case is designed to determine the revenue requirements necessary to permit the utility to recover its reasonable expenses of operation, plus earn a fair return on assets devoted to providing utility service. The rate adjustment required is measured by the difference between the utility's anticipated revenue requirements and the projected revenue that would be produced by the utility's current rate tariffs. The regulator will usually suspend the utility's request for an increase to conduct an investigation of the data supporting the utility's request. The investigation is usually conducted in a public hearing format, where all qualified persons have an opportunity to present evidence or cross-examine utility witnesses about details of the utility's request.

Test Period

For purposes of determining a utility's reasonable cost of operation, a regulatory body usually requires the utility to present details of its actual experience during a 12-month "test period." This test period represents the results of actual experience during the period presented. Alternatively, the test period can be prospective in nature and represent a period in the future based on the utility's forecasts and projections. Although revenues and expenses for the test period will initially be historical by nature, the utility will propose certain adjustments, known as *pro-forma adjustments*, to "normalize" conditions in the test period and to provide for certain "known and measurable changes" that have occurred and need to be reflected in rates of future periods. Normalizing represents adjustments to the test period to reflect the effects of changes that the utility knows will occur if those changes had taken place at the beginning of the test period. For example, if a utility negotiated a new agreement with its union for an increase in pay that will take place in the middle of the test year, the utility will make adjustments to payroll expense to reflect this agreement as if it takes place for the entire year. Thus rates will be set to recover all costs of this new agreement in future periods.

Selection of an appropriate test year is important because the utility must ensure that the test period is representative of its costs of doing business. If all costs are not properly included, rates may be set lower than needed, resulting in possible liquidity concerns. There are advantages and disadvantages of both historical and prospective test years. The advantage of the historical approach is that the regulator can review known costs that the utility has incurred and evaluate them as to whether or not they were prudently incurred. The historical costs can then be adjusted to reflect known changes. These known changes can be evaluated by the regulator and intervenors to determine whether or not they are reasonable and prudent. Under the prospective filing, the regulator must assess the utility's ability to budget and forecast—a subjective process. However, under the prospective reporting methodology, a better recovery of current costs is provided for the utility.

Rate Case

When a utility files a rate case, the regulatory body accepts the filing and, in certain instances, appoints an administrative law judge or hearing examiner to hear the case. In other jurisdictions, the commissioners themselves hear the case. Prehearing conferences are held and schedules are set for the case, including dates for intervenors and other people to become involved. Affected parties intervene and request information from the utility. This is called the "discovery stage." An analysis of the case is prepared by the regulatory agency's appointed staff. Direct testimony of the intervenors and witnesses are filed and rebuttal testimony of all witnesses is filed. Hearings are held and witnesses are cross-examined by attorneys. Attorneys prepare briefs of issues and suggested findings and reply briefs. If an administrative law judge is involved in the case, he or she issues an order or report.

Attorneys then file exceptions to the report. The attorneys present oral arguments before the commission and finally the commission issues its order. The utility can petition for reconsideration on issuance of the order and the petition is then ruled on by the commission. A legal appeal process can follow if the utility or intervenors do not agree with the commission's final order.

Rate Base, Cost of Service, and Cost of Capital

Three basic components are decided on in a rate case. These components are rate base, cost of capital, and cost of service. Each of these will be discussed in more detail in the following paragraphs. Again, these rate elements are those generally associated with private utilities. Readers should consult AWWA Manual Ml, *Water Rates,* for revenue requirement issues usually associated with governmental water utilities.

Rate Base

Rate base represents the amount of capital invested by the utility in order to provide utility services. It is often referred to as the amount of investment "used and useful" in serving the public. The determination of "used and useful" plant is intended to encourage a utility to design and build the appropriate amount of plant to serve current needs plus a reasonable amount of capacity for future needs, but to discourage the construction of excessive capacity beyond that which can be used during some reasonable future period. A typical determination of rate base includes utility plant in service, less accumulated depreciation, less accumulated deferred income taxes, less contributions in aid of construction, plus a working capital allowance. Net utility plant in service is frequently included in the rate base on an "average basis." Thus average basis could be a 13-month average balance, a 12-month average balance, or another method used by the regulator. One alternate method permits end-of-test-period balances. In certain instances, in order to protect the financial integrity of the utility, construction work in progress is included in the rate base. Contributions in aid of construction are deducted from the rate base because they represent assets that have been contributed to the utility but which the utility did not have to fund with utility resources. Therefore, the utility should not earn a return on those assets.

How much working capital is necessary for operations can be determined in many different ways, based on the jurisdiction in which the utility operates. Working capital can be a simple balance-sheet method, which would include current assets less current liabilities. Some jurisdictions use a one-eighth of cash operating expenses methodology or 13-month averages to determine working capital. Others use "lead lag" studies to estimate the amount of investor money needed to sustain operations until payment is received. A utility provides service before revenue is collected, which creates a lag between expenditures and revenue; at the same time, the utility normally receives goods and services considerably before it pays for them. When these leads and lags are combined, they reflect the amount of working capital needed to cover cash flow.

The determination of the rate base is an essential part of the rate case because it represents the assets on which the utility will be allowed to earn a return.

Cost of Service

The second aspect of a rate case is the determination of the cost of service. The cost of service represents reimbursement of utility costs, such as operations and maintenance, depreciation, taxes, and other general utility costs. These costs are determined using historical information. They are adjusted for any known and measurable changes. There is a significant amount of judgment involved in determining these changes. There can also be many questions as to whether costs are properly classified as utility costs and therefore included in the cost of service. Cost of service includes depreciation, which is the recovery of assets invested in providing utility services.

Cost of Capital

The final component of the revenue requirement calculation is the determination of the cost of capital and rate of return. This is frequently the most debated item in a utility's rate case. It involves a considerable amount of subjectivity in its calculation. Return is what the utility shareholders receive for the use of their money. Return is designed to provide the recovery of interest and equity costs, including preferred and common dividends. The appropriate overall rate of return is based on the weighted cost of the various sources of capital reflected in the utility's capital structure. An example of the development of an overall rate of return would include long-term debt and preferred and common stock of the company. The amount of each one of these sources of capital is multiplied by its percentage of the total amount of its capital and then multiplied by the cost of the capital. Refer to Table 9-1 for an example.

The costs of long-term debt and preferred stock are often easily attainable because most debt and preferred stock have a stated rate. The most debated issue in the cost of capital is the cost of common equity. There are no stated rates for the cost of common equity and this area involves the most judgment. The concept of the cost of capital as an opportunity cost is consistent with the standards of fair rate of return that were

Table 9-1. Cost-of-capital example

	Amount	Percent of Total	Cost (percent)	Weighted Cost of Capital (percent)
Long-term debt	$100,000	50	9	4.5
Preferred stock	20,000	10	6	.6
Common equity	80,000	40	13	5.2
	$200,000	100	28	10.3

formulated in 1923 in *Bluefield Water Works and Improvement Company v. Public Service Commission of West Virginia* (262 U.S. 679,692). In that case, the court ruled:

> A public utility is entitled to such rates as will permit it to earn a return on the value of the property which it employs for the convenience of the public equal to that generally being made at the time and in the same general part of the country on investments in other business undertakings which are attended by corresponding risks and uncertainties.

Additionally, in 1944, in *Federal Power Commission v. Hope Natural Gas Company* (320 U.S. 591), the court found that the standards of a fair rate of return require that the return be (1) commensurate with the return to enterprises of corresponding risks, (2) sufficient to maintain the credit and financial integrity of the regulated company, and (3) adequate to allow the company to attract capital.

Generally, two common methods are used to determine return on equity—comparable earnings and discounted cash flow. The comparable earnings technique consists of developing (1) historical earnings by various comparison groups, with consideration given for relative risks and uncertainties; and (2) the level of earnings needed to attract capital, including data regarding interest coverages and bond ratings. The principal problem in applying the comparable earnings test is in selecting an acceptable sample of comparable companies.

The discounted cash flow technique for determining return on common equity is a formula approach based on the fact that the price of the common share is equal to the present value of the investor's expectation of all future income to be received from such share. The number of assumptions required to solve for the required discounted return, such as projecting what investors expect when they purchase the stock, does not make this method any more reliable than the comparable earnings approach.

Some regulators will include other items in determining the cost of capital, such as accumulated deferred income taxes, accumulated deferred investment tax credits, customer deposits, and short-term debt.

The overall rate of return is multiplied against the rate base to determine the return requirement. Return requirement is added to the utility's cost of service to arrive at an overall revenue requirement. The revenue requirement is compared to the revenues generated from the current rate structure to determine the revenue increase or decrease that will result from the rate proceeding.

Once the total revenue requirements have been established, an equitable distribution of the cost to the various customer classes must be devised. The cost of serving each customer class is different, depending on the type of facility being served and the usage pattern of each class. Generally, these are broken up into residential, commercial, and large industrial users. There also may be separate classifications for municipal or other governmental usage.

The final step in the rate-making process is to set rates that reflect the results of the allocation cost study and collect the authorized revenue requirement. This process is called *rate design*. The rate design process applies information obtained from the cost study to the class billing data to develop the rate charge for each service offered.

The cost-of-service studies are usually based on one or two methodologies, embedded or marginal. An embedded cost-of-service study represents the total historical or forecasted cost of serving each consumer group. A marginal cost study looks at the cost of providing each consumer group with an additional increment of service.

Reporting

Regulators may impose various reporting requirements on the utility. Many regulators require annual financial reports to be filed. These reports generally include year-end financial statements and detailed supporting financial and operating statistics. The purpose of the reports is to enable the regulator to monitor the financial and operating performance of the utility. If a utility is operating at levels significantly above or below results expected from its last rate hearing, the regulator may require the utility to file a rate case in order to adjust rates appropriately. Annual reports are completed based on a prescribed format so that regulators can compare utilities and easily identify required data.

In addition to annual reports, a regulator may require special reports related to monitoring specific data, such as cost conservation efforts, construction, or compliance with agreements. Reports may also result from rate hearings in order to provide additional or continued information on subjects of interest to the regulator.

This page intentionally blank.

Part 4

Accounting Cycle Implementation and Management

This page intentionally blank.

Chapter 10

Revenue and Rates

Maintaining an adequate level of revenue, which is collected equitably from all classes of customers using water service, is a major responsibility of water utility management. Other secondary considerations gaining increased public attention are attempts to use the water rate structure to promote water conservation and to provide low-cost water service to low-income, elderly, or other specific customer classes. Whether the water utility is governmental or private, total revenues must be sufficient to enable the utility to (1) provide adequate customer service to maintain and perpetuate the water system, (2) pay taxes or make payments in lieu thereof when required, (3) earn an appropriate return, and (4) have a financial position adequate to borrow funds at reasonable cost for system expansion or improvement. Adequate revenues result from establishing and charging appropriate rates for the water sold and fees for services furnished by the utility.

Customer payments for water service provide the main source of revenue for most water utilities. Maintaining an adequate and continuing flow of cash to the utility requires effective planning, management, and control of revenues and funds on hand by water utility management. Sources of revenue are usually constrained by the enabling legislation, charters, governing ordinances, or board or commission policy. State public utility commissions must generally approve revenue proposals of private utilities before the proposals can be implemented and (in some states and under some circumstances) must also approve rates charged by municipal utilities. Governmental water utilities are usually subject to an elected or appointed board or commission rather than a state public utilities commission.

The revenues of a water utility are divided into the following two broad categories, depending on their source: "operating revenues" and "nonoperating revenues." (See the 1996 NARUC system of accounts for Class A water utilities in appendix A.) Operating revenues include revenues derived from the sale of water and from other activities closely allied to the sale of water. Sources of nonoperating revenues may include one-time payments from new customers intended to recoup at least a portion of the capital costs incurred to develop new capacity (often called *system development charges, availability fees, capacity fees,* or some similar name, depending on the locale). The sources of nonoperating revenue may include rents derived from nonutility property; interest and dividends earned; recreational fees; and revenue for providing supervision, management, engineering, and similar services to other organizations. Ordinarily, revenues from merchandising, jobbing, and contract work are also classified as nonoperating. Nonoperating revenues, together with the nonoperating expenses incurred in obtaining the revenues, are usually classified in the "other income" section of the income statement.

Operating Revenues

Water Sales

Revenues derived from the sale of water represent the major source of operating revenue to the water utility. Water sales should be categorized to match the significant revenue flows arising from services provided by the utility, such as general customer water sales, fire protection service, wholesale, irrigation, or other special classes of service. Sales to general customers are often broken into categories such as residential sales, commercial sales, industrial sales, and sales to public agencies. Categories are usually based on the type of customer and the use made of the water supplied to the customer. Residential sales include all sales of water service to individuals for home or domestic uses and often for smaller multifamily accounts (e.g., duplexes, triplexes, etc.). Commercial sales include uses by multiple-family, master-metered accounts (e.g., apartment or townhouse complexes, some condominiums, etc.); retail and wholesale businesses; and occupants of office buildings. Industrial sales include sales of water to manufacturing firms for use in manufacturing. Sales to public agencies include sales of water to municipal, state, and federal government units for services billed under general service classifications, as opposed to special contracts or agreements. Customers in various classes may have similar or the same rates, as classes are sometimes assigned to identify types of use rather than as groupings of customers with similar demand and usage patterns. As a general rule, customers with similar demands or usage patterns should have similar rates.

Metered and Unmetered Sales

Sales of water to general customers may be metered or unmetered. Under the category "metered sales to general customers," the charge to the customer is based on a rate schedule applied to the amount of water delivered through each meter or combinations of meters. Under the category of "unmetered sales to general customers," the charge to the customer is based on a flat rate per period of time per housing unit, footage of frontage on the water main, or some other measure. Although the flat-rate basis is still used, meter-based rates are more widely employed and are generally considered to result in more equitable charges to consumers. In addition, when compared with unmetered service, metered service promotes conservation and results in more economical use of a water plant by reducing unaccounted-for water and waste by customers caused by leaks or excessive irrigation.

Fire Protection Service

Fire protection service can be broken into two categories, private fire protection service and public fire protection service. Private fire protection service includes charges for service availability (i.e., for maintaining sufficient pressure and capacity to fight fires even though such capacity is rarely used) plus fees for water delivered to customers through specific facilities, such as hydrants, that can be either privately or publicly owned, provided the service is billed under separate fire protection rate schedules.

Public fire protection service includes revenues obtained from municipalities or other public authorities for fire protection service rendered to the general public. In the case of private water utilities, charges for public fire protection typically are levied against the municipality on the basis of the number of hydrants, miles of mains, or "inch-foot" calculations (where "inch" refers to the diameter of mains and "foot" refers to the length of mains). In the case of governmental water utilities, a charge for public fire protection may be levied against the municipality or directly against property owners on the basis of assessed valuation. The latter procedure is an equitable way of distributing the cost of public fire protection among those benefiting from such service. Another common means to allocate the costs of a water system between potable water service and fire protection is the use of engineering-derived formulae such as the "Maine Formula," which takes into account such factors as the size of the utility when allocating such costs.

Public Agencies

The "sales to the public agencies" category includes revenues from municipalities or other governmental agencies for such purposes as supplying water to public buildings, parks, swimming pools, fountains, and median strips. Sales to public agencies can be made under special contracts or agreements that call for the application of either metered or flat-rate schedules.

Irrigation

In some utilities, sales to irrigation customers may comprise a significant portion of total water sales. The "sales to irrigation customers" category includes revenues for water supplied for commercial irrigation purposes such as sod farms. These revenues are generally billed under rate schedules applicable solely to irrigation customers and can be either metered or unmetered.

Resale

The "sales for resale" category includes revenues from water supplied to private water utilities or to other municipal utilities for resale, including water supplied for standby or for mutual assistance agreements. Water supplied for resale is usually billed under special rate schedules or contracted agreements.

Interdepartmental

The "interdepartmental sales" category includes amounts charged for water supplied to other departments of the governing entity under specified rate schedules. An example would be a case in which the water department sold water to the electric utility or wastewater treatment department of the same city.

Other Sales Revenue

There may be other special sales of water that, if significant in amount and billed under special rate schedules, should be classified separately. These special sales include revenues from water supplied for commercial air conditioning or cooling towers, refrigeration, large industrial users, or institutions that consume a significant portion of the total water delivered by the utility and that are billed under special rate schedules or agreements (e.g., a large college or university located in a small town). In addition, revenues from water furnished to builders or contractors during construction and to other customers who use water for a limited time without permanent connections should be classified separately if their consumption is significant.

Other Operating Revenues

Although revenues derived from the sale of water represent the major source of operating revenues, other operating revenues may also be significant. For example, ad valorem taxes for a governmental water utility and power sales can provide a significant source of revenues for some utilities. The sources of other operating revenues should be reported separately when their impact is meaningful to the operations of the utility.

Some of the classifications suggested clearly have limited impact on many utilities. For example, forfeited discounts include the amount of billed water-revenue discounts forfeited and the amount of additional charges to customers who do not pay their water bills within a specified time. This may or may not be significant to a utility. However, "miscellaneous service revenues" include items such as fees for changing or reconnecting service and charges for maintenance of appliances, piping, or other installations on customers' premises. Such fees could provide a significant revenue base to cover the cost of these services. Rents from "water property and interdepartmental rents" include rents received from other organizations or departments for use of property devoted to water operations. "Other water revenues" include revenues incidental to water operations and not included in any of the previous accounts, such as income from the sale of material and supplies not ordinarily purchased for resale and commissions on the sale or distribution of water of other utilities.

Operating Revenue Accounts

State public service commissions generally require private utilities to maintain separate accounts and subsidiary records for each specified type of operating revenue. At a minimum, separate accounts and subsidiary records are generally required for each type of operating revenue discussed in the preceding sections (shown in the system of accounts presented in appendix A). In addition, operating revenue derived from other sources, if significant in amount, should also be classified in separate operating revenue accounts.

The careful maintenance of detailed operating revenue accounts (including the division of sales to general customers in terms of residential customers, commercial customers, industrial customers, and public authorities) is essential to water utility management and to regulatory authorities for determining and establishing rate schedules. Water utility management can use the information contained in the detailed operating revenue accounts to analyze trends in revenue and to aid in forecasting future water requirements. Trends and forecasts of water revenue requirements can, in turn, affect management decisions regarding the amount and type of capital expenditures to be undertaken by the utility, the securing of additional water rights and franchises, and other preparations for expansion.

Projecting Operating Revenues

Sound planning on the part of water utility management is a prerequisite to obtaining an adequate level of revenue. Total operating revenues must be sufficient to enable the water utility to provide adequate water service. The operating budget ("operating and maintenance budget," or "O&M budget") is an important planning aid to water utility management. It allows management to develop plans to meet the water utility's revenue requirements or costs of providing service. The nature of revenue requirements differs among water utilities. In the case of private utilities and governmental water utilities subject to rate regulation by state commissions, revenue requirements customarily include operating expenses and an allowance, as measured by operating income, intended to provide a fair and reasonable return on a defined rate base. In the case of governmental water utilities not subject to commission jurisdiction, the revenue requirements of the utility are frequently a function of "cash needs" analogous to the budgetary basis used by municipalities for budgeting and financial reporting. The composition of "cash needs" varies. Cash needs typically include, but are not limited to, operation and maintenance expenses, debt service requirements, outlays for normal plant replacements, extensions, and improvements and contributions to reserves.

Developing the Operating Budget

An early step in the development of the operating budget is to estimate the revenue component of the budget. The statement of estimated operating revenues will show the projected revenues by major components, generally forecasted for a budget period of one year or more. Operating revenues are a function of the demand for water service and the rate ("tariff") schedule applied to this demand. In turn, the demand for water service in a given locality is a function of factors such as the population level, industrial concentration, weather conditions, and economic conditions.

Operating revenues should be estimated for each category of service to which a separate rate schedule applies (sales to general customers, public and private fire protection service, wholesale, and any other significant revenue category). Forecasting revenues by residential, commercial, industrial, and public authority components is recommended if the accuracy of the forecast can be materially improved by separately forecasting the revenue to be derived from each component. Forecasting by residential, commercial, industrial, and public authority components could improve the accuracy of the forecast if the historical water-consumption pattern for each of these classes of general customers reflects a different trend in water usage or when future trends may be expected to diverge. In addition, if a water utility serves more than one community or district, each of which is subject to different rate schedules or reflects different water usage characteristics, then operating revenues should be estimated for each community or district served. To increase the accuracy of the forecast, large-use customers or customers having extraordinary demands for service may be requested to supply estimates of their probable demands for water during the budget period.

Because sales to residential customers typically produce the greatest portion of total operating revenues, it may be desirable to forecast residential sales by components, such as single-family houses, multifamily houses, and apartment houses. The extent to which the revenue forecast is made by separate customer classes and by components of classes depends on (1) the extent to which different customer classes and components of classes are subject to differing rate schedules, (2) the extent to which different classes and components of classes reflect differing consumption characteristics, (3) the degree of accuracy desired in the operating revenue forecast, and (4) the availability of historical and projected consumption data accumulated at the appropriate level of detail.

The preparation of a statement of estimated operating revenues may be considered as a two-step process. In the first step, an estimate must be made of either the quantity of water required by each customer class and the projected number of accounts in each customer class, or other quantity measures used as a basis for applying rate schedules. In the second step, the existing rate schedules must be applied to the estimated quantity components to determine the estimated revenue obtainable from each customer class.

Interrelation of Operating Budget and Capital Expenditures Budget

The forecast of demand for water service is the starting point of the entire budgetary process; that is, estimated customer demand for water service is the basis for quantification of the entire water utility operations plan. The estimate of the quantity of water required by customers will in turn affect the level of budgeted operating revenues (assuming that at least a portion of customers' water usage is metered).

The estimated amount of water required by customers will also affect the level of some budgeted operating expenses. Many of the operating expense items of a water utility do not vary in amount in response to changes in operating activity by the utility (e.g., labor expenses are relatively fixed). Meter reading, billing, and collection expenses do not vary directly with consumption but can vary to some degree with the number of customers served by the utility. Accountants call such costs "fixed." There are other operating expenses that do vary directly in proportion to changes in operating activity. The accounting term for this group of costs is "variable." Electricity or fuel expenses (for pumping) and chemical expenses (for treatment) are examples of expenses that vary in relation to the quantity of water produced in response to customer demands.

In addition to serving as a basis of budgeting operating revenues and some operating expenses, a forecast of future water consumption is used by water utility management in planning a capital improvements program (CIP) that will provide facilities sufficient to meet future demands for water. Total system capacity must be provided to meet the peak hourly demand placed on the system during the year by general customers, and additional capacity must be available to provide adequate public fire protection service even during times of peak demand by general customers. The impact of planned additional facilities on operating expenses (including the level of preventive maintenance and improvements) and on revenue requirements must also be considered. In order to be an effective capital budgeting tool, the forecast of annual customer water requirements should be made in detail for at least a five-year period, and should include anticipated peak demands for service. Longer-term water demands must also be developed for at least a 25- to 30-year period, since the lead time for implementation of major capital improvements (that is, the time from initial planning until the date the facility is actually in service) can easily stretch for 20 years. Inasmuch as the forecasts for the period beyond the first year are not used as a basis for the current operating budget, the long-term forecasts need not be as detailed in terms of customer or service components.

Forecasting Sales of Water to Metered Customers

Historical water consumption information accumulated from individual customer records may be used as a basis for estimating the amount of water to be sold to each class of metered customer, or component thereof, during the budget period. For example, if the water utility uses a tiered rate structure for pricing, the unit price of water changes with the amount of water used. The rate for quantities between x and y gallons will be different from the rate for quantities between y and z. Each of these specified ranges is called a *block*. Managers can track and chart the amount of water sold within each block for each customer class. A trend line can then be fitted to the historical data. The trend line can be extrapolated in order to estimate the amount of water to be sold to the class of customer or class component for the budget period. If, in addition to the block-rate schedule, a service charge or minimum charge is levied on customers, an estimate must also be made of the revenue to be obtained from service charges or minimum charges. The estimate of the revenue from service charges or minimum charges involves forecasting the number of customers who will be subject to the charges. This forecast can be made on the basis of historical information in the same manner as the forecast of water consumption. If the service charge or minimum charge is based on the size of meter or other measure, then the historical data must be assembled on that basis.

Forecasting Unmetered Sales

Unmetered sales charges to a particular class of customer are based on quantity components or measures other than the amount of water consumed. Thus, budgeted revenue for a particular unmetered customer class depends on (1) the estimated number of customers in the class and (2) the estimated number of units on which water charges are based. Such units might include dwelling units, front footage on the main of the customers' premises, or hydrants. Customer records should provide historical data for these factors, which can then be extrapolated.

Modification of Historical Trends

Historical data, such as per-capita consumption records, should be examined to ensure that underlying conditions have not changed. Economic and social conditions in the service area of the utility can change, causing corresponding changes in the number of customers in a particular class, the quantity of water sold within each block of a block-rate schedule, the number of meters of various sizes, or other demand and revenue factors. Projections based on historical consumption trends may need to be adjusted to account for changing conditions in the service area. Specifically, the estimated number of customers should be modified to reflect increases resulting from building permits projected to be issued, the number of new houses to be built, and other similar factors. Likewise, historical projections of the quantity of water sold within each block of a block-rate schedule should be adjusted for the estimated effects of changes in pricing policies, advertising and other promotional activities, and general and local socioeconomic conditions.

Applying the Rate Schedules

After the quantity components are estimated, they must be related to the appropriate rate schedule in order to determine total projected revenues. For example, in the case of metered sales from a block rate structure, the estimated quantity of water to be sold is matched to and multiplied by the appropriate rate in the block structure to arrive at estimated revenues from each block. Total estimated water sales revenue is derived by adding estimated water sales revenues from each block of the pricing structure and across all classes of customers (residential, commercial, industrial, and others) if different classes of customers have different rate structures. If a service charge or minimum charge is levied on metered customers, then the appropriate charge must be multiplied by the estimated number of customers (or number of meters, if the charge is based on meter size) to determine the total estimated revenue obtainable under the service charge or minimum charge.

To determine the budgeted amount of revenue from unmetered sales, the appropriate flat-rate schedules are applied on the basis of some common denominator, such as housing units, bedrooms, front footage, or hydrants used by each customer class.

Ultimately, the adequacy of forecasted operating revenues should be judged in terms of covering the cost of providing water service. In an inflationary and capital-expansion environment, the existing rate schedule may be judged inadequate for meeting the various costs of providing water service (revenue requirements). In such instances, either the existing rate schedule should be increased to reflect the inflationary environment or a rate study undertaken to develop an alternative rate schedule that will generate the necessary revenues.

Developing the Rate Schedule

The particular rate-making procedure to be followed in establishing a rate schedule for a water utility depends on many factors, including differences in the form of ownership (private or governmental), differences in regulatory control over water rates (control by a state public service commission or by a local authority), and differences in individual viewpoints or preferences concerning the appropriate procedure to be followed to meet local conditions and requirements. Nevertheless, there are basic considerations involved in developing a rate schedule for almost any water utility. (Refer to AWWA Manual Ml, *Principles of Water Rates, Fees, and Charges,* for specific information and principles of water rate structure design.)

The development of an adequate rate schedule represents a joint effort among various experts, particularly accountants and engineers. The accounting records (property and expense records) supply the basic data for the cost-of-service study. From these records, the accountant must develop pro-forma expense forecasts. The accountant or engineer is generally responsible for converting original cost records to rate-base values (when applicable) that fall somewhere between original cost less depreciation and replacement cost less depreciation. Subsequently, the accountant and engineer must work together to allocate utility plant and operating costs to each class of customer in order to develop an equitable water rate schedule. Water rates should be established at levels that will produce sufficient total revenue to allow the water utility to (1) operate and maintain the water system in a manner that will provide adequate service, (2) meet financial obligations, (3) attract capital to maintain and improve facilities, and (4) provide additional facilities required by customer demand.

Depending on the circumstances under which the water utility operates, total revenue requirements are determined in accordance with the "utility basis" approach, the "cash needs" approach, or a combination of both. In order to attain reasonable equity, differences in rates and charges for water service applicable to different classes of customers and users should be based, insofar as possible, on the cost of serving the different customer classes and uses.

Revenue Requirements Under the Traditional Public Utility Approach

In the case of private utilities subject to rate regulation by state public service commissions, revenue requirements are generally established by applying the traditional public utility or "utility basis" approach. Under the public utility approach, the total revenues must be sufficient to permit a given return on a defined rate base. In instances where state regulatory bodies have jurisdiction over rates of governmental water utilities, the approach to the determination of revenue requirements can vary. In some cases, the public utility approach is employed, whereas in other cases, the "cash needs" approach is required. The usual exemption of governmental water utilities from a state commission regulation does not necessarily hold when the utility renders service to customers located outside the municipality's borders or outside designated service areas. When commissions do regulate outside-service-area water charges, the related revenue requirements are generally determined using the traditional public utility approach.

In the case of governmental water utilities not subject to rate regulation by state public service commissions, the determination of revenue requirements according to the traditional public utility approach also provides an alternative to the use of the "cash needs" approach. The public utility approach recognizes that the water utility is the property of the citizens of the municipality and that outside users should be charged amounts to cover operation and maintenance expenses, depreciation expense, local taxes, and a reasonable return on the value of all property devoted to providing service to the suburban user who is not at risk of otherwise contributing to the funding of the utility (i.e., not subject to the possibility of subsidizing the utility via general fund transfers of citizen's taxes paid).

If the public utility approach is used inside the service area, as is required of private utilities and of some governmental water utilities subject to commission regulation, then differences between inside-the-service-area and outside-the-service-area rates may be justified on the basis of variations in the cost of serving the two groups of customers. Rates developed under the "cash needs" approach will often result in rates that may be lower than rates developed under the public utility approach because the "cash needs" approach does not generally include a return on the rate base.

There is almost always some time between the date an application for new rates is prepared and submitted to the state public service commission for approval and the date the new rates become effective; this delay is generally referred to as "regulatory lag." If rates are predicated on past or present costs and if operating expenses increase markedly, then the revenues derived from the new rate schedule may become inadequate shortly after it goes into effect. Therefore, a realistic forecast of expenses should be based on past operation and maintenance expenses, depreciation and amortization charges, and taxes, all adjusted for known or anticipated changes for the applicable future period. Recent trends favor regular rate increases to cover the impact of inflation and the often sharply increasing marginal costs of service as available water supplies become more difficult and costly to develop. Although periodic changes in rates are necessitated by changing requirements, too frequent changes in rates could be undesirable because of the cost incurred in conjunction with rate cases and the adverse effect on customer relations. However, regular annual rate increases that reflect inflationary costs in current dollars are most equitable to both current and future customers.

Properly matching costs with revenues will assure that current customers pay only their fair share of costs of services incurred by the utility. However, in the case of water utilities subject to public service commission regulation, the rate base and operating expense figures are usually historical in nature and generally are developed for a "test year." The test year is typically the 12 months prior to the rate study, adjusted for conditions that are expected to prevail in the future. The amount of the rate base and rate of return to be allowed on the defined rate base are established by the public service commission for those water utilities subject to its jurisdiction. The determination of rate base differs between states. Methods employed by public service commissions may be original cost less depreciation, replacement cost less depreciation, or some combination of the two approaches. In any event, a rate base and a rate of return must be established to ensure a regulated water utility an income sufficient to attract the capital necessary to maintain and improve the facilities as required by customer demand.

Revenue Requirements Under the "Cash Needs" Approach

Most governmental water utilities elect, or may be required by law, to use the "cash needs" approach to rate determination. Depending on local policy and conditions, there is a wide variation among governmental water utilities as to the types of cash outlays that are to be covered by revenues. The rate study, in accordance with the "cash needs" approach, generally would determine the amount of operating revenue needed to cover operation and maintenance expenses; debt-service requirements, including revenue bond coverage requirements, if any; plant replacements; and normal plant extensions and improvements not otherwise funded by bonds. In some instances, operating revenues may also be required to cover other cash outlays, such as appropriations for major improvements, contributions to other municipal funds, and payments in lieu of taxes. The emphasis on cash needs in determining the revenue requirements for a governmental water utility not subject to commission regulation is primarily a result of two factors. First, major utility plant improvements for most governmental water utilities are financed by revenue bonds that require annual debt service payments from cash generated from water sales. Second, governmental water utilities are ordinarily expected to recover the cost of service (measured in terms of normal annual cash outlays) through operations but are not expected to earn a profit. Governmental water utilities may, however, be required to maintain debt-service and other management reserves. Further, the "cash needs" approach is similar to the budget basis used by other municipal departments or agencies and, therefore, may be more easily explained and justified to municipal administrators.

It should be noted that, in accordance with the "cash needs" approach, no explicit provision is made for depreciation expense. Depreciation charges are noncash expenditures and, as such, are properly excluded. However, the use of the "cash needs" approach does not imply that depreciation expense should be ignored in determining utility operating income. The application of sound accounting principles requires that provisions be made for depreciation and other noncash or multiperiod expenses in the financial statements. Multiperiod expenses include items that can benefit more than one accounting period, such as prepaid insurance or bond issue discounts. Typically, in a "cash needs" approach to developing rates as a substitute for depreciation expense, the principal portion of debt service is included as are contributions to various reserves (operating reserve, repair/renewal reserve, etc.) that would not be included in a utility basis approach to rate setting.

Revenue requirements under "cash needs" should be based on the average requirements for the period to which the new rate schedule will apply. Operation and maintenance expenses should be forecast as described in chapter 12. Forecasted debt-service requirements should include payments on principal and interest to be made on outstanding debt and on any borrowing expected to take place during the budget period. Coverage requirements on revenue bond debt service also may necessitate attention in establishing revenue requirements.

The amounts estimated for contributions to repair and replacement reserves should be sufficient to provide for current renewals and replacements of water utility property over time that is no longer serviceable. This ensures that current customers do not receive service at costs below the long-term average cost of providing service. The requirement for normal extensions and improvements should provide for small main extensions, services, meters, hydrants, and other minor items. The amount of funds needed for major extensions and improvements often is not included in the estimate, since it is assumed that major improvements will be financed by new customers. Required contributions to other municipal funds, particularly if made as a payment in lieu of taxes (PILOT) or as a return on investment, should also be included in the computation of cash basis revenue requirements. If the policy of a utility is to minimize or avoid debt, operating revenues may be required to cover the cost of major extensions as well as improvements not otherwise financed from contributions.

Determining the Rate Schedule

The definition of *rate base* varies from one public service commission to another, as does the definition of *allowable rate of return*. Consequently, the level of rates in rate schedules developed by two similar water utilities subject to regulation by two different public service commissions may vary. In the case of governmental water utilities not subject to the jurisdiction of state public service commissions, the level of rates in rate schedules also may vary markedly depending on the source of supply, density of water distribution system infrastructure, the relative infrastructure age and amount of recent infrastructure reinvestment, the capital structure of the utility, the requirements for payments of taxes (or payments in lieu of taxes or return on investment), and capital financing policies. Historically, many water utilities employed a rate schedule of three to seven blocks applicable to all general customers (residential, commercial, industrial, and public authorities). Under the block-rate schedule, charges per unit of water consumed by customers vary depending on the amount of water consumed within successive consumption blocks. Separate rate schedules are often provided for private fire protection, public fire protection, sales for resale, and other classes of use.

Historically, block-rate schedules often provided for decreasing incremental charges to customers as consumption increases. This type of rate design is called a *declining block rate*, presumably because it reflects the cost structure of water production and delivery. It is argued that it costs less to produce and deliver large quantities of water to large customers, and the ratio of peak demand to average demand typically is smaller for the large water user than the small user. Therefore, the extra capacity costs necessary to meet peak demand are relatively less for large users. A counter argument would be that the plant and delivery system have to be built to meet the needs of the larger users and their peak demands, regardless of the variation between their peak and average usage. Building a delivery system capable of fulfilling the needs of the larger users may offset the economies of scale in production. Moreover, the declining rate structure encourages consumption rather than conservation and effectively makes the unit cost of water higher for small users.

Recent legal, regulatory, and social trends have reduced the number of consumption blocks contained in rate schedules. Some utilities have settled on a single volume rate per unit of water. Agencies anticipating inadequate sources of water, which could result from drought conditions or rapid growth without ready access to new supplies, often implement increasing ("inclining block-rate") or seasonal rate structures as an attempt to limit water consumption. The success of these inclining rate structures depends on a number of variables such as the design of the block structure, significance of the water bill to the customer, local weather conditions, and public education. The residential demand for indoor water needs is relatively inelastic with respect to price (estimates are that as price goes up, water usage goes down about 10 to 15 percent, although academic studies vary in their estimates). Outdoor residential uses, such as lawn watering, are more responsive to price, and there is more responsiveness to price over the long term than the short term, as people replace plumbing fixtures with models that offer lower water use and change their outdoor landscaping to less thirsty varieties. Industrial water use is more sensitive to price than domestic usage, in part because such users have other options, such as recycled water and changing industrial processes. In short, while factors other than price may be more important in conserving water, there is sufficient responsiveness to price over the variety of users and over the long run to support in declining block rates when water shortages occur and conservation measures are desirable.

Developing an equitable schedule of rates and charges applicable to various classes of customers and uses requires periodic cost-of-service studies. The process often involves three major steps: (1) allocation of the costs of service to cost functions, (2) allocation of the functional costs to customer classes, and (3) development of the rate schedules. For more detailed information about cost-of-service and rate design, refer to AWWA Manual Ml.

Monitoring Revenues

A general rule for accrual-basis accounting is that revenue is recognized at the time possession, title, or use of a product or service is transferred to the customer. Under accrual accounting, the major item of revenue for a water utility—sales of water—is recognized on the basis of customer billings. (If a utility is required to follow cash-basis accounting, then revenue is recognized when cash is received from customers.) Revenue from other sources should also be recognized, to the extent practicable, as it is earned during the accounting period.

The use of meters for measuring the quantity of water delivered to customers results in a lag between the time that water is consumed and the time that meters are read. There is an additional interval between the time a meter is read and the time the bill is rendered to a customer. These lags result in some inaccuracies in assigning revenues to accounting periods. As remote reading systems become practicable, such lags may be reduced. In an effort to decrease inaccuracies, some utilities currently estimate the amount of water delivered to customers but not represented by meter readings, and determine the prospective billing based on monthly pumping figures and customers' past consumption records. This method may be particularly useful if a water utility reads customers' meters every two months but prepares a monthly statement of revenue. Even if all meters are read and all customers billed during the accounting period, revenues from the sales of water service based on meter readings and billings during the period will be understated by the amount due to the utility for water service rendered between the time meters are read and the end of the accounting period. For example, if meters are read regularly throughout the month, the deficiency is approximately equivalent to 15 days' revenue. The deficiency may be largely offset by water service that was delivered to customers during the preceding accounting period but that is represented by meter readings and billings during the current accounting period. Variations in customer consumption from one accounting period to another, therefore, make reported revenue somewhat inaccurate, but the inaccuracy is seldom considered to be material or large enough to mislead users of water utility financial statements.

Comparing Budgeted and Actual Revenue

Actual revenues usually differ to some extent from budgeted revenues. Budgeted revenue estimates serve as useful standards only to the extent that they are valid and reasonable. Variations from budgeted revenue figures are to be expected; however, significant variations in actual revenues from budgeted revenues should be investigated to determine the reason and if management action is necessary. In some cases, variations arise from faulty budgeting procedures. In other cases, managers or employees have failed to follow the operating plan. Random events that cause variation, such as weather, tend to average out over time.

Revenue totals should be reported to management on a frequent and periodic basis, typically at monthly intervals. Revenue statements should be designed to display results both in total and in detail by geographical area and customer classes. During each year, monthly statements should present both actual and budgeted data.

Variations in revenue from the budget standard caused by unanticipated changes in the volume of water used by customers may be largely beyond the control of management. Sometimes it is not the amount of water produced that varies, but the gap between production and billing, which can be caused by a large fire, unmetered use of fire hydrants, main breaks, faulty meters, or unauthorized use of unmetered water (spraying children in hot summer months from fire hydrants?). While large fluctuations may not be predictable, it is usually possible to minimize or at least account for unmetered usage.

For revenue control purposes, water utility management is primarily interested in assuring that (1) user demands for water are met, (2) the water produced is actually used by customers, and (3) metered customers are billed correctly for the amount of water that they use. User demands for water are met primarily by ensuring that plant capacity is adequate to meet the water requirements of all customers and by remedying customer complaints concerning water service. Control over water use and billing for this use is discussed in the following section.

Accounting for Water Output

The control of water produced and delivered to the distribution system is closely allied with the control of revenues. This control assists a water utility in increasing the effectiveness and efficiency of its operation. The difference between water delievered to the distribution system (measured, for example, by a master meter installed in the mains that supply the distribution system with treated water) and water used by customers (metered use and estimated flat-rate use) is considered "unaccounted-for water." Determining customer use of water is improved when all users are metered. Even in a completely metered system, some estimate of use is necessary because all meters cannot be read simultaneously. In addition, water used through unmetered hydrants, to fight fires, or lost when mains break also results in "unaccounted-for water." Residential, commercial, and industrial use is metered by the majority of water utilities. Public use, with the exception of fire protection, should also be metered.

In order to account for all treated water, unmetered water use should be estimated. Estimates of water use for firefighting could be based on the number and size of hose streams, pressure, and the length of time water is used. Estimates of water used by street department water trucks, if not metered, may be based on the capacity of each truck and the number of tank loads used. Unmetered, treated water used by the utility itself, for example, to clean filter beds, can also be estimated.

The ratio of total water used by customers to total water delivered to the distribution system provides one index to the efficiency of utility operation. In addition to the immediate concerns related to revenue, it should be kept in mind that leakage may allow the backflow of groundwater into the mains, resulting in contamination of the treated water before it reaches the customer. Factors influencing the ratio of unaccounted-for water include the age and condition of the distribution system (including meters), ground conditions, pressure, and source of supply. A program of systematic meter reading, testing, and repair; leak control; maintenance of operating statistics; and controlling unauthorized use will help a utility attain or maintain an acceptable percentage of accounted-for water in relation to total treated water delivered to the distribution system.

In summary, the increasing cost of expanding water utility plant capacity and the limited supply of water make it imperative that existing plant capacity be used efficiently and effectively. The total accounted-for water (or revenue-producing water) in relation to the total water delivered to the distribution system is an effective measure of the efficiency and effectiveness of operations. By increasing the ratio of accounted-for water to water delivered, the need for expensive programs to increase plant capacity may be minimized. Increased net income or a decrease in customer water rates should also result from reducing unaccounted-for water.

This page intentionally blank.

Chapter 11

Operation and Maintenance Expenses

Operating income is computed by subtracting operating expenses (expenses applicable to the furnishing of water utility services) from operating revenues (revenues derived from the normal operations of a water utility). Planning and controlling revenue items are discussed in chapter 10. Planning and controlling operating expense items are the subjects of this chapter.

A water utility's expenses are classified by regulatory bodies as "operating expenses" and "nonoperating expenses." Operating expenses include all expenses applicable to the furnishing of water utility services. Nonoperating expenses include expenses not associated with a utility's normal business of supplying water. Such expenses typically are small in relation to operating expenses.

Operating expenses are usually subdivided into operating expenses, maintenance expenses, depreciation expenses, amortization expense, taxes other than income taxes, and income taxes. Planning and controlling operation and maintenance expenses are discussed in this chapter; planning and accounting for depreciation and amortization expenses are discussed in chapter 12; and planning for taxes is discussed in chapter 13.

Nature and Classification

Operation expenses for a water utility include the expenses incurred in operating the source-of-supply and pumping facilities, water treatment facilities, and transmission and distribution facilities. In addition, operation expenses include customer accounts expenses. Examples of customer accounts expenses include meter reading, maintaining customer records and collections, uncollectible accounts, and miscellaneous expenses incurred in maintaining customer accounts. Customer accounts expenses also include customer service costs related to supervision, labor, and providing customer service and informational activities to encourage the safe and efficient use of a utility's service, to promote conservation of water, and to assist customers in answering specific questions regarding the proper and economical use of a utility's service and of customer's equipment that uses the service. Operation expenses also include the administrative and general expenses of a utility that have not been charged directly to a particular operating function and sales expenses in promoting the use of water service.

Maintenance expenses for a water utility include maintenance of the source of supply and pumping, water treatment facilities, transmission and distribution facilities, and general plant facilities. In general, expenses for repairing a water utility plant, or for replacing parts of structures and equipment of a size less than that of a "retirement unit" for the purpose of maintaining a utility plant, are called maintenance expenses. The state utility regulatory agency or the utility generally will define retirement units. The cost of replacing significant parts of a water utility plant that prolong the useful life of the asset should not be charged to maintenance expense accounts but should be capitalized. See chapter 12 on capital assets.

The operation-expense and the maintenance-expense accounts, which are summary accounts, are supported by subsidiary operation and maintenance expense accounts. Subsidiary operation and maintenance expense accounts are designed to show in detail a portion of the cost of rendering water service to customers.

Functional Classifications: What Is Included in Operation and Maintenance?

The NARUC classification of detailed operation and maintenance accounts reflects the fact that many water utilities are enterprises subject to rate regulation. As illustrated by the chart of accounts presented in appendix A, detailed operation and maintenance expense accounts are provided for each functional division of the utility. The functional expense categories are as follows:

- Source-of-supply and pumping expenses:
  —Operation maintenance
- Water treatment expenses:
  —Operation maintenance
- Transmission and distribution expenses:
  —Operation maintenance
- Customer accounts expenses
- Administrative and general expenses

The uniform system of accounts developed by NARUC allows regulators to distinguish capital expenditures from operating and maintenance expenses and to separate utility activities from nonutility operations. In applying this uniform system, an individual utility may add accounts and subaccounts as needed.

Expense Classification for Planning and Control

Each member of the water utility's management team must be responsible for planning expenses under their control. Each manager's plan for expenditures should be expressed in terms of wages and salaries, materials and supplies, and other natural classifications, such as contractual services. For example, Table 11-1 shows the comparison of budgeted operating expenses with actual expenses for a water utility's meter

Table 11-1. Meter maintenance operating expenses

Operating Expense Control Report — Meter Maintenance Shop						
	Month of June			Year to Date		
	Actual	Budget	Over (Under)	Actual	Budget	Over (Under)
Salaries and Wages:						
Foreman	$430	$410	$20	$2,695	$2,575	$120
Meter repairmen	1,155	1,090	65	7,185	6,720	465
Laborers	740	740	0	5,090	5,055	35
Total Salaries and Wages	$2,325	$2,240	$85	$14,970	$14,350	$620
Materials and Supplies:						
Small Tools	$10	$20	($10)	$105	$100	$5
Maintenance Materials and Supplies	910	890	20	5,325	5,450	(125)
Other	480	510	(30)	175	355	(180)
Total Materials and Supplies	$1,400	$1,420	($20)	$5,605	$5,905	($300)
Other Expenses:						
Maintenance of Meter Testing Equipment	$5	$20	($15)	$115	$105	$10
Utility Services	25	30	(5)	180	180	0
Incidental Expenses	15	10	5	40	60	(20)
Total Other Expenses	$45	$60	($15)	$335	$345	($10)
Total Operating Expenses	$3,770	$3,720	$50	$20,910	$20,600	$310

maintenance shop. Note that the expense items shown in Table 11-1 are at a level of detail beyond that provided by the NARUC classification of accounts.

Planning

Within the framework of the major objectives and policies established for the water utility, management must plan and control the utility's operation and maintenance activities. As noted in chapter 10, a forecast of demand for water service is the starting point for the entire budgetary process. Demand for water service (in terms of both volume of water and number of customers) is an important factor in determining the level of operation and maintenance activities.

Evaluation of Alternatives

The first step in planning any activity is to determine if relationships that existed in the past continue. Assuming an activity is still needed, there may be alternatives for how it should be performed. Managers may need to examine these alternatives and cost them out. Consistent with forecasted demand for water service, each alternative (including the alternative presently employed) for performing an operation or maintenance activity must be translated into, and evaluated in terms of, estimated requirements for personnel, material, and plant facilities. Frequently, each alternative requires a different combination of personnel and labor skills, materials, and other resources. For example, using computers to perform the customer accounting functions requires a different mix and type of personnel, material, and equipment than does the use of manual procedures. After selecting alternatives to be followed during the budget period, estimates of required personnel, material, and other operating and maintenance expenses become the basis of operating budgets. If selected alternatives require facilities not currently available, then acquisition or construction of facilities must also be included in the proposed equipment and/or capital expenditures budget.

Estimating Costs

A number of techniques are used to project costs for the budget year. Many of them rely on historical records of accounting data, plus expert knowledge of changes in the community or in the market from which goods and services are being purchased. For some purposes, average costs over a number of years are most appropriate; for others, trend data are likely to give the best estimate of spending for the next year. Some expenditures are formula or contract driven, and hence are more predictable. The more managers know what drives costs, the better their predictions of expenditures are likely to be.

The Use of Historical Data

Many budget projections are built up from analysis of unit costs—how much has it cost the utility to perform this task in the past. This analysis works well if there is no reason to suspect that costs or quantities are likely to change. For example, in cases where it is reasonable to establish a physical standard of performance (such as the number of labor hours required to paint a given number of fire hydrants), past performance is a helpful guide for setting the standard. The standard can then be used to estimate labor or material requirements for the level of the operation or maintenance activity expected to be attained during a budget period. Since the number of hydrants to be painted is within managerial control, a fixed number can be chosen, perhaps a given percent of all hydrants, and the costs calculated with reasonable accuracy.

Historical data are useful for developing price components such as unit costs for materials and supplies. Trends in cost for particular supplies can be useful in predicting the coming year's prices. With those trends in mind, managers can develop a good estimate for budgeted expenditures by multiplying expected unit prices by estimated quantities to be used.

For some cost items, the immediate past is a good predictor, especially if any changes for the budget year are already known. Thus the amount of money to be spent on rentals of property or equipment is likely to reflect the current year's costs, and increases are likely to be known well in advance. Similarly, the costs of renewing contracts for service are likely to be known in advance, and depending on contract language, may be equal to the cost in the current year plus a factor for inflation; or there may be step increases in charges from one year to the next that are included in contract language. Some contracts may pass along cost increases to the contractee, in which case water utility managers have to estimate them in advance based on their own knowledge of the drivers of cost increases and the past history of increases.

In using history to come up with spending projections, at times managers may want to use averages, at times they will want to look at trends, and at still other times, they will want to use only the last year or two of data. Averages are useful when the costs jump around a lot from year to year, up and down, perhaps in accordance with the weather; in such cases averages taken from data that cover a number of years may be the best guess of what will happen the following year. Trend lines, which measure whether something is going up or down over time, can be useful in predicting the next year's levels, so long as items are clearly trending upward or downward, and are not random. For example, insurance costs may be going up from year to year, and the rate of change in recent years may give a reasonable estimate of what will happen in the following year. Similarly, the costs of chemicals may be increasing from year to year at a rate that is easily determined by looking at past purchases. If there is no change in vendor prices or quantities purchased (large quantity purchases may be cheaper per unit than smaller purchases) or method of purchasing (as part of a larger consortium or independently), this historical data may be all that is needed to help estimate the future cost of chemicals.

Formulas

Sometimes it is not past history that managers need to work with, but formulas or contracts. Labor costs may be specified in contracts, wage increases may be determinate—a given percent of the last year's wages, for example. If there are cost-of-living increases included, then managers may need to refer to recent increases in whatever index of cost of living is specified in the contract. These indexes tell you what has happened in the current year and give a percent figure to multiply times the wage base. Generally cost-of-living indexes are too broad to be used for most of the operating items in a water utility budget. Indexes that measure inflation for the goods and services local governments purchase may be more useful, and the history of changes in specific items, such as chemicals, may be more useful yet. When contracts for service build in inflation increases, it is important to note which index they are using.

In general, figuring out how much to budget for expenditures is a matter of calculating the likely price and multiplying by the likely quantities, whether labor or parts or supplies. To the extent that past circumstances are not expected to exist in the future, there may be little or no historical data on which to rely, or historical data may need to be modified to come up with estimates of cost. Maintenance costs for new equipment, for example, may be unknown; to come up with an estimate may require reviewing the specs, calling the manufacturer, finding others who have bought this equipment and asking about their experiences, or guessing based on similar equipment about which the utility does have data.

Cost Behavior

Figuring out likely expenditures is much easier if managers know why particular costs rise and fall. Such knowledge is also useful for control purposes. Many operation and maintenance expense items do not vary in amount in response to changes in volume of water sold. For example, the level of materials and supplies expense for maintenance purposes depends to a large degree on the size of a water utility plant rather than the quantity of water sold. Of course, the level of maintenance materials and supplies expense in relation to the physical size or cost of plant assets varies among particular types of utility plant assets. For example, for such plant items as source-of-supply tunnels and reservoirs, the level of materials and supplies expense normally is small in comparison to plant items such as distribution mains. The level of expense for wages and salaries depends primarily on the number of permanent employees required to operate and maintain water utility facilities. The level of customer accounts expenses depends more on the number of customers than on the volume of water sold. Some major expense items, such as chemicals and fuel or other sources of power for pumping, vary with the volume of water produced for customer use.

Many of the factors that influence cost behavior are interdependent. The number of employees depends on the size of the water utility plant and the number of customers served. The size of the water utility plant depends on the number of customers served and the volume of water produced for customer use. Therefore, for the purpose of understanding and determining cost behavior, expense items should be related to those factors that both directly and indirectly affect the level of the expense items.

Considerations in planning major categories of water utility operation and maintenance expenses are discussed in the following sections.

Source-of-Supply and Pumping Expenses

Major items of expense incurred in operating and maintaining source-of-supply facilities include labor, materials, and supplies. Operation expenses also may include purchased water and rent of leased source-of-supply facilities. Major items of expense incurred in operating pumping facilities include labor, materials and supplies, fuel or power used for pumping, and rent. Major items of expense incurred in the maintenance of pumping facilities include labor, materials, and supplies.

Labor

Source-of-supply and pumping labor expense is a product of personnel requirements and wage and salary levels, both of which must be forecast in the budget process. The number of employees required to operate and maintain source-of-supply and pumping facilities effectively depends on the physical conditions, design, and extent of the facilities. The personnel requirements for operation activities are largely unresponsive to changes in the amount of water demanded by customers; within wide ranges of water production, personnel requirements for pumping facilities are fixed. The introduction of new pumping facilities incorporating the latest technological developments, or increases in the size of pumping facilities, will probably cause changes in personnel requirements. Historical data concerning operating personnel requirements for the operation of facilities during a budget period will provide a basis for forecasting labor expense.

The number of employees required to maintain source-of-supply and pumping facilities is a function of utility maintenance policy. In the language of operations researchers, a proper maintenance policy is one that minimizes the total cost of maintaining a facility plus the cost of not maintaining the facility. The cost of maintenance is a familiar concept; the cost of not maintaining includes those costs incident on an interruption of service supplied by the facility. Within the framework of this overall maintenance policy, a maintenance program based on the physical condition, design, and extent of facilities and on replacement policy, must be established for each budget period. Maintenance personnel required to fulfill the budgeted maintenance program are thus determined. Practical experience shows that personnel must be provided for emergency maintenance as well as routine maintenance.

Existing wage and salary schedules, modified by expected changes in the schedules and expected changes in the number of employees at each level in the schedules, serve as a basis for translating personnel requirements into labor budgets.

Materials and Supplies

The usage of materials and supplies for operation and maintenance purposes depends on the physical condition, design, and extent of source-of-supply and pumping facilities and the estimated or scheduled workload. Historical data concerning materials and supplies usage, adjusted for anticipated changes in the nature and extent of the workload, are useful for budgeting requirements. The estimated usage then must be multiplied by anticipated unit prices of materials and supplies in order to arrive at a budget figure for materials and supplies expense.

Purchased Water

The cost of purchased water, if any, also must be budgeted. Depending on the utility's supply sources and related supply contracts, the estimated amount of water to be purchased depends on the difference between the estimated volume of water demanded by customers (as forecast by procedures discussed in chapter 10) and the estimated amount of water to be supplied by a utility's source-of-supply facilities. The amount to be supplied by utility facilities is based on historical data adjusted for anticipated changes in the capabilities of source-of-supply facilities to meet the demand for water. An estimate of the cost of purchased water during a budget period is then obtained by applying the appropriate rate schedule to the estimated volume of water to be purchased for resale.

Fuel and Power

A water utility may (1) purchase fuel for use in producing its own power to operate pumps, (2) purchase fuel or power to operate pumps, or (3) employ a combination of methods. The amount of fuel (such as coal and/or natural gas) used in the production of power to operate pumps and the amount of fuel or power (such as diesel fuel or electricity) used directly in the operation of pumps depends largely on the amount of water produced for customers.

Historical data concerning the amount of fuel and power required to pump 1 million gal (or 1 million L) of water serve as a basis for forecasting fuel and power requirements for a budget period. Forecasted fuel and power usage during a budget period is determined by multiplying historical fuel and power usage per 1 million gal (1 million L) pumped by estimated pumpage (in terms of millions of gallons [liters]) for the budget period. Estimated fuel and power usage must then be multiplied by anticipated unit prices to arrive at a budget figure for fuel and power expense.

Consistent with the capabilities of the pumping facilities, forecasted fuel and power expense should reflect the least-cost combination of fuel and power sources available for use during a budget period.

Rent

Rent expense depends on the extent to which property of others is used in connection with the source-of-supply system. A budgeted figure for rent expense, applicable to source-of-supply facilities, can be determined from existing or anticipated lease agreements. Rent expense applicable to other facilities can be estimated in a similar manner.

Before a water utility commits itself to leasing property, the advantages and disadvantages of leasing as opposed to purchasing should be considered. Purchasing has the advantage of allowing the cost of the property to be included in the rate base and, for private utilities, the advantage of tax savings from the additional depreciation expense. Disadvantages of purchasing include those normally accompanying ownership, such as the expenses of property taxes, insurance, maintenance, and the cost of having to finance the purchase. The advantages of leasing include eliminating the problems of financing the purchase and, for private water utilities, the tax savings from the treatment of rental payments as deductible expenses. Disadvantages include the lack of flexibility to changing conditions resulting from the commitment to a long-term fixed obligation and the lack of any interest in the residual value of property on termination of the lease. The choice of leasing as opposed to purchasing depends on the circumstances surrounding a particular item of property.

Water Treatment Expenses

The major items of expense incurred in operating and maintaining water treatment facilities include labor, materials and supplies (other than chemicals), chemicals, and rent.

Labor, Materials, and Supplies

Water treatment labor expense is a product of personnel requirements and wage and salary levels. Materials and supplies expense incurred in the operation and maintenance of water treatment facilities is a product of usage and unit prices of materials and supplies.

As with source-of-supply and pumping facilities, the number of persons employed and the usage of materials and supplies (other than chemicals) for operation and maintenance activities depend largely on the physical condition, design, and extent of the water treatment facilities. Requirements for personnel, materials, and supplies (except chemicals) for operation and maintenance activities are largely unresponsive to changes in the amount of water demanded by customers, at least within wide ranges. Technological changes incorporated into new water treatment facilities, or the enlargement of existing facilities, will affect personnel, materials, and supplies requirements.

The earlier discussion about forecasting personnel requirements, wage and salary levels, and materials and supplies expense (see "Source-of-Supply and Pumping Expenses") is equally applicable to planning and forecasting water treatment labor, materials, and supplies expense for a budget period.

Chemicals

The level of chemical usage is dependent, to a large extent, on the volume of water produced for customer use. The amount of chemicals used also is affected by the quality (in terms of purity) of raw water received for treatment from the source-of-supply facilities.

Historical data concerning chemicals used per 1 million gal (or 1 million L) of water produced serve as a useful guide for determining chemical usage during the budget period. The historical data should be adjusted for anticipated changes in the level of chemical usage caused by changing raw-water quality. For each type of chemical used, the estimated usage per 1 million gal (or 1 million L) of water is multiplied by the estimated volume of water to be supplied to customers in order to get total chemical usage. Total usage for each chemical is multiplied by the anticipated per-unit cost for that chemical to obtain budgeted chemical expenses.

Transmission and Distribution Expense

Labor, materials, supplies, and rent are among the major items of expense incurred in operating and maintaining transmission and distribution facilities.

Labor

Transmission and distribution labor expense is a product of personnel requirements and wage and salary levels, both of which must be forecast in the budget process. The number of persons employed for operation and maintenance activities depends largely on the physical condition, design, and extent of transmission and distribution facilities. The growth of a transmission and distribution system will, of course, affect personnel requirements. Personnel requirements for operating storage facilities, transmission and distribution mains, and fire mains generally are not subject to wide fluctuation. Historical data concerning personnel requirements for operating the facilities, adjusted for contemplated changes, serve as the basis for forecasting personnel requirements during a budget period.

Personnel requirements for maintaining customer meters depend on the numbers of customer services and meters installed, removed, relocated, turned on, and shut off. Historical data concerning personnel requirements for the handling of customer meters, adjusted for anticipated changes in the number of customer meters and services to be installed, removed, relocated, turned on, and shut off, serve as a basis for forecasting personnel requirements during a budget period. The number of employees required to maintain transmission and distribution facilities is a function of the utility maintenance policy. Within the framework of the overall maintenance policy, a maintenance program must be established for a budget period. The extent of the maintenance program will depend on (1) the physical condition, design, and extent of distribution reservoirs and standpipes; (2) the physical condition, size, and length of transmission and distribution mains and fire mains; (3) the physical condition, size, and number of customers' services, meters, and hydrants; and (4) the replacement policy. Maintenance personnel requirements for a budget period are forecast based on the scheduled maintenance program and on estimated emergency repairs.

Existing wage and salary schedules, modified by expected changes in the schedules and expected changes in the number of employees at each level in the schedules, serve as the basis for translating personnel requirements for transmission and distribution activities into labor budgets. Based on past experience, utility management may desire to budget at overtime rates the probable number of labor hours expected to result from emergency repair work on transmission and distribution facilities.

Materials and Supplies

The usage of materials and supplies for operation and maintenance purposes depends on the physical condition, design, and extent of the transmission and distribution facilities, and on the estimated or scheduled workload. Historical data concerning materials and supplies usage, adjusted for anticipated changes in the nature and extent of the workload, are useful for budgeting materials and supplies requirements. The estimated usage must then be multiplied by anticipated unit prices of materials and supplies in order to arrive at a forecast of expense for a budget period.

Billing and Customer Relations

Amounts billed to customers for operation and maintenance work performed on customer service connections and meters also should be estimated for a budget period. The estimated billings then should be credited against the costs incurred in performing the work to determine estimated net expense incurred by the water utility during the budget period. Historical data, adjusted for anticipated changes in work billed to customers, serve as a basis for forecasting customer billings for work performed during a budget period.

The components of billing and customer relations include the maintenance of accounts, which encompasses incentives for and education about conservation and responding to inquiries and complaints. Estimates of cost depend on labor, material and supplies, and rent, but in this portion of operations, the cost of unpaid bills also needs to be estimated. Prior history is the guide, with alterations based on economic and social conditions as well as changes in policy and workload. Various degrees of automation may influence labor costs.

Customer accounts activities include opening and closing customer accounts, meter reading, billing, collecting, maintaining customer records, and handling customer complaints and requests for information. Major items of expense incurred in performing customer accounts activities include supervision, labor, materials and supplies, losses from uncollectible utility revenues, and expenses associated with the use of data processing equipment. As noted previously in this chapter, the purpose of these expenditures is to encourage the safe and efficient use of water, to promote water conservation, and to assist present customers by answering specific inquiries as to the best use of the utility's service and the best use of customer's equipment that uses the service.

The careful use and preservation of all scarce natural resources have become increasingly important in recent years. Many municipalities have found it necessary to ration water during periods when sources of supply have been drawn to very low levels or depleted. The increasing use of newspapers, television, and the internet to promote conservation in water consumption and to educate the general public about the limitations of water supply sources has resulted in a relatively new cost classification for many water utilities. Therefore, attempts to forecast customer service expense should include particular attention to water utility plans regarding future public education programs designed to promote water conservation and more efficient water usage.

The level of customer accounts expenses largely depends on the number of customers served. Customer accounts activities should be organized to minimize expenses for a given number and type of customer served. The attempt to minimize customer accounts expenses involves evaluating alternative procedures for conducting customer accounts activities. As an example, by extending the period covered by meter readings and billings, personnel requirements and labor expenses can be reduced. However, the savings in labor expense from extending the billing period would be offset at least partially by the cost of additional working capital required to tally unbilled water sales, the increased loss from uncollectible accounts, the overall reduction in available cash flow, and the increased loss of sales of water resulting from the lack of timely correction of under registration of meters. Moreover, extending the billing period mutes the pricing signal sent to encourage conservation. The practice of billing large customers (such as industrial customers) more frequently than small customers (including residential customers) may minimize the unfavorable effects of extended billing periods. Also, if meters are read every two months, then estimated bills may be rendered in alternate months to reduce the unfavorable effects cited above.

Within the context of a given meter-reading and billing schedule, there are a number of alternatives available for conducting customer accounts activities. In the case of meter reading, the method of recording metered water usage (for example, by using meter sheets instead of meter sensing cards) and the location of meters (for example, locating meters in outside pits instead of basements) will affect equipment and personnel requirements.

Labor

Historical data concerning personnel requirements for performing customer accounts activities serve as a useful guide in forecasting needs during a budget period. Historical personnel requirements must be adjusted for anticipated changes in the nature and extent of the workload resulting from changes in procedures for conducting accounts activities and from estimated changes in the type and number of customers served during a budget period. Existing wage and salary schedules, modified by anticipated changes in the schedules and expected changes in the number of employees at each level in the schedules, serve as a basis for translating forecast personnel requirements into a labor expense budget for customer accounts activities.

Materials and Supplies

Materials and supplies expense also can be estimated from past experience. Historical data concerning materials and supplies expense should be adjusted for anticipated changes in usage due to changes in the nature and extent of the workload for a budget period. The estimated materials and supplies usage must then be multiplied by anticipated unit prices in order to determine a budget figure for materials and supplies expense.

Rent

A budget figure for rent expense should be based on existing or anticipated lease agreements.

Uncollectible Utility Revenues

Uncollectible utility revenue is a function of the water utility's credit and collection policies. Unless credit and collection policies are to be changed during a budget period, past experience, in terms of bad debts as a percentage of accounts receivable or of operating revenues, serves as a basis for estimating uncollectible water utility revenues for the budget period. Anticipated changes in local economic conditions or demographic composition during a budget period and anticipated rate increases should also be considered in estimating uncollectible revenues.

Administrative and General

Administrative and general expenses typically comprise a significant portion of operation and maintenance expenses. Major administrative and general expense items include the following:

- Salaries and bonuses of officers, executives, and office staff employed in connection with the general administration of a water utility's operations
- The cost of outside services (for example, legal, accounting and auditing, engineering, labor negotiating, and similar services) generally applicable to all operating functions

- Property insurance expense incurred to protect against losses and damages to property employed in a utility's operations
- Insurance expense incurred to protect a water utility against injury and damage claims of employees or outside parties, and expenses incurred in settlement of injury and damage claims
- Payments under employee pension plans and payments with respect to other employee benefits (for example, employee accident, sickness, hospital, and death benefits)
- Rent charges with respect to property employed in performing administrative and general functions
- Assessments against a water utility to cover expenses incurred by state public service commissions
- Labor, materials, and supplies expense incurred for the maintenance of general plant facilities

Administrative and general expenses may vary significantly from one accounting period to another as a result of the performance of nonroutine functions, such as the preparation and presentation of rate cases before a public service commission. Note that many commissions require that costs of preparing and presenting rate cases be deferred and amortized over a stipulated time period. Expenses also vary because of the use of outside services on other than a routine basis. Expenses incurred in performing these nonroutine activities, to the extent that they can be foreseen, should be reflected in the operating expense budget. Administrative and general expenses also vary in settlement of injury and damage claims. Other expense items are incurred on a routine basis and can be budgeted on the basis of past experience. Such items include salaries, bonuses, office supplies, the cost of legal or other services used on a continuing basis, property insurance, insurance against injury and damage claims, costs of pension plans and other employee-benefit programs, rent, labor, and material expense for general plant maintenance. Some of these routine expense items are detailed below.

Labor

Personnel requirements for performing administrative and general functions are relatively fixed over reasonably long periods of time. Therefore, personnel requirements for a budget period can be based on past experience. The introduction of new office equipment during a budget period may, of course, require adjustment of past experience regarding personnel needs. Existing wage and salary schedules for administrative personnel, modified by changes in the schedules and expected number of employees at each level in the schedules, serve as a basis for translating personnel requirements into a labor expense budget for administrative personnel.

Office Supplies

Estimates for office supplies expense can be reasonably based on past experience and historical trends; adjustments may be required for changes in the nature and extent of workload and for anticipated changes in unit prices applicable to each office supply item.

Contracts for Service

The expense associated with outside services also may be estimated from past experience, adjusting for anticipated changes in use of services and for changes in fees and expenses paid under contract for services.

Property Insurance

The level of property insurance expense depends on the risk exposure, on the one hand, and the amount of coverage desired (that is, the amount of risk the utility is willing to retain) on the other. Risk exposure in turn depends on the size and value of water utility plant facilities as well as on known hazards and management policies to reduce or live with those risks. Property insurance expense can be estimated by referring to existing or proposed insurance contracts, modified by monitoring current insurance industry trends. To the extent that property insurance coverage is not purchased from an insurance firm but provided on a self-insured basis, a reasonable allowance for expected property loss may be budgeted on the basis of past experience.

Injuries and Damages

Insurance expense incurred to protect a water utility against injury and damage claims of employees and outside parties also can be estimated by referring to existing or proposed insurance contracts. To the extent that insurance coverage is not purchased from an insurance company but provided on a self-insured basis, a reasonable allowance for expected losses due to injuries and damages to employees or outside parties may be budgeted. The budget is based on past experience and, in the case of litigation in progress, on the advice of attorneys. The budgeted loss as a result of injuries and damages serves as the basis for making a charge to the injuries and damages expense account, with a corresponding credit being made to the injuries and damages reserve account.

Employee Pensions

Water utilities, both investor owned and government owned, operate a variety of pensions, sometimes in combinations, and each has its own characteristics and budget requirements. These include 401K plans, Social Security, defined contribution pension plans, and defined benefit pension plans. Managers need to know what plans they are operating, the characteristics of those plans, and how to budget for the employer's contributions to those plans.

Social Security is the federal pension plan to which employees and employers are required to contribute. The contributions are based on a percent of wages or salary of each employee up to a given maximum. Utility contributions for other retirement programs such as 401K and pension plans are usually controlled by utility policy, union contract, and/or actuarial calculations.

401K plans are more variable. The employee may contribute up to a given limit each year of pretaxed and post-taxed money. The employer may match the employee contribution, up to a given limit. The level of the match is up to the employer and the plan in place. Although employees may change the level of their contributions, they are unlikely to do so multiple times in a year and so their contributions should be relatively stable and predictable, and hence the employer match should also be reasonably predictable. Since the limits are fixed each year and known in advance, employers are unlikely to be caught with a large unfunded share.

401K plans are a form of defined contribution plan, that is, the employer puts in a given amount each year that is determined in advance and often is regulated by the pension plan or a labor contract. Most defined contribution plans are expressed in terms of a percent of wages. One of their great advantages is the ease of calculating how much the employer needs to contribute.

The most difficult pension contributions to calculate are the defined benefit plans. In these plans the employer is guaranteeing a percent of the employee's final salary (which may be based an average of several near-retirement years or only the last day of employment) for the employee's entire post-retirement life. The final salary under the terms of the pension life expectancy, and predicted rate of return on investments (discount rate) are educated guesses based on actuarial data. These elements are used to calculate an annual required contribution (ARC). The employer is expected to contribute each year an amount that when invested at a given rate of return, will in 40 years (some pensions use a shorter window of 30 years) produce the targeted amount of money. Usually the pension managers and or a hired actuary tell managers what the ARC is. Complications occur when the stock market declines, because then the contribution of the employer is expected to increase to make up for the decrease in value of the pension assets. An increase in the number of employees, or the wage scale, or the longevity of retirees can also cause a larger ARC. The amount of the required contribution can also go down if market returns rise. To prevent major shocks, it is a good idea to hire an actuary at regular intervals to make sure the utility is contributing as much as it needs to.

Payments under a pension plan depend on the terms of the pension contract or agreement and on the number of water utility employees covered by the plan. If accruals are made to a reserve account to provide for future pensions, then employee pension expense, based on actuarial studies, is equal to the amount of the accrual made during the accounting period. A pension fund from which pension payments are made also may be established and maintained through contributions to the fund equal in amount to the periodic reserve accruals. If pension payments are made to retired water utility employees by an insurance company, employee pension expense is determined by the payments to be made by the water utility to the insurance company during the accounting period. In cases where accruals are not recorded in a pension reserve or where annuities are not purchased, employee pension expense is determined by direct payments made by the water utility during the accounting period to, or on behalf of, retired employees.

While past experience may be useful in estimating employee pensions expense during a budget period, adjustment in historical data will be required for changes in contract terms, for new actuarial studies, for changes in the number of employees covered, and for changes in other factors influencing pension expense.

Other Employee Benefits

Expenses associated with other employee-benefit programs (for example, accident, sickness, hospital, and death benefits) also can be estimated by referring to the appropriate contracts or agreements giving rise to the benefit plans and by using past experience regarding the cost of these plans. Historical data will require adjustment for changes in the terms of the contracts, changes in the number of employees covered, and changes in other factors affecting the cost of the employee-benefit plans.

Here trends may be more important than prior levels of expenditure, as medical inflation is running faster than inflation generally. There are usually estimates available of the industrywide cost increases for the future year. While individual health insurance plans have different coverages and may not track exactly the national trends, mapping the water utility's health insurance costs against national trends can be helpful in projecting annual costs. Again, if the water utility self-insures, decisions must be made about the amount of retained risk and some plan for catastrophic events. Managers need to be familiar with any changes in their state's Workers' Compensation plans and costs, and budget accordingly.

Other Administrative and General Expenses

Rent expense associated with property used for administrative and general activities can be estimated by referring to existing and proposed lease agreements. Assessments to cover the expenses incurred by state public service commissions and labor, materials, and supplies expense incurred for the maintenance of general plant facilities may be estimated by projecting historical trends. Adjustments of historical data will be required for extraordinary changes in factors influencing the level of these expenses.

Centrally Provided Services

A water utility organization typically includes certain centralized entities that provide services to other segments of the organization. Examples of such entities are a central garage that provides transportation services and a central stores department that receives and issues materials and supplies. Since each centralized unit represents a responsibility center, costs associated with rendering centralized services should be budgeted for each centralized activity. Actual costs associated with rendering centralized services are accumulated in clearing accounts and allocated to particular operation and maintenance activities and to particular capital expenditure projects. Allocation of centralized activity expenses is discussed later in this chapter. Depending on the size and the complexity of the utility organization, separate clearing accounts may be established for the expenses of transportation, power-operated equipment, stores, fuel stock, shops, and similar activities.

To illustrate the budgeting process associated with centralized activity expenses, the remaining discussion in this section is devoted to forecasting two of the more common types of centralized activity expenses: transportation expenses and central stores expenses.

Transportation

Transportation services are primarily used by operation and maintenance personnel in the transmission and distribution division, meter reading and bill collecting personnel, and supervisory personnel. The size of the central garage depends on the requirements of the entire water utility organization for transportation services.

Based on the anticipated needs of a water utility for transportation, the personnel, equipment, and materials and supplies requirements must be determined for a budget period. Wages and salaries of the garage supervisor, equipment operators, and equipment maintenance personnel may be budgeted in a manner analogous to the budgeting of other wages and salaries expense previously described in this chapter. Other expenses incurred in operating and maintaining equipment (for example, gas, oil, maintenance materials and supplies, depreciation of equipment and garage, and taxes on equipment) may be estimated by using historical data regarding each individual piece of equipment modified in accordance with anticipated changes in equipment.

Central Stores

In the case of central stores, the major items of expense include wages and salaries, and materials and supplies. Requirements for personnel to operate central stores and the level of materials and supplies needed to perform central-stores activities depend on the requirements of a water utility organization for the services rendered by central stores. Adjustments in historical data may be required because of anticipated changes in factors affecting the expense items.

Controlling Operation and Maintenance Expenses

Effective control over operation and maintenance expenses is mandatory from the standpoint of avoiding frequent requests for changes in water utility rate schedules in response to increasing expenses. Unless operation and maintenance expenses are kept in strict control, frequent and costly rate studies may become necessary, and there is no assurance that rate increases will always be approved.

Comparing Budgeted and Actual Expenses

Effective control of operation and maintenance expense requires that actual results be compared with planned (budgeted) expenses on a routine basis. The comparisons should be made by developing a system of monthly comparative reports of actual and budgeted operation and maintenance expenses for each responsibility segment of a water utility organization. Table 11-1 presented earlier in this chapter provides an example of a monthly control report for a meter maintenance shop. Similar reports should be prepared for each segment of the utility.

Significant variations between budgeted and actual amounts should be investigated to determine needed corrective action. For example, an unfavorable variation between actual and budgeted chemical expenses might be explained by unanticipated price increases of various kinds of chemicals, an unanticipated increase in the volume of water supplied to customers, or lower-than-expected-quality raw water being received for treatment.

In the case of significant unfavorable variations between actual and budgeted figures, the manager or supervisor in charge of the organizational unit experiencing the variation should be required to indicate on the monthly report what corrective action, if any, is being taken to alleviate the problem. In no case should a manager or supervisor in charge of a responsibility segment of the water utility be held responsible for expenses over which he or she has no control. For example, expense variations caused by inefficiency in a centralized activity (such as a central garage or central stores) should be attributed to the management of the centralized activity and not to the serviced segments as a controllable variance.

Use of Unit Cost Standards Based on Historical Data

For certain types of work performed by various segments of a water utility, unit cost standards or benchmarks can be developed to judge the efficiency of work performed. Unit cost standards also allow for distributing certain expenses (such as those incurred by central garages and central stores) among operation and maintenance activities and among construction projects.

The efficiency of operations is best measured by the relationships between costs incurred and amount of work accomplished. Work is usually measured in terms of physical units, the cost per unit being determined by dividing total costs applicable to a number of units of work performed by the number of units. The procedure for developing unit cost standards is (1) to establish units of work for the activity, (2) to compile all the elements of cost entering into the performance of the work, and (3) to divide the total cost by the number of units in order to arrive at the cost per unit. Unit cost standards are usually developed from historical cost data for a particular period of time. Periods reflecting abnormal operating conditions should be eliminated from consideration.

If managers calculate the unit costs of painting fire hydrants, the standard cost per hydrant can be used to evaluate the efficiency of current performance of this activity. In so far as practical, unit standards should be developed for all other maintenance activities that involve a significant annual expense. These unit costs also allow for possible comparisons among water utilities, and benchmarking, that is, comparing the utility against industry standards. If the costs are considerably higher than industry standards or benchmarks, the question would be why and whether some changes are needed.

Unit cost standards also may be used to judge the performance of pumping and water treatment activities. For example, the current cost of chemicals used per 1 million gal (or 1 million L) of water pumped could be compared with standard unit costs. In addition, customer accounting costs over a period of time could be compared on a per-customer basis. The cost of operating and maintenance transportation and other power-operated equipment could be compared on a per-mile (or per-kilometer) or per-hour-operated basis.

It should be noted that unit cost standards require periodic updating. For example, changes in wage and salary levels and changes in the cost of materials and supplies affect the applicability of existing cost standards for that activity and will necessitate changes in the cost standards. Further, increases in productivity resulting from improved technology or improved management techniques also may affect the applicability of existing cost standards associated with particular activities and, therefore, require the determination of new cost standards.

Reconciling Expense Classification for Planning and Control With Functional Expense Classifications

If managers are going to be able to monitor the implementation of the budget in terms of expenditures and control spending, the accounting system has to echo the budget and be responsive to the administrative structure and functional division of work. There are some expense classifications used for management planning and control purposes that are directly comparable with the functional classification of expenses shown in the suggested system of accounts in appendix A. Included among these expense classifications are chemicals expense (for water treatment) and fuel or power-operated equipment, which could be compared on a per-mile-driven or per-hour-operated basis. For other expenditures, the one-to-one match between budget, administrative unit, and accounting data may not be so clear. As a result, managers may need to allocate expenses to administrative units or responsibility centers and the accounting system must record expenses by these same units. The result should be more accurate records of what is spent by what units for what work.

Wages and Salaries Expense

Records must be maintained for the amount of wages and salaries expense incurred for specific activities and jobs performed by each responsibility segment. Generally, wages and salaries expense is allocated among various jobs and activities on the basis of time expended by employees performing particular activities or jobs. The time expended is recorded and maintained on individual or group time sheets. Normally, not all wages and salaries paid to employees of a water utility will be classified as expense. If construction work is performed by the utility, the wages and salaries paid to employees engaged in construction activity should be capitalized.

Materials and Supplies Expense

As in the case of wages and salaries expense, records must be maintained for each responsibility segment regarding the amount of materials and supplies expense incurred for specific activities and jobs performed. Generally, the cost of materials and supplies used is allocated among activities and jobs on the basis of information contained in stores requisition forms. As in the case of labor costs, a portion of the cost of materials and supplies used may require capitalization in the "construction work in progress" accounts, whereas the remaining portion is allocated to the various operation and maintenance expense accounts shown in the suggested system of accounts (appendix A).

Centralized Activity Expenses

The expenses incurred in performing centralized service functions must also be allocated to particular activities and jobs, including those related to stores, fuel stocks, transportation, power-operated equipment, and shop expenses.

Stores expense represents the cost of handling materials and supplies. As materials and supplies are charged to activities and jobs, a portion of the stores expense should be allocated to each activity and job. The amount to be charged is arrived at by applying a predetermined percentage to the cost of materials used. Estimated or actual total stores expenses are divided by the total estimated or actual cost of materials and supplies handled in order to determine the applicable percentage. Fuel-stock expenses are allocated to activities and jobs in a similar manner.

Transportation expenses and power-operated equipment expenses must also be allocated to specific activities and jobs. The wages and salaries of equipment operators are allocated to activities and jobs on the basis of information contained on time sheets. The costs of operating and maintaining equipment (for example, costs of gas, oil, maintenance materials and supplies, maintenance labor, depreciation of equipment and garage, taxes on equipment, and general overhead) typically are allocated to activities and jobs on the basis of a rate established for each piece of equipment. That is, an individual equipment record sheet is maintained for each piece of equipment to record the costs of operating and maintaining the piece of equipment. Each activity or job is then charged the cost of operating and maintaining the equipment on the basis of a rate per-hour or per-mile operated.

Shop expenses include all the costs connected with operating a central shop. Labor costs and shop overhead may be charged to activities and jobs on the basis of an hourly rate. The cost of materials and supplies may be charged on the basis of an hourly rate or on the basis of actual costs incurred for each activity or job.

Administrative and general expenses ordinarily are not allocated to other functional expense accounts. However, administrative and general expenses directly traceable to construction activity should be transferred to construction costs and capitalized in construction work-in-progress accounts.

Summary of Planning Operation and Maintenance Expenses

Effective planning requires that alternative procedures for conducting operation and maintenance activities be evaluated. The combination of procedures that is expected to result in the most efficient use of resources should be the one selected. After determining the procedures to be employed, operation and maintenance expenses should be budgeted for each organization responsibility segment, including those performing centralized service activities (such as central garages and central stores) and those

Figure 11-1. Structure of an annual operating budget

Statement of Estimated Revenues and Expenses Budget, 20XX	
Summary	
Operating Revenues	$6,930,000
Operating Expenses	
Operation and Maintenance Expense	$2,009,700
Depreciation and Amortization Expense	485,100
Taxes	2,564,100
Total Operating Expenses	$5,058,900
Utility Operating Income	$1,871,100
Operation and Maintenance Expenses	Budgeted Cost Center Amount, 200Y
Office of the General Manager	$36,400
Production Division	748,370
Transmission and Distribution Division	324,850
Commercial Division	268,960
General and Administrative Division	631,120
Total Budgeted Operation and Maintenance Expenses	$2,009,700
Transmission and Distribution Division Budgeted Expenses	Budgeted Cost Center Amount 200Y
Office of the Division Manager	$23,200
Operations Section	116,485
Maintenance Section	185,165
Total	$324,850
Detail of Maintenance Section Budgeted Operating Expenses	Budgeted Cost Center Amount, 200Y
Maintenance Supervision	$12,480
Maintenance of Mains and Storage Facilities	61,120
Maintenance of Customer Services	70,365
Maintenance of Meters	41,200
Total	$185,165
Detail of Budgeted Operating & Meter Maintenance Expenses	Budgeted Cost Center Amount, 200Y
Salaries and Wages:	
Foreman	$5,150
Meter Repairers	13,435
Laborers	10,105
Total Salaries and Wages	$28,690
Materials and Supplies:	
Small Tools	$200
Maintenance Materials and Supplies	10,900
Other	710
Total Materials and Supplies	$11,810
Other Expenses:	
Maintenance of Meter Testing Equipment	200
Utility Services	300
Incidental Expenses	200
Total Other Expenses	700
Total Budgeted Meter Maintenance Expenses	$41,200

directly involved with the operation and maintenance of water utility plant facilities, customer account activities, sales promotion and advertising activities, and administrative and general activities.

The end result of planning operation and maintenance activities, as described in the preceding sections of this chapter, is an annual budget of operation and maintenance expenses such as that shown in Figure 11-1.

Chapter 12

Capital Assets

Capital is a major portion of the cost of operation of any water utility, but the costs for capital are typically not recorded all at once when the outlay is made but rather are spread out over time. To plan for such expenses, managers need to know how to report those expenditures. The major tools are depreciation and amortization. The basic idea is that when a capital purchase is made, there is no change in the balance sheet because an asset has been acquired that is of the same value as the outlay, but the value of that asset declines over time. That decline in asset value is recorded through depreciation.

Nature and Significance of Depreciation

Depreciation of utility plant assets is an economic fact that must be given explicit and systematic recognition, by both private and governmental utilities, as a cost of rendering water service. In order to plan appropriate procedures for distributing the cost of a depreciated asset over its estimated service life, it is helpful to understand the forces that tend to limit the service life of the asset.

Causes of Depreciation

Both physical factors and functional factors affect the usefulness of water utility plant assets. Physical deterioration of an asset is caused either by wear and tear resulting from use of the asset, or by decay, rot, rust, and corrosion resulting from the action of time and the elements. Physical deterioration generally can be observed. However, observation may sometimes be difficult, as in the case of water mains.

The physical lives of water utility plant assets are also related to the extent to which maintenance is carried out with regard to the assets. Maintenance limits depreciation by reducing the effects of the physical causes of depreciation. For example, failure to make even minor repairs on pumping equipment would quickly terminate the useful life of the equipment. A preventive maintenance policy will greatly prolong the physical life of many water utility plant assets. Therefore, the estimated physical life of plant assets is, to a large extent, a function of the maintenance policy discussed in chapter 11.

Functional or nonphysical causes of depreciation are external to the operation of a water utility plant. Functional depreciation occurs when utility plant assets are no longer usable as originally intended. Included among the functional causes of depreciation are obsolescence, inadequacy, and the actions of government authorities. Obsolescence indicates a lack of economic usefulness as a result of new designs, inventions, and other improvements. Inadequacy occurs when facilities are no longer large enough to meet the demand for water service. Actions of government authorities, including regulatory commissions, may require that water utilities make changes in serviceable property (affecting, for example, safety, convenience, or appearance) so that the welfare of the general public, water utility customers, or utility employees is improved. Property relocation because of urban renewal or highway construction projects is an example.

As the preceding discussion indicates, there are a number of factors that limit the useful life of a plant asset. To the extent that the factors can be forecast with a reasonable degree of accuracy, they should be given consideration in determining the service lives of plant assets.

Significance of Depreciation Expense to Interested Parties

Depreciation is important to a number of groups interested in the affairs of a water utility. The groups that are particularly interested in depreciation include public service commissions, management, customers, taxing authorities, and investors (bondholders and stockholders). Although the discussion in this section emphasizes the significance of depreciation expense associated with a utility plant, it is equally applicable to amortization expense.

Depreciation is of interest to public service commissions, management, and customers associated with private utilities primarily because depreciation expense, as a cost of rendering water service, is an important factor in establishing the structure and level of rate schedules. The annual depreciation expense must be equitably apportioned among customer classes in order to develop a rate schedule based on the cost of supplying water service to each class (see the section in chapter 16 about planning rate schedules). In addition, depreciation is important for establishing rates because accumulated depreciation is an element to be deducted from the original cost (or other value concept) of a utility plant in determining the rate base. Depreciation is not as important for rate-setting for governmental utilities using the "cash basis" for determining rate revenue requirements. However, the amount of annual depreciation can be compared to the amount of capital investment associated with system rehabilitation and replacement to provide a rough assessment of the adequacy of rehabilitation and replacement budgets.

In the case of investors, appraisals of security values by bondholders and stockholders depend on the asset values and earnings information included in accounting reports, and on the maintenance of the capital invested in the water utility. Depreciation accounting helps to determine appropriate balance-sheet values for assets, to determine periodic earnings, and to maintain invested capital by allocating the costs of tangible plant assets over the service lives of the assets. The credit standing of a water utility, as well as future earnings, may be affected if current income measurement is based on incorrect depreciation charges.

The credit worthiness of governmental systems using the "cash basis" is less dependent on depreciation because credit worthiness is significantly influenced by the ability to generate adequate revenues and these revenues are not determined in whole or in part by the amount annual depreciation.

Depreciation expense is of interest to management as an element in determining net income. It also is an important factor in the analysis and budgeting of cash flows. Depreciation charges are noncash expenses, thus must be added back to net income to determine cash flow resulting from operations. It should be emphasized that depreciation charges are not, by themselves, a source of cash. The accounting recognition of depreciation expense does not in itself directly produce additional funds. However, the recognition of depreciation expense by management does indirectly influence cash flows because it is a factor in setting rates. In addition, management recognition of depreciation expense indirectly influences cash flow to the extent that such recognition prevents disbursements for dividends (in the case of private water utilities) or to the general fund (in the case of governmental utilities) that would otherwise be made from fictitious earnings resulting from inadequate depreciation charges. Further, depreciation expense, to the extent permitted by tax authorities, will influence cash flows by reducing the income tax liability of private water utilities. Because depreciation charges are allowable deductions in establishing an private water utility's liability for income taxes, procedures for calculating depreciation charges and the amount of such charges are necessarily of interest to tax authorities. The determination of depreciation charges for income tax purposes is discussed in a later section of this chapter.

Differences Between Private and Governmental Utilities

In the private sector, the ability to record the cost of and depreciation of capital assets has been of critical importance, especially perhaps in regulated industries, where the rates permitted have depended on what is considered a fair return on capital. Depreciation has also been important in calculating taxes due. Because of its importance in the private sector, and the desire of investors, financial advisers, and bond raters to be able to read financial statements across sectors, there was a major push to require the public sector to also use the same or similar formulas to estimate the value of and depreciation of capital. The result was GASB's accounting standard 34, which requires public-sector organizations to estimate the value of their capital investments, including depreciation.

The result has not always been logical, as the reasons for emphasizing the recording of capital in the private sector do not necessarily hold in the public sector. Rates for water utilities in the public sector generally are not based on a return on capital, so much as on all the costs required to produce the water to meet public demand. Public sector organizations do not pay taxes where calculations of depreciation matter. Estimating the value of capital is less relevant as well because the likelihood of selling assets to pay for liabilities is much less.

Opponents of GASB 34 argued that governmental units pay for major maintenance and capital replacement in order to maintain the physical plant and keep it in good working order, and hence do not need to depreciate their capital; it maintains its worth. As a result, GASB has offered governmental agencies an alternative to traditional estimates of capital and depreciation. This alternative also has difficulties in application to water utilities, but it has the advantage of focusing attention on creating a standard for how much improvement should be made to facilities to keep them updated and in good working order, and measuring the percent of that ideal that is actually being invested. Thus it focuses less on recording capital outlays and more on planning and budgeting for capital, especially for maintaining capital facilities.

This chapter discusses the different treatment of capital outlays in private and governmental water utilities.

Governmental Water Utilities

The goal of GASB 34 is to make the true financial condition of governmental utilities more transparent to investors and to the public more generally. If a utility is drawing down its capital, that is, not replacing or repairing major elements of the system in order to keep rates low, then its financial condition is deteriorating and that shortcoming should show up somewhere on its books. If a government entity can demonstrate that it is keeping its infrastructure in good condition and has paid what it needs to pay, then investors should find it a more attractive target for their money, and hence be more willing to lend at more moderate rates. To make its physical condition more transparent, GASB requires either a traditional estimate of value of capital investments plus a record of major updating or improvements minus depreciation, or a plan that includes the ideal level of maintenance and investment and regular reports as to the actual expenditures compared to this plan.

Business accounting does not record initial capital outlay as an expense, because what is purchased is of equal value to the outlay. The expenditure is recorded and appears on the books only as the items purchased or investment is depreciated, over its lifetime. The investment thus loses some percent of its value each year until it is worth nothing. While businesses do not record the initial outlays, they still have to know what they are in order to depreciate them.

Assume, for example, that a length of pipe lasts 50 years; accountants would depreciate or record one-fiftieth of the cost each year, until on the accounting records, there was no value left in the pipe. The cost is thus spread across the years of any investment's useful life.

There are problems with this approach when applied to public-sector water utilities. For one thing, the useful life of infrastructure of a water utility seen as a whole is not a fixed and known duration; it depends on the maintenance and replacement of key elements of the system. It is not clear what depreciation might mean in this circumstance or over what period depreciation should occur. Properly maintained key elements can last a very long time. Second, this approach does not tell investors how well the infrastructure is being taken care of. Nor does it give any clue to the replacement costs, because it omits concern for inflation, and it is the replacement costs that must concern managers. An agency may report low costs, because capital items have reached near the end of their useful lives, with rates determined only to cover costs, while a large unfunded capital need for replacement is pending but invisible in the financial reports.

The alternative approach that GASB allows to public-sector agencies records the actual cost of maintaining the infrastructure, not depreciation. This approach requires the agency to figure out what it should cost annually to keep the system in good condition, and report that number, and then evaluate actual infrastructure condition at regular intervals, compared with the ideal. This approach requires an asset management system. Evaluating condition of the entire physical plant and equipment and delivery system at least every three years is burdensome, however, especially since portions of it do not require such frequent inspection. Expenditures may be lumpy as well. Coming up with a single number to evaluate the condition of many different parts of the system may be confusing to say the least.

It is possible under GASB 34 to combine approaches, depreciating capital for the balance-sheet numbers and also providing an asset management system. (This material relies on a paper by Ken Harlow of Brown and Caldwell, "GASB 34—An Infrastructure Heresy," online at *www.bcwaternews.com/assetmgt/AM02_Heresy.pdf*.). More on how to calculate depreciation is provided below in the portion of the chapter on private utilities. Where governmental utilities differ from the investor owned utilities, such differences are noted.

Private Utilities

The following sections of the chapter deal with planning and accounting for depreciation and amortization expenses as elements in determining revenue requirements for rate-making purposes, for determining income, and in analyzing and budgeting cash flow for private utilities. For a further discussion of the subject of utility depreciation accounting, refer to the National Association of Regulatory Utility Commissioners' (NARUC) publication *Public Utility Depreciation Practices.*

Definitions and Concepts

Depreciation

NARUC defines *depreciation* as the loss in service value not restored by current maintenance, incurred in connection with the consumption or prospective retirement of utility plant in the course of service from causes that are known to be in current operation and against which the utility is not protected by insurance. Among the causes to be given consideration are wear and tear, decay, action of the elements, inadequacy, obsolescence, changes in the art, changes in demand, and requirements of public authorities.

For the purpose of clarifying the preceding definition and the remainder of this chapter, the following NARUC definitions are presented:

- *Service value* is the difference between the original cost and the net salvage of a utility plant.

- *Original cost,* as applied to a utility plant, is the cost of such property when first devoted to public service.
- *Net salvage value* is the salvage value of property retired less the cost of removal.
- *Salvage value* is the amount received for property retired, less any expenses incurred in connection with the sale or in preparing the property for sale. If retained, salvage value is the amount at which the material recoverable is chargeable to materials and supplies, or other appropriate accounts.
- *Cost of removal* is the cost of demolishing, dismantling, tearing down, or otherwise removing the utility plant, including the incidental costs of transportation and handling.
- *Property retired,* as applied to a utility plant, is property that has been removed, sold, abandoned, destroyed, or that for any cause has been withdrawn from service.
- *Service life* is the time between the date a utility plant is in service or leased to others, and the date of its retirement. If depreciation is accounted for on a production basis rather than on a time basis, then service life should be measured in terms of the appropriate unit of production. (For example, if a pump wears out after a given number of gallons of water rather than a given number of months or years, calculating depreciation per 1,000 gal may make more sense than depreciation per year.)

In view of the NARUC definition of depreciation, and the definitions of associated terminology, the term *depreciation* is limited to the accounting for original cost. Depreciation accounting for water utilities involves procedures whereby the original cost less net salvage value of the tangible utility plant (excluding land) is distributed over the estimated useful life of the assets in an orderly and rational manner. In addition, the depreciation expense for a particular period of time is the portion of the original cost (less net salvage value) of the tangible water utility plant that is allocated to that particular period.

It should be made clear that depreciation, from the standpoint of accounting, is defined in terms of cost. The economic concept of depreciation, conversely, involves the process of valuation. In this case, depreciation (or appreciation) is measured in terms of the loss (or gain) in value of property. The engineering concept of depreciation is established by comparing the present physical condition of a depreciated asset against the physical condition of the asset when new.

Amortization

NARUC defines *amortization* as the gradual extinguishment of an amount in an account by distributing such amount over a fixed period, over the life of the asset or liability to which it applies, or over the period during which it is anticipated the benefit will be realized.

This definition of amortization is very broad in scope, referring to the orderly extinguishment, over time, of amounts in balance-sheet accounts in general. Although the NARUC definition of amortization refers to both assets and liabilities, the discussion in this chapter emphasizes the process of amortizing amounts in asset accounts classified within the "utility plant" category. Nevertheless, the term *amortization* also applies to the distribution among accounting periods of amounts in other balance-sheet accounts, such as those associated with nonutility property, debt discount and expense, and debt premium.

Note that, from an accounting viewpoint, a broad definition of asset amortization encompasses the concept of depreciation. Depreciation refers to a particular type of asset amortization—that associated with the allocation, among accounting periods, of the original cost of tangible utility plant (excluding land). In regard to the utility plant, amortization usually is employed more narrowly to describe the process of allocating, among accounting periods, the amounts commonly referred to as intangible assets. The costs of such intangibles, such as water rights, would be spread across years, even though the water rights did not wear out or lose value.

Depreciation and Amortization Expense Accounts

The NARUC system of accounts for water utilities establishes a number of accounts for the purpose of recognizing depreciation and amortization. With regard to the income statement, and for the purpose of determining operating income, five accounts within the "operating expense" category are devoted to depreciation and amortization expense. A brief description of the five expense accounts (listed with their account numbers as shown in appendix A) is as follows:

- **Depreciation Expense (403).** This account includes the amount of depreciation expense associated with all classes of depreciated utility plant in service. However, depreciation expense applicable to transportation and work equipment, shop equipment, tools, and other general equipment may be charged to clearing distribution of expenses between construction and operation. In addition, depreciation and amortization expenses applicable to utility plant leased to others should be charged to account 413, "income from utility plant leased to other."
- **Amortization of Utility Plant Acquisition Adjustments (406).** When authorized by a state regulatory body, this account is used by private utilities and is charged or credited with amounts representing the periodic amortization of the balance in utility plant account 114, "utility plant acquisition adjustments." A utility plant acquisition adjustment is represented by the difference between (1) the cost to the acquiring water utility of utility plant acquired as an operating unit or system and (2) the original cost of such property less accumulated depreciation and amortization and less any related contributions in aid of construction.
- **Amortization of Limited-Term Utility Plant (407.1).** This account includes amortization charges applicable to utility plant accounts for

limited-term franchises, licenses, patent rights, limited-term interests in land, and expenditures for improvements on leased property where the service lives of the improvements are less than the term of the lease (the cost of such improvements allocated to a particular accounting period is considered as depreciation expense).

- **Amortization of Property Losses (407.2).** This account includes the periodic charge for amortization of the balance in deferred debit account 182, "extraordinary property losses," when a state regulatory body authorizes such a balance to be amortized through charges to operating expense.
- **Amortization of Other Utility Plant (407.3).** When authorized by a state regulatory body, this account is used by private utilities and includes the periodic change for amortization of intangible or other utility plant in service that does not have a definite or terminable life and that is not otherwise subject to charges for depreciation expense. Periodic depreciation and amortization expenses associated with nonutility operations and with nonutility rental properties should be excluded from the above accounts. Such amounts should be charged to other income and deductions account 426, "miscellaneous nonutility expenses."

Typically, the total amounts that are recognized over time for depreciation and amortization of a utility plant, and that represent accumulated write-offs of asset costs, are accounted through the use of contra-asset accounts. A contra asset account is a separate account on the balance sheet that shows additions or reductions to the value of the main asset or liability account. The purpose in this case would be to show the original value minus the reductions taken so far through depreciation. In the case of amortization, such totals would show how much of the original cost had already been recorded. For this purpose, the NARUC system provides six "accumulated provision" accounts related to utility plant. These six accounts, together with account numbers, are as follows:

- Accumulated provision for depreciation of utility plant in service (108.1)
- Accumulated provision for depreciation of utility plant leased to others (108.2)
- Accumulated provision for depreciation of property held for future use (108.3)
- Accumulated provision for amortization of utility plant in service (109.1)
- Accumulated provision for amortization of utility plant leased to others (109.2)
- Accumulated provision for amortization of property held for future use (115)

For the same purpose, but with regard to nonutility property, the NARUC system establishes account 122, "accumulated provision for depreciation and amortization of nonutility property."

Alternative Methods for Recording Depreciation Expense for Governmental Entities

Governmentally owned water utilities need to account for both noncontributed and contributed assets such as grants or shared revenue. According to the *Governmental GAAP Guide** two alternatives are available for recording depreciation expense. In the first alternative, depreciation expense on only the noncontributed assets is included with operating expenses and closed directly to retained earnings. This method is most like that of a commercial entity. In the second alternative, depreciation expense on contributed assets is closed directly to the contributed capital account that was created when the restricted grant, entitlement, or shared revenue was received and the noncontributed asset depreciation expense is closed directly to retained earnings. Depreciation expense on contributed assets is still included as an operating expense on the Statement of Revenues, Expenses, and Changes in Retained Earnings, but will be added to net income to determine the change in retained earnings for the period.

Determining Depreciation Expense

Once the decision has been made to purchase or construct depreciable assets, management planning of annual depreciation charges is limited to determining the appropriate portion of the cost of the assets that should be allocated to each accounting period in the form of periodic depreciation expense. The determination of periodic depreciation charges involves the following four steps: (1) estimating the service lives of the depreciable assets, (2) estimating the net salvage value of the assets, (3) selecting a depreciation formula to distribute the cost of assets over their estimated service lives, and (4) applying the selected depreciation formula to the service value of the depreciable property.

In some instances, the water utility may not have sufficient retirement experience or sufficient records of asset retirements to estimate the service life of an asset or group of assets. In such cases, retirement experience of other water utilities, information concerning service lives provided by equipment manufacturers and regulatory commissions, and/or special engineering studies conducted by the utility may be used in making service-life estimates.

Estimated service life based on retirement experience or other information described in the preceding paragraph must be adjusted in light of available information regarding probable future conditions affecting the service life of the depreciable asset. Future conditions may alter the relative effect of causes (physical and functional) of depreciation that existed in the past. In brief, estimates of future service lives of assets are subjective and can reflect only the best informed judgment.

* Available from the US Government Bookstore, 1961 Stout St., Denver, CO 80204.

Estimating Net Salvage Value

Because the amount of a periodic depreciation charge is the function of the service value (original cost less the salvage value net of cost of removal) of the depreciable asset, it is necessary that the net salvage value also be estimated. Estimated net salvage value may be based on historical information and adjusted for probable future conditions affecting the salvage value and cost of removal.

Selecting a Depreciation Formula

A number of depreciation formulas can be used to distribute the depreciable cost (or service value) of an asset over the estimated service life of an asset. Characteristics of the various methods are discussed below.

Straight-Line Method

The straight-line method of depreciation distributes the depreciable cost of an asset in equal amounts to each of the accounting periods comprising the total estimated service life of the asset. Under this method, the depreciation rate per period may be determined by dividing the depreciable cost or service value (original cost less net salvage value), expressed as a percentage of original cost, by the total number of estimated time periods (either months or years) in the service life of the asset. Table 12-1 presents a simplified example of the application of the straight-line method; the example is in the form of an equipment ledger card. With regard to most depreciated water utility plant assets, the straight-line allocation method of recognizing depreciation is the predominant method used for reporting to water utility management and external groups (except to the US Internal Revenue Service [USIRS]), and for determining annual depreciation expense and accumulated provisions for depreciation to be used in rate studies.

The straight-line method assumes that time expiration is the sole factor, other than asset cost and net salvage value, determining the depreciation charge. It is unlikely that the service value of an asset will expire uniformly throughout the service life of that asset; physical and functional factors that limit service life may cause more loss in service value of an asset in one period than in another. However, unless there is sufficient evidence that the rate of service value expiration differs substantially from one period to another (such as where service value expiration is caused by primarily wear and tear from use), the assumption of uniform service life expiration is not unreasonable. In addition, the straight-line method is the easiest depreciation method to apply and therefore the most acceptable from an administrative point of view. In contrast to other depreciation methods, the straight-line method readily permits the recalculation of depreciation charges-based on changing estimates of service lives or net salvage values.

Method Based on Use

For some water utility plant assets, depreciation is more a function of actual use than of time expiration. As examples, depreciation of transportation equipment may be closely related to vehicle miles driven, and depreciation of pumping equipment may be closely related to hours operated. In such cases, a method that allocates depreciable cost among

Table 12-1. Application of straight-line method

PLANT ASSET AND ACCUMULATED DEPRECIATION	
ITEM	Flatbed truck
PRIMARY ACCOUNT CLASSIFICATION	Vehicles and Equipment
DESCRIPTION	Ford F350
FROM WHOM ACQUIRED	Downtown Ford
SERIAL NUMBER	F3501234567W
DATE PURCHASED	7/1/2012
ESTIMATED SERVICE LIFE	10 years
WHERE LOCATED OR STORED	Maintenance yard
COST	$20,000
PERSON RESPONSIBLE FOR ASSET	Fleet Manager
SALVAGE VALUE	$2,000 (10%)
DEPRECIATION RATE (YEAR)	$1,800 (9%)
(MONTH)	$150 (0.75%)

		Asset Account			Accumulated Depreciation			Net Book
Date	**Description**	**Dr.**	**Cr.**	**Bal.**	**Dr.**	**Cr.**	**Bal.**	**Value**
July 1, 2012	Purchase of Asset	$20,000		$20,000				$20,000
Dec. 31, 2012	Annual Depreciation					900	900	19,100
Dec. 31, 2013	Annual Depreciation					1,800	2,700	17,300
Dec. 31, 2014	Annual Depreciation					1,800	4,500	15,500

Computations:*

Original Cost	= $20,000	(100%)
Less Salvage Value	= (2,000)	(10% of original cost)
Depreciable Cost (Service value)	= $18,000	(90% of original cost)

Annual Depreciation Rate $= \dfrac{90\%}{\text{Estimated Service Life}} = \dfrac{90\%}{10} =$ 9% of *original* cost (or $1,800 per year)

Monthly Depreciation Rate = 9% / 12 = 0.75% of *original* cost (or $150 per month)

*Alternatively, the straight-line rate may be expressed as a percentage of depreciable cost or service value, an annual rate of 10% in this case (the annual depreciation charge is the same, 10% of $1,800, or $180).

accounting periods, based on asset use during each period, may be considered appropriate. Such a method is commonly referred to as a *unit-of-production method.* Table 12-2 presents an example of the application of a depreciation method based on use.

Sum of the Years' Digits Method

The sum of the years' digits (SYD) method for recognizing annual depreciation charges is used by many private water utilities in determining taxable income. It is acceptable

Table 12-2. Application of a depreciation based on use

End of Year	Miles Operated	Depreciation Charge	Accumulated Depreciation	Net Book Value
1	16,000	$640	$640	$3,360
2	12,000	480	1,120	2,880
3	18,000	720	1,840	2,160
4	20,000	800	2,640	1,360
5	14,000	560	3,200	800

Computations:

Cost of service truck	$4,000
Net salvage value	800
Depreciable cost (service value)	$3,200
Estimated Service Life	80,000 miles
Depreciation Rate ($3,200 ÷ 80,000 miles)	$0.04 per mile

to the USIRS as a legitimate depreciation method for income tax purposes. However, this accelerated method may not presently be acceptable to public service commissions as an appropriate method for determining the depreciation expense portion of a utility's operating expenses for general financial reporting purposes or for rate determination purposes. Under the SYD method, annual depreciation expense is determined by applying a constantly declining fraction to the depreciable cost (service value) of an asset. The fraction to be applied in each year is determined as follows: (1) the years of service life of the asset are numbered in reverse order (1 for the last year, 2 for the next-to-last year until all years in the service life are assigned a number); (2) the sum of the numbers thus assigned is determined; and (3) the applicable fraction for each year has as its numerator the number assigned to the year in question and as its denominator the numbers assigned to all years. Table 12-3 presents an example of the application of the SYD method.

Since the SYD method attributes a greater amount of cost to the early years of the service life of an asset than to the later years, there is a presumption that service value expires more rapidly in the early years than in the later years. Therefore, the method recognizes the fact that, in some cases, a plant asset makes a greater contribution to revenue when it is new than when it is old. Nevertheless, the fractional allocation to each year of the service life of the asset is rather arbitrary and, in most cases, will not match actual service value expiration.

Double Declining Balance Method

As an alternative to the SYD method, the double declining balance (DDB) method also is used by private water utilities to recognize depreciation on an accelerated basis for income tax determination purposes. As in the case of the SYD method, the DDB method may not presently be acceptable to public service commissions as an appropriate

Table 12-3. Depreciation using the sum-of-the-years'-digits method

(1) Year	(2) Annual Depreciation Rate	(3) Depreciable Cost	(4) Charge to Depreciation Expense (2) x (3)	(5) Annual Credit to Accumulated Provision for Depreciation	(6) Balance in Accumulated Provision for Depreciation Account	(7) Net Book Value After Annual Charge
0						$1,800.00
1	5/15	$1,500.00	$500.00	$500.00	$500.00	1,300.00
2	4/15	1,500.00	400.00	400.00	900.00	900.00
3	3/15	1,500.00	300.00	300.00	1,200.00	600.00
4	2/15	1,500.00	200.00	200.00	1,400.00	400.00
5	1/15	1,500.00	100.00	100.00	1,500.00	300.00
		$1,500.00	$1,500.00			

Computations:

Cost of asset	$1,800.00
Net salvage value	300.00
Depreciable cost (service value)	$1,500.00
Service Life	5 years

Sum of the Years' Digits:

Year 1	=	5
Year 2	=	4
Year 3	=	3
Year 4	=	2
Year 5	=	1
		15

Table 12-4. Depreciation using the double declining balance method

(1) Year	(2) Annual Depreciation Rate	(3) Undepreciated Cost Before Annual Charge	(4) Annual Charge to Depreciation Expense (2) x (3)	(5) Annual Credit to Accumulated Provision for Depreciation	(6) Balance in Accumulated Provision for Depreciation Account	(7) Net Book Value After Annual Charge
0						$2,000.00
1	.20	$2,000.00	$400.00	$400.00	$400.00	1,600.00
2	.20	1,600.00	320.00	320.00	720.00	1,280.00
3	.20	1,280.00	256.00	256.00	976.00	1,024.00
4	.20	1,024.00	204.80	204.80	1,180.80	819.20
5	.20	819.20	163.84	163.84	1,344.64	655.36
6	.20	655.36	131.07	131.07	1,475.71	524.29
7	.20	524.29	104.86	104.86	1,580.57	419.43
8	.20	419.43	83.89	83.89	1,664.46	335.54
9	.20	335.54	67.11	67.11	1,731.57	268.43
10	.20	268.43	68.43*	68.43	1,800.00	200.00

Computations:

Cost of asset	$2,000.00
Net salvage value	$200.00
Service life	10 years

$$\text{Annual straight-line rate}^{\dagger} = \frac{100\%}{\text{service life}} = \frac{100\%}{10} = 10\%$$

Double straight-line rate = 10% x 2 = 20%

*Note that depreciation expense in year 10 is not the product of columns 2 and 3. The amount charged to depreciation expense in year 10 is an amount sufficient to reduce the cash value of the asset at the end of year 10 to an amount equal to estimated salvage value. In order to accomplish this, depreciation expense in year 10 is slightly higher than in year 9. To avoid the need for increasing depreciation expense in the last year, a formula is available for computing a fixed rate to apply each year to undepreciated asset cost. The computed rate, when applied annually to the undepreciated asset cost, will accumulate depreciation expense over the service life of the asset exactly equal to the depreciable cost of the asset. The fixed rate formula is:

$$r = 1 - \sqrt[n]{S/C}$$

Where

r = constant rate

n = number of periods in the estimated service life

S = net salvage value

C = cost of the asset

Applying the formula to our example results in the following fixed rate, which is slightly greater than the straight-line rate:

$$r = 1 - \sqrt[10]{\$200/\$2{,}000} = .2057$$

†Annual straight-line rate must be computed without adjustment for estimated net salvage value. Compare with Table 12-1 where annual straight-line rate is computed after consideration of net salvage value.

method for calculating the depreciation expense portion of a utility's operating expenses for general financial reporting purposes or for rate determination purposes. Under the DDB method, annual depreciation is determined by multiplying the undepreciated balance of asset cost by a percentage that is twice the annual rate (computed without adjustment for net salvage value) associated with the straight-line method. Table 12-4 presents an example. Like the SYD method, the DDB method serves rather arbitrarily to attribute a relatively greater portion of an asset's depreciable cost to the early years of the service life of the asset than to the later years.

Two other methods of recognizing depreciation charges make use of the "time value of money" concept. These two related methods are the compound interest and the sinking fund methods. While the two methods have some theoretical merit, they are more complex than the other depreciation methods discussed here and are infrequently employed in practice.

Methods of Applying Depreciation Formulas

Depreciation formulas may be applied in a number of ways to the cost of depreciable assets. Depreciation expense and accumulated provision for depreciation may be accounted for by individual depreciable property items, groups of property items, functional groups of plant accounts, or the utility plant as a whole.

Accounting for Depreciation by Individual Property Items

Accounting for depreciation by individual property items requires that depreciation rates be fixed separately for each individual unit of property. Such a procedure is reasonable for large items of property, such as pumps and vehicles. When an individual item is retired, the recorded cost of the item is credited to the primary plant account in which the cost of the item is included, and the accumulated provision for depreciation account is charged with the amount of accumulated depreciation related to the retired property item.

Generally, a gain or loss from the disposal of the property item will result, measured by the difference between the net book value of the asset (original cost less accumulated depreciation) and the net salvage value. NOTE: Table 12-1 presents an example of accounting for depreciation by individual property unit. In cases where many similar items of property are involved, accounting for depreciation by individual property items includes providing detailed information concerning accumulated depreciation related to the retired property item.

Accounting for Depreciation by Groups of Property Items

Classes of property consisting of numerous small units having the same or similar service life expectancies (such as meters) are generally accounted for by groups rather than individual units. In effect, each group is considered as one asset. Consequently, it is necessary to determine an average service life for each group. The aggregate cost of a group of property items having similar service life expectancies is represented by the balance in a primary plant account such as "services, meters or hydrants." Based on the average service life and the cost of the group of similar property items, periodic depreciation expense is determined for the group by applying one of the depreciation formulas described in the preceding section. Typically, straight-line depreciation is employed in conjunction with the group method, and a composite depreciation rate is determined for the group (or primary account). The amount of depreciation expense for any period is obtained by applying the composite depreciation rate to the balance in the primary account.

When an individual property item is retired, its cost is credited to the primary plant account in which the cost of the item is recorded and the accumulated provision for depreciation account is charged for the cost of the item less net salvage value. No recognized gain or loss will result from the disposal of individual property items when they are accounted for on a group basis. This procedure for accounting for retirements of depreciable property is basically the one required by the NARUC system of accounts. As discussed in chapter 7, this NARUC procedure avoids fluctuations in the rate base that would otherwise occur when property is retired and not immediately replaced.

The use of the group method is most logical when primary account balances consist of the cost of individual property items having similar service life expectancies. However, the use of the group method can be extended to other primary accounts, such as "structures and improvements," which have balances composed of the cost of a variety of property items that are not similar in nature and do not have the same estimated life.

Accounting for Depreciation by Functional Groups of Accounts and By the Utility Plant as a Whole

Use of the group method also can be extended to functional groups of primary plant accounts (source-of-supply pumping, water treatment, transmission and distribution, and general plant), and even to the depreciable cost of the utility plant as a whole. NARUC recommends that water utilities maintain subsidiary records showing the amount of accrued depreciation (as well as the book cost of property retired, and the cost of removal, salvage, and such other items as recoveries from insurance) for each functional group plant account. Retirements of depreciable property would be handled in the manner described in the preceding section concerning accounting for depreciation by groups of property items.

Using the straight-line method, Table 12-5 presents the calculation of a composite rate for a group of assets. Each asset may be considered as (1) an individual property item with the composite rate applicable to a primary plant account, (2) a primary account with the composite rate applicable to a functional group of primary accounts, or (3) a functional group of accounts with the composite rate applicable to the cost of depreciating utility plant as a whole.

Table 12-5. Computation of depreciation using a composite rate for a group of assets

Asset	Cost	Net Salvage Value	Depreciable Cost	Estimated Service Life	Annual Depreciation Expense
A	$100,000	$10,000	$90,000	30	$3,000
B	50,000	1,000	49,000	10	4,900
C	60,000	4,000	56,000	16	3,500
D	200,000	0	200,000	40	5,000
	$410,000	$15,000	$395,000		$16,400

Composite Rate on Cost: $16,400 ÷ $410,000 = 4 percent.

Reevaluating the Adequacy of Periodic Depreciation Charges

Because the service value and service life of an asset or group of assets are based on estimates of future conditions, the service value and service life chosen for use in the depreciation computation may prove inaccurate. Thus, service life estimates and net salvage value estimates should be reviewed periodically to determine their reasonableness in light of current knowledge and experience.

Depreciation Studies

The purpose of depreciation studies is to review a water utility's present depreciation rates in order to establish their adequacy and to recommend changes where appropriate. Depreciation studies, which may be conducted by water utility staff and/or outside consultants, represent an in-depth analysis of plant depreciation policies and procedures. Typically, the studies make use of accounting records of a utility, including historical service-life evidence, field inspections of selected properties, consultations with utility personnel, and information concerning conditions expected to exist in the future that will influence physical and functional depreciation.

The primary component of depreciation studies is the estimate of average service lives of property groups. Such estimates of future service lives, which necessarily require some degree of judgment, typically are founded on a study of past retirement experience. In the ideal situation, the continuing property records of a water utility provide the information concerning installation and retirement dates. However, since a large part of a water utility plant is long-lived, there often is an insufficient quantity of retirement data available to make a meaningful study. In such cases, a technique using survivor curves may be employed. In general, this technique involves a comparison of the water utility's own retirement experience with additional industry data (survivor curves) in order to project estimates of service lives. Under this approach, information concerning the water utility's own retirement history is required but not on as detailed a basis as in the ideal situation.

Remaining-Life Method

The remaining-life method serves to update depreciation charges with respect to a depreciable asset or group of assets. The method is particularly useful in cases where it is difficult to determine with any degree of exactness the service lives of utility properties at the time of their purchase or construction.

The remaining-life method emphasizes estimated remaining service life as opposed to the estimate of total service life. Under this method, an estimate of the remaining service life of an asset or asset group is made periodically. The new estimate of service life is then applied against the undepreciated cost less estimated net salvage value of the asset to determine an appropriate depreciation expense figure applicable to future periods. The depreciation expense computed by the remaining-life method is compared with the depreciation expense computed in accordance with the method currently in use in order to determine (1) an appropriate depreciation expense figure applicable to future periods and (2) whether current charges are reasonable or if adjustments need to be made.

Depreciation Based on Replacement Cost

Conventional depreciation accounting for water utilities reflects a process of historical or original cost allocation. In recent years, caused largely by the presence of substantial inflation, concern over the adequacy of historical cost-based depreciation charges has increased. At issue is the question of whether or not current depreciation practices can ensure maintenance of the original capital invested in a water utility. In connection with the concern over maintenance of invested capital, it has been suggested that depreciation charges should be based on the cost of replacing the water utility plant as opposed to the original cost of the plant.

In December 1986, the Financial Accounting Standards Board (FASB) issued Financial Accounting Standards Number 89 (SFAS 89), "Financial Reporting and Changing Prices." This statement encourages (but does not require) a business enterprise to disclose supplementary information on the effects of changing prices. Entities are not discouraged from experimenting with other forms of disclosure.

The practical justification for measuring depreciation in terms of replacement cost can be appreciated by water utility treasurers and controllers who have had to secure funds for plant replacement, improvement, and expansion in the face of rising price levels. One purpose served by depreciation accounting based on replacement cost is to permit a more meaningful calculation of actual water utility operating expenses and income in order to establish realistic rate schedules and to permit capital maintenance. Depreciation accounting based on replacement cost is not at present generally accepted for financial reporting purposes in the United States or Canada, nor is it accepted by tax authorities or regulatory authorities in either country. Nevertheless, it is a concept that should be considered by water utility management, regulatory authorities, and other interested groups.

Determining Amortization Expense

The determination of periodic amortization expense related to assets and deferred debits generally presents little problem. The service lives of the assets and deferred debits are established by law or contract (as in the case of limited-term interests in land and improvements on leased property where the service life of the improvements is terminable by action of the lessee) or are established by regulatory commissions (as in the case of utility plant acquisition adjustments and extraordinary property losses). The straight-line depreciation method generally is employed to compute the amortization expense.

Utility Plant Acquisition Adjustments

NARUC recommends that water utilities acquiring properties from another utility record such property at the original cost to the first utility devoting it to public service. If the purchase price differs from the original cost, the difference is recorded separately in account 114, "utility plant acquisition adjustments." As approved or directed by state public service commissions, the "utility plant acquisition adjustments" account balance may be amortized over a period of time (generally as recovered through rates) with a corresponding charge to an amortization expense account.

Extraordinary Property Losses

Account 182, "extraordinary property losses," is provided by NARUC to record extraordinary losses on property abandoned or otherwise retired from service, losses that could not be reasonably anticipated (and therefore could not be avoided through greater accumulated provisions for depreciation or amortization), and that are not covered by insurance. The amounts to be included in this account are authorized or directed by state public service commissions. The period over which the extraordinary property loss is to be amortized or otherwise disposed of is also subject to the approval or direction of the regulatory commission.

Depreciation Expense for Income Tax

Under certain circumstances, the US Internal Revenue Code permits private water utilities to use accelerated depreciation methods for income tax purposes. The accelerated methods, which were originally authorized as a result of the 1954 revision of the federal income tax laws, may be applied to the cost of water utility property purchased, constructed, or reconditioned after 1953. The accelerated methods provide for the depreciation of a particular item of property at a faster rate than under the straight-line allocation method, thus resulting in larger deductions for tax purposes during the early years of the service life of the property and smaller deductions during later years. The accelerated depreciation methods permitted include the sum of the years' digits method (see Table 12-3 and related discussion) and the double declining balance method (see Table 12-4 and related discussion). In addition, the federal tax law provides guidelines for determining depreciate lives to be used for income tax purposes. These tax lives may differ from the service lives used by the water utility for purposes other than tax determination. It should be apparent that depreciation charges for tax purposes may differ from depreciation charges for other purposes if (1) an accelerated depreciation method is used for tax purposes and the straight-line method is used for other purposes and/or (2) the depreciate lives employed for tax purposes differ from the estimated service lives of assets used for determining depreciation expenses for other purposes.

Effect of Tax Depreciation on Cash Flows

The use of accelerated depreciation methods for tax purposes has implications for private utilities both from the standpoint of increasing cash flows (assuming normalization) and from the standpoint of rate determination. With regard to an individual property item, the use of accelerated depreciation for tax purposes (as opposed to the straight-line method) will result in lower income taxes in the early years of the property life and higher taxes in later years. This will result in additional funds for working capital or plant investment during the early years of the life of the property. In later years, however, cash flows will decrease because of the smaller deduction for depreciation and the resulting increase in taxes. Therefore, accelerated depreciation results in a tax deferral as opposed to a tax saving. From the standpoint of the water utility as a whole, accelerated depreciation will result in a permanent tax saving only if the utility experiences a continual growth in plant investment sufficient to permit high depreciation charges on new plant investment to offset the lower depreciation charges on older plant investment.

Flow-Through Method

For IOU rate-making purposes, actual income taxes paid are considered as the income tax expense and are included in the cost of service; however, depreciation expense for rate-making purposes is based on the straight-line method. This approach to the treatment of income taxes resulting from accelerated depreciation is known as the "flow-through" approach. The benefits received from electing to use accelerated depreciation methods for tax purposes are allowed to flow through to water customers as reduced rates resulting from the reduction in income taxes.

Normalization

Considered as a tax deferral, if accelerated depreciation methods are employed for tax purposes, the actual income tax paid must be adjusted or "normalized" by recomputed income tax expenses on the basis of the straight-line depreciation. The amount of income tax computed by using the straight-line method represents the income tax figure for financial statement and rate-making purposes. The difference between the income tax computed using the straight-line method and the actual tax liability as determined using accelerated depreciation methods is credited to a balance-sheet account for accumulated deferred income taxes (see account 282, "accumulated deferred income taxes—liberalized depreciation," in appendix A). The accumulated deferred income tax account balance is increased or decreased each year as necessitated by the difference between the normalized tax expense and the actual income tax liability.

Table 12-6. Example utility schedule of funds—revenues, expenses, and changes in retained earnings

For the period of July 1, 2010, through June 30, 2011

	System Fund	Internal Service Fund	Debt Service Fund	Reserve Fund	Renewal and Replacement Fund	Project Fund	Combined Total
Operating Revenues							
Water System Revenues	$60,325,527						$60,325,527
Wastewater System Revenues	78,126,058						78,126,058
Chilled Water and Steam System Revenues	2,925,532						2,925,532
Reuse System Revenues	1,978,235						1,978,235
Total Operating Revenues	143,355,352	0	0	0	0	0	143,355,352
Operating Expenses							
Personal Services Contractual	32,834,823	(702,280)					32,132,543
Services, Materials, and Supplies Other	33,573,293						33,573,293
Charges Interfund Transfers Internal	8,666,993						8,666,993
Internal Service Fund	17,028,833						17,028,833
Service Fund—Net (gain)	(11,009,752)						(11,009,752)
Total Operating Expenses Before Depreciation	81,094,190	(702,280)	0	0	0	0	80,391,910
Depreciation Expense	37,452,499	1,020,291					38,472,790
Total operating expenses	118,546,689	318,011	0	0	0	0	118,864,700
Operating income	24,808,663	(318,011)					24,490,652
Nonoperating Revenues							
Interest Earned and Miscellaneous	2,800,378	0	676,153	1,973,146	153,519	1,079,142	6,682,338
Total nonoperating revenues	2,800,378	0	676,153	1,973,146	153,519	1,079,142	6,682,338

(Continued next page)

Table 12-6. Example utility schedule of funds—revenues, expenses, and changes in retained earnings (continued)

For the period of July 1, 2010, through June 30, 2011

	System Fund	Internal Service Fund	Debt Service Fund	Reserve Fund	Renewal and Replacement Fund	Project Fund	Combined Total
Nonoperating Expenses							
Amortization of Refunding Bond Expense	48,192						48,192
Write-off of Capital Project	168,108						168,108
Interest Expense: Revenue Bonds	(1,044,045)		39,008,326				37,964,281
Installment Notes	3,651						3,651
Loss / (Gain) on Sale of Fixed Assets	35,352						35,352
Amortized Discount Expense	595,713						595,713
(Gain) on Sale of Investment	(1,239,222)						(1,239,222)
(Gain) on Escrow Account				(6,915)			(6,915)
Reorganization							
Total Nonoperating Expenses	(1,432,251)	0	39,008,326	(6,915)	0	0	37,569,160
Income (loss) Before Operating Transfers	29,041,292	(318,011)	(38,332,173)	1,980,061	153,519	1,079,142	(6,396,170)
Operating Transfers In (Out)	36,352,112		38,332,173	(1,980,061)			
Net Income (Loss) — Carried Forward	(7,310,820)	(318,011)	(76,664,346)	3,960,122	153,519	1,079,142	(6,396,170)
Retained Earnings, July 1, 2010	159,342,198	10,807,960	3,717	41,200,687	42,820,207	21,493,697	275,668,466
Residual Equity Transfers In (Out)	(34,069,660)		15,481,102	2,574,495	16,014,063		
Transfers to the City	(2,470,142)						(2,470,142)
Contributions in Aid of Construction	(16,508,002)				16,508,002		0
Retirement of Revenue Bond Principal	15,375,000		(15,375,000)				0
Expenditures for Plant Additions	63,087,955				(44,991,898)	(18,096,057)	0
Retained Earnings, June 30, 2011	177,446,529	10,489,949	(76,554,527)	47,735,304	30,503,893	4,476,782	266,802,154

Chapter 13

General and Income Taxes

Planning and controlling tax expense are of greater concern to private water utilities than to governmental water utilities since the latter are exempt from paying federal income taxes and often from paying state and local taxes. Tax expenses are a significant portion of private water utility revenues, making a thorough knowledge of taxes important.

In the case of a governmental water utility, direct tax payments may not be the real measure of the utility's total tax burden. Rather, "payments in lieu of taxes" may be applicable in addition to any direct tax payments.

The US Internal Revenue Code is very complex and is constantly changing. Therefore, this chapter only presents an overview of federal income taxes as they relate to private water utility operations.

Types and Descriptions of Taxes

Water utilities, particularly private utilities, are subject to a wide variety of taxes. Income taxes usually get the most attention because of their complexity and accounting challenges. However, in total dollar amounts, other taxes can represent a larger portion of a utility's total tax expense.

Federal Income Taxes

Governmental water utilities are generally exempt from federal income taxation. Further, governmental water utilities are exempt from most state and local taxation. As a result, tax reporting requirements faced by governmental water utilities are fewer than those faced by private water utilities, which are subject to federal, state, and local taxes. However, governmental utilities may be required to provide free water service to other governmental departments as an alternative to paying local taxes, or they may be required to transfer cash to the general fund as a "payment in lieu of taxes."

Preparing and filing federal income tax returns involve more than reporting taxable income and the related tax liability. The tax return must be accompanied by supporting information or statements required by regulations or instructions. An private utility's financial statement net income may differ from the taxable income shown on the federal income tax return because the accounting treatment of certain income and expense items differs from the tax treatment. Income tax laws are written with feasibility of collection and enforcement in mind and don't necessarily agree with generally accepted accounting principles. Tax payments made during a particular accounting period may not always coincide with the tax expense for that period. Some payments, for example, are classified as prepaid taxes allocable to a future period; other payments, for taxes properly classified as expenses of the current period, are not made until a future period. The National Association of Regulatory Utility Commissioners (NARUC) accounts provide for income tax expense, for prepaid and deferred taxes, and for accrued tax liabilities.

For private utilities, recognizing revenues and expenses for financial reporting purposes differently than income tax purposes may create differences between the income tax liability for a particular period and the income tax expense for the same period. For example, using an accelerated depreciation method for tax purposes and the straight-line method for financial reporting purposes may cause such a "timing" difference. These differences are recorded on the balance sheet by establishing accumulated deferred income tax accounts.

Federal tax laws are extremely complex and change frequently in response to new or amended federal tax legislation. Utilities should employ qualified specialists in tax law and accounting. Even though a utility may have experienced staff on hand, the use of external consultants may also be necessary.

State and Municipal Income Taxes

State and municipal income taxes are becoming increasingly important as a source of revenue for state governments and municipalities. Private utilities should verify the tax filing requirements for each locality in which they generate revenue. Some state and municipal income tax returns correspond to the federal income tax return; in these cases, state and municipal income tax returns usually can usually be prepared from the federal return and supporting schedules. In other cases, even though the state and municipal income tax is patterned after the federal tax, income subject to taxation and deductions allowed may differ somewhat from that reported on the federal return. In such a situation, the income tax return for the state or municipal government may still use the taxable income figure derived from the federal return, with adjustments being made on the return itself or on a separate schedule for the difference between federal, state, or municipal taxable income.

Property Taxes

Taxes based on the value of property are a major source of revenue for state and municipal governments. A utility may be required to pay several different types of property taxes and may pay property taxes to many different tax authorities, including state, counties, school districts, cities, or any other tax districts. The term "property tax" generally means an ad valorem (that is, in proportion to the value) levy on real and personal property. In general, a property tax in its true form is a tax on all property not specifically exempt. Theoretically, all property is valued uniformly and taxed at a uniform rate. Property is typically classified as real property, or tangible and intangible personal property. Each class of property is individually valued and a tax rate (which may be the same or may be different for each class of property) is applied to each class. The basis for valuing real property and tangible and intangible personal property varies widely among various taxing jurisdictions. The basis for valuation may be established by law or regulation as original cost less depreciation, reproduction cost less depreciation, cash value, or some other value.

Frequently, a utility's tangible and intangible personal property is valued on a going-concern basis, as opposed to a piecemeal assessment of specific items of property. In some instances, the assessed value may be determined by the total market value of securities outstanding or by capitalizing utility net income. Once the value of all property subject to tax is assessed, the tax rate per unit value of property, such as per $100 or per $1,000, is fixed. Property tax returns typically include information concerning the class of property subject to the tax, a listing of such property, the assessed value of the taxable property, and the tax liability on the assessed valuation.

Gross Receipts Taxes

These taxes are levied on the revenue or receipts of the utility. They may be based on all operating revenue; on revenue from sales to particular classes of customers, such as residential and commercial; or on all revenues, both operating and nonoperating. Taxes actually levied on revenue or receipts may carry different descriptive titles among different tax jurisdictions. For example, they may be called *franchise taxes*, *privilege taxes*, *occupational taxes*, or *license taxes*. A gross receipts tax return may include data on total receipts, sales originating in the taxing jurisdiction, and sales by class of customer.

Sales Taxes

Sales taxes are based on sales of utility services to customers. They usually are levied on retail sales (sales to final water customers). A tax also may be levied on sales for resale in some instances. Whereas gross receipts taxes are levied on water utilities, sales taxes are levied on the utility's customers, with the utility serving as a collecting agency. Sales taxes are normally stated as separate items on bills for service and are neither expenses nor revenues to the utility. Water utilities must collect the taxes, maintain appropriate records, and make periodic reports and payments to the tax authorities. A sales tax return typically includes data concerning gross receipts from taxable sales to customers, as well as data regarding sales for resale and sales to governmental authorities, which are usually exempt from taxation.

Payroll Taxes

Payroll taxes include Social Security and Medicare (FICA) taxes, Federal Unemployment (FUTA) taxes, State Unemployment (SUTA) taxes, Federal Income Tax (FIT) and possibly local taxes such as state income taxes and disability taxes.

FICA taxes are taxes on employee salaries to finance a federal program providing workers and their dependents with benefits. Social Security taxes fund old-age, survivors, and disability insurance, whereas Medicare taxes fund the hospital insurance part of FICA. An private utility's employees participate in this program. Governmental water utilities may also be subject to FICA taxes if the utility's employees have been brought into the Social Security program through agreements with the US government. Taxes are paid both by the employer and by the employee.

FUTA and SUTA taxes on employee salaries finance the joint federal and state unemployment insurance program. FUTA is paid by the employer but not by the employee. In most cases, SUTA, too, is paid by the employer but not the employee.

Private water utilities generally are subject to FUTA and SUTA taxes. The federal act establishing unemployment compensation insurance excludes employees of governmental water utilities from mandatory coverage since, under the US Constitution, the federal government cannot tax state and local governments or their instrumentalities. Nevertheless, most states participate in the unemployment compensation program through legislation that affords some form of unemployment insurance coverage for employees of governmental utilities, either on a compulsory or voluntary basis.

Other Taxes

Many other types of corporate taxes are levied on water utilities by state governments and municipalities. These include franchise taxes based on flat annual fees and capital stock taxes.

Utilities also pay Workers' Compensation insurance premiums either to a state fund or a private insurance company. This premium is computed on payroll dollars but is not a tax and should be included in the appropriate operating expense account that includes the cost of insurance or reserve accruals to protect the utility against injuries and damage claims of employees or others.

Accounting for General Taxes

The total amount of taxes applicable to a given accounting period is not always charged immediately to expense, because a portion of the tax liability may be assigned to various asset accounts. Any capitalized tax payments are expensed when the assets are subsequently depreciated or amortized in subsequent accounting periods. Examples of tax payments properly charged to asset accounts include:

- Taxes, including payroll taxes, specifically applicable to construction work should be considered as a cost of construction and charged to the applicable plant account
- Special assessments for street and similar improvements should be included in the appropriate utility plant account
- Gasoline and other sales taxes should be charged when practicable to the account that includes the cost of the materials on which the tax is levied

Only those taxes assessed directly against the utility are accounted for as part of the utility's own tax expense. There are some taxes levied against customers and employees where the utility collects the tax and remits the amount collected to the appropriate tax authorities. Examples of taxes remitted by the utility but not classified as tax expense include:

- Sales taxes levied against customers and collected from customers on the basis of separate charges designated on the bills for service
- Amounts withheld from employees for federal and state income tax liabilities
- Amounts withheld from employee wages as the employees' FICA tax contribution

Property taxes have been recorded in various periods, including the year paid (the cash basis method of accounting), the year during which the assessment date falls, and the fiscal year of the levying governmental body. When determining which period to record the expense in, the important consideration is consistency from year to year.

In some cases, the final determination of tax activity cannot be made until after the end of the accounting period in which the tax expense is assignable. In such cases, the tax expense and tax asset or liability must be estimated for financial statement purposes. If estimates are recorded to the tax expense accounts and to balance-sheet accounts, then when the actual tax activity becomes known, adjustments will be required to account for any differences between estimated and actual tax activity. In addition to the use of estimates of tax activity to prepare financial statements, tax expenses must be estimated to complete the operating budget.

Anticipating Tax Implications

Private utility management and their governing bodies must consider the tax implications of alternatives before decisions are finalized and implemented.

Decisions regarding utility plant expenditures will affect property taxes (by increasing total assets subject to valuation) and income taxes (because depreciation and property taxes are deductible expenses for income tax purposes). When evaluating whether to lease or purchase property, proper recognition must be given to the tax advantages and disadvantages associated with each alternative. In addition, evaluating financing alternatives must consider the tax effects associated with each option. For example, interest payments on debt are tax deductible whereas dividend payments on stock are not. For rate-making purposes, decisions regarding the revenue requirement also depend on the anticipated tax rates (since taxes are a cost of rendering water service). The estimated tax expense also depends on decisions regarding financing and capital expenditure projections.

Management cannot make proper decisions regarding the activities of the utility without knowledge of the tax implications associated with alternative courses of action. Management may be kept aware of these tax implications through the use of capable tax experts who provide advice concerning the tax effects associated with the proposed alternatives.

For operating budget purposes, forecasting the asset or liability and expense associated with any particular type of tax requires applying an estimated tax rate to estimated taxable income or loss to obtain estimated tax asset or liability and estimated tax expense. Forecasting the major types of taxes incurred by water utilities is discussed in the following sections.

Estimating Taxes

Federal Income Taxes

Estimating federal income tax expense for the budget period requires that taxable income or loss be forecast. The appropriate tax rates expected to be in effect during the budget period are then applied to estimated taxable income or loss to determine the estimated federal income tax expense for the period.

Taxable net income does not necessarily coincide with book net income as defined by the NARUC *Uniform System of Accounts* nor does it necessarily conincide with net income as shown in audited financial statements. Taxable net income is a legal concept that may be defined as gross income (revenue) not specifically exempt from taxation, less deductions (expenses) permitted by law. Revenue and expense items as described in the Uniform System of Accounts do not necessarily mirror revenue and expense items includable for federal income tax purposes.

Estimating Gross Income

The major sources of total income as defined for income tax purposes include operating revenues, nonoperating revenues, and gains and losses from the sale or exchange of property and investments. Nonoperating revenues includable in gross income include such items as interest and dividends earned. Historical data, adjusted for anticipated changes in revenues during the tax period, are used to estimate total income for income tax purposes.

As noted in the preceding paragraph, gains and losses from the sale or exchange of property and investments are part of total income for income tax purposes. However, for financial accounting purposes, these items may not affect operating income. If these gains and losses are considered to be extraordinary, the associated tax effects should be classified with the extraordinary items in the utility's income statement, in accordance with the NARUC Uniform System of Accounts.

The amount of gain or loss and related income tax effect from the disposition of assets may be difficult to determine. The advice of qualified tax consultants (certified public accounts, lawyers, or members of utility tax staff) should be obtained before any decision is made regarding the sale or exchange of assets.

Estimating Deductions

Allowable expenses for income tax purposes, as specified by the Internal Revenue Code, occasionally differ from expenses as determined for general accounting purposes. For instance, no gross income deduction is allowed for estimated property losses and injury and damages claims not covered by insurance. (Deductions are limited to actual losses during the tax year not covered by insurance.)

In general, budgeted operation and maintenance expenses are used to forecast deductions from gross income for tax purposes. Expense estimates included in the operation and maintenance expense budget require adjustment when the basis for estimating a particular expense item is inconsistent with the basis employed for federal income tax purposes.

The amount of depreciation expense included as a deduction from gross income for tax purposes may differ substantially from that computed for book purposes. Factors giving rise to this difference include:

- A depreciation method, such as straight-line, may be used for financial accounting purposes, whereas an accelerated depreciation method, such as double declining balance or sum of the years' digits, may be used for income tax purposes.
- Estimated service lives of depreciable assets for financial accounting purposes may differ from depreciable lives used for tax purposes.
- The cost basis of property may differ between that used for tax purposes and that used for book purposes.

Clearly, two separate estimates of annual depreciation expense may be required—one estimate for financial accounting purposes and one for tax purposes.

For tax purposes, depreciation expense may be accounted for by individual property items, by groups of property items, or by total depreciable property as a single asset. Depreciation by individual property items requires that individual depreciation rates be established for each asset. Depreciation by asset groups requires that group rates be established and applied to the cost of each group of assets. Depreciation of property as a single asset requires that a composite rate be developed and applied to the total cost of utility property.

The amount of income taxes determined payable for a period does not necessarily represent the appropriate income tax expense determined for financial accounting purposes for that same period. The problem of properly matching income tax expense with accounting income is resolved through an accounting process known as "interperiod" tax allocation or most commonly referred to as "accrued" or "deferred income tax accounting." Generally accepted accounting principles require that accrued or deferred income tax accounting be used to account for the tax effects of transactions that involve timing differences. This practice is referred to as "normalization." If the differences between book and tax income are ignored and there is no provision for deferred income tax to be paid in the future, this accounting method is referred to as "flow-through accounting." Accrued or deferred income tax entries may arise from book and tax differences other than depreciation, although depreciation usually is the largest difference between book and tax income.

The earlier discussion concerning the components of gross income and the types of allowable deductions from gross income provides only an overview of forecasting taxable income; it is not a comprehensive study of all the considerations involved in estimating or determining taxable income. Federal tax laws and procedures for determining taxable income are extremely complicated and subject to frequent change. The advice of qualified tax consultants or members of the utility's tax department is required for planning and control of taxable income.

Estimating Tax Rates and Determining Tax Liability

The estimated income tax liability is a product of estimated income tax rates and estimated taxable income (gross income less allowable deductions) less any permissible tax credits. Federal income tax rates are set by the US Congress and may vary from year to year. Normally, the best guide as to rates of the budget period is to use rates in effect at the time of budget preparation. However, when legislative bodies are contemplating revisions in income tax rates, the best available information concerning the revisions should be used in estimating tax rates to be applied.

Estimating the Investment Tax Credit

The Tax Reform Act of 1986 repealed the investment tax credit as of Dec. 31, 1985. Currently, though the investment tax credit still exists, it is comprised of only a few areas, including the rehabilitation tax credit and the business energy investment tax credit. The investment tax credit is a component of the general business credit and is subject to the limitations, carry-back, and carry-forward rules that apply to the other components of that credit.

Though the investment tax credit has been greatly reduced in scope, ever-changing tax laws can reinstate this credit at some point in the future.

State and Municipal Income Taxes

The discussion of estimating income taxes has been primarily targeted at the federal level. In many locations, state and municipal income taxes are patterned after the federal income tax. Taxable income estimated for federal tax purposes generally can be used as a basis for income subject to state and municipal income taxes. The estimated state and municipal income taxes depend on the tax rates expected to be in effect for the budget period. Current state and municipal tax rates, adjusted for anticipated changes in the rates, serve as the basis for estimating rates applicable to the budget period.

Property Taxes

Because a water utility has a large investment in plant facilities, property taxes typically comprise a large portion of the utility's tax burden.

Property taxes are based on the assessed valuation of property held as of a given date. (Property not held on that assessment date is not subject to property taxes.) The assessed value is multiplied by the tax rate per unit of assessed value (such as per $1,000 of assessed value) to obtain the property tax liability.

Estimating Assessed Valuation

The bases for valuing property vary widely among the various taxing jurisdictions. Assessment of public utilities may be done by state agencies or by local assessors.

Typically, not all property of a water utility is reassessed on an annual basis. Rather, property is valued once as a whole, and then adjusted on an annual basis to account for additions and retirements.

In estimating the valuation to be assigned to properties owned in order to arrive at an estimated property tax liability, assessed value from the preceding year serves as a beginning point. Utility management must adjust the prior year's assessed value for anticipated additions and retirements of properties owned during the budget period.

Utility management may take or time certain actions to minimize property taxes. For example, management may plan to accomplish retirements of property items before the assessment date while delaying property acquisitions until after the assessment date. To the extent practicable, management may also save taxes by minimizing inventories of materials and supplies held on the assessment date.

Estimating Property Tax Rates

Property tax rates often vary from year to year. Nevertheless, the best guide to the property tax rate for the budget year is the rate in effect during the current period. Utility management must be aware of new rates being considered by governmental bodies that might be enacted during the budget period. If historical data show a trend line of increasing taxes, the budget period might be based on this historical trend.

Other Taxes

Other major taxes to which a water utility may be subject are the revenue tax, or gross receipts tax, and payroll taxes.

Revenue Taxes

The revenue tax is easy to administer in comparison with the property tax, and for that reason it is sometimes levied in lieu of the property tax. Revenue taxes may be levied on all operating revenue or on a particular class of operating revenue, such as residential sales or commercial sales. Forecasted operating revenues for the budget period serve as the basis for determining estimated revenue or gross receipts taxes. In addition to the estimate of operating revenues subject to the tax, revenue tax rates must be estimated. Although rates may vary from year to year, revenue tax rates applicable to the current period serve as the basis for estimating tax rates during the budget period. Adjustments in current rates may be called for if there is evidence that revenue tax rates will be changed by the legislative body imposing the tax.

Payroll Taxes

The major types of payroll tax expenses are Social Security taxes and unemployment insurance taxes. Under the federal Social Security program, FICA taxes are levied on both employee and employer. Only that portion of the tax levied on the water utility is treated as a tax expense. The FICA tax expense is determined by the number of employees, the

FICA tax rate, and the amount of each employee's wages subject to the tax. However, the FICA rate and the wage base to which it applies are subject to periodic and frequent upward revisions.

Under the FUTA, a tax on the employer is levied based on each employee's income. States have similar taxes, but the wages subject to the tax and the rates differ in most instances from the federal wages and rates. However, a credit against the FUTA is allowed for employer contributions to a state plan. State unemployment tax laws contain a merit rating provision under which a reduction in the state contribution rate is allowed to employers who show a favorable and steady employment record.

The estimated payroll as forecast serves as the base against which the unemployment tax rate is applied to forecast unemployment tax expense applicable to the budget period. This forecast payroll is reduced by the amount of salaries and wages that exceed the taxable base for federal and state for each employee. The product of the estimated taxable payroll and the estimated tax rates for the budget period (consistent with the anticipated merit rating for the utility) results in the budget estimate for the tax expense.

Other Taxes

There are many other varieties of taxes to which a water utility may be subjected, such as franchise taxes based on a flat annual fee or other basis. These taxes must also be forecast for inclusion in the annual operating budget. For minor taxes, historical data may act as a sufficient guide in estimating for the budget period.

Summary

The number and variety of taxes levied on water utilities, as well as the financial impact taxes have on operating expenses, require that water utility management maintain effective control over the determination and incurrence of tax expense. The existence of a tax department within the utility organization is typical of large water utilities. The tax department is responsible for the efficient planning and control of tax expense.

The tax department of the utility must ensure that managers are aware of the tax implications of operating and capital budgeting decisions. The tax department is responsible for keeping abreast of current tax developments in order to minimize tax payments within the context of existing tax regulations and requirements. In addition, the tax department is responsible for meeting tax reporting and tax payment deadlines in order to avoid the incurrence of legal penalties associated with noncompliance. It is important that appropriate tax records be maintained for use in justifying the amount of tax payments made, disputing deficiency assessments, and settling tax claims with tax authorities.

If the utility does not have qualified tax experts within the organization, tax consultants should be retained to advise the utility staff as required.

Periodic reviews comparing actual taxes with budget estimates may prove helpful in discovering errors in tax computations. Further, such reviews may reveal areas requiring additional or more effective tax planning.

Chapter 14

Capital Improvement Programs

Water utilities depend on their equipment and physical plant for water production. Property that lasts more than a year (the public sector usually uses a minimum of two years) and that costs a substantial amount of money to purchase is normally considered part of capital, though the line between capital purchases and maintenance can be fuzzy at times. Machines wear out and need to be replaced, pipes break and sometimes need to be replaced, and technology changes and needs to be updated. Meters that are remotely readable may make billing quicker and less expensive, for example. New equipment may be more fuel efficient or use less electricity, lowering operating costs; different water purification systems may have less impact on the environment or be safer and simpler. Water utilities sometimes need to expand to serve new neighborhoods or businesses or even neighboring towns. For all these reasons—replacement, updating, expanding, reducing operating expenses, and minimizing environmental impacts—capital improvement programs are a necessary part of any water utility, whether government or investor owned. Managers need to plan and budget for capital improvements, they need to finance such projects, and they must record the expenditures in the appropriate fashion.

For the purposes of rate making and to facilitate planning and budgeting, it is important to be able to distinguish capital from operating expenditures. To determine the cost of service related to assets, the cost of operating, maintaining, and depreciating such assets should be considered. NARUC has made this distinction very clear by listing all the water utility plant accounts. If the expenditure in question falls in one of the following categories, it is considered capital.

Organization (301). All fees expended during organization or incorporation of the utility.

Franchises (302). Fees paid to governmental agencies or political subdivisions that allow the utility to operate in certain jurisdictions in perpetuity or for a specified term. Annual or other periodic payments under franchises shall not be included.

Land and land rights (303). The cost involved in acquiring and placing land in a condition in which it can be used by the utility. The land or land rights will be identified for all uses in this account. The account can be subdivided for source of supply, pumping, water treatment, transmission and distribution, and general plant.

Structures and improvements (304). This account will include the cost of all structures and improvements connected with the utility plant. The account can be subdivided for source of supply, pumping, water treatment, transmission and distribution, and general plant.

Collecting and impounding reservoirs (305). The cost of the structure used to collect and store water.

Lake, river, and other intakes (306). All costs associated with the construction of intakes that will be a source of the water supply.

Wells and springs (307). All costs associated with the installation of wells and springs that will be a source of the water supply.

Infiltration galleries and tunnels (308). All costs associated with the construction of infiltration galleries and tunnels used as a source of the water supply.

Supply mains (309). The cost associated with the installation of mains, canals, aqueducts, tunnels, and their appurtenances used to transport water from the source to the water treatment facility.

Power generation equipment (310). The cost incurred with the installation of power generation equipment. Normally, the equipment will be used for the production of power used in pumping operations.

Pumping equipment (311). The cost of pumps and motors used to move water. The equipment may be driven by electric power, diesel engines, steam engines, or hydraulic water methods.

Water treatment equipment (320). The cost of apparatus and equipment used during the treatment of water.

Distribution reservoirs and standpipes (330). The cost associated with the construction of facilities used to store treated water.

Transmission and distribution mains (331). The cost incurred in the installation of the mains and appurtenances used to move treated water to the customer's service line.

Services (333). The cost associated with installing service pipes from the distribution main to the customer.

Meters and meter installation (334). The cost incurred in the installation of meters used to measure the quantity of water delivered to the customer.

Hydrants (335). The cost associated with the installation of fire hydrants that the utility owns.

Other plant and miscellaneous equipment (339). The cost of intangible source of supply, water treatment, pumping or transmission, and distribution plant not properly classified in another account.

Office furniture and equipment (340). All costs of office furniture and equipment devoted to utility service. Normally these items will not permanently attach to buildings.

Transportation equipment (341). The cost associated with vehicles used for transportation of equipment, material, and personnel.

Stores equipment (342). Cost of all equipment used for receiving, shipping, handling, and storing of materials and supplies. Each location that the utility has for storage will have the assets maintained separately.

Tools, shop, and garage equipment (343). The cost of tools, implements, and equipment used in construction and maintenance not includable in other accounts.

Laboratory equipment (344). All costs associated with the laboratory equipment used for general laboratory purposes.

Power-operated equipment (345). The cost of power-operated equipment used for the construction and maintenance of the various assets of the utility.

Communication equipment (346). The cost associated with telephone, telemetry, and wireless communication equipment.

The Capital Expenditures Budget

The capital expenditures budget is a plan for all changes to the existing utility plant, including both additions and retirements. In order to facilitate coordination of long-range and short-range plans, the capital expenditures budget should be prepared for a period of at least five years. The process of developing a five-year capital expenditures budget should integrate all aspects of the planning function, including design, financing implications, and the impact the facilities would have on assignment of personnel and the use of material. The effect of the capital expenditures budget on personnel and material requirements serves as the basis for planning the operating and construction activities to be performed by a utility. The capital expenditures budget enables management to develop a financing program to meet the cash requirements of the budget and allows management to time its activities in money markets in order to minimize the cost of money. In addition, the capital expenditures budget serves as a management control mechanism over capital expenditures.

Expenditures in the capital budget are limited to those items approved by management and policy-making groups as necessary to meet the demands of customers for water service. The construction budget usually has its origin in requests from division heads to the general manager of a utility for approval of specific projects, presented in the form of individual project budgets. It is the responsibility of the general manager and his or her staff to evaluate individual project requests and to consolidate those projects approved by the general manager. The consolidation of individual projects aids the general manager in coordinating the activities of the individual departments of the water utility. The budget is then submitted to the policy-making group (city council or board of directors) for final approval.

In the case of governmental utilities, the capital expenditures budget may become a legally binding document on approval by the city council or other policy-making group. The approved capital expenditures budget serves as the authorization to issue commitment documents and to incur expenditures in the amount appropriated (approved) by the city council or other policy-making group. In the case of private water utilities, the capital expenditures budget, although ordinarily requiring approval by the board of directors, is not a legally binding document. It is generally agreed that appropriations for capital expenditures should be stated in broad terms to provide reasonable latitude for water utility management consistent with the broad control needs of the policy-making group.

To be useful as a planning and control mechanism, a summary of budgeted capital expenditures, such as that shown in Table 14-1, should be based on a carefully prepared and detailed analysis of individual projects. It is useful to classify capital expenditure projects as "major projects" and as "blanket projects." Major projects include proposed additions to and retirements of the utility plant that involve relatively large outlays and are of a nonroutine nature. Examples of major projects include the construction or retirements of a water treatment plant, a pumping station, a standpipe, transmission mains, and other similar large additions or retirements of a water utility plant. Each of these projects is of sufficient size to warrant individual attention and consideration by top management and policy-making groups (the city council or board of directors).

Blanket projects include proposed additions to and retirements of the utility plant that are routine in nature. Examples of blanket projects include the installation and retirement of customer meters and hydrants. The individual items included in blanket projects are so numerous, so similar in character, and so small in cost relative to major projects that individual attention and consideration by management is unwarranted.

The summary of budgeted capital expenditures is supported by individual project budgets, for both major projects and blanket projects. Typically, each individual project budget includes a project number, a description of the project, the purpose and necessity of the project, scheduled starting and completion dates for the project, estimated cost of the project, estimated incremental operating revenues and expenses associated with the project, and estimated return on the investment. Individual project budgets should be prepared for uncompleted major projects (carryover projects from the prior and/or current years) as well as for new projects.

A work order system serves as an instrument to assist management in planning and controlling capital expenditure activities. Separate work orders may be prepared for additions to and retirements of the utility plant, or retirements may be included with additions on the same work order, provided that all items related to retirements are kept separate from those relating to additions.

Specific management approval is customarily required in order to begin work on each individual project. A work order, when approved, serves as the authorization to commence a specific unit of work, places responsibility for the execution of the work, and serves as a review of a proposed expenditure at the time the request for authorization to make expenditures is received by management. In addition, the work order is the basis for accumulating costs, which are later transferred to appropriate plant accounts and continuing property records when the work is completed. A separate work order is sometimes issued for each primary plant account that will be affected by a particular capital expenditure project. Other utilities may provide only one work order

Table 14-1. Five-year capital expenditures* budget summary

The Willing Water Utility Five-Year Capital Expenditures Budget Summary 20B1 to 20B5

Project Number	Brief Description of Projects	Estimated Expenditures or Retirements*	Expenditures or Retirements as of Dec. 31, 20CY	Expenditures or Retirements Required to Complete	Budgeted Expenditures or Retirements				
					20B1	20B2	20B3	20B4	20B5
	Source of Supply Plant								
307	Purchase of Reservoir Land—Expenditures	$41,000		$41,000	$41,000				
308	Extension of Roadway on Reservoir Land—Expenditures	20,000		20,000		$15,000	$5,000		
309	Replacement of Bridges and Culverts								
	Expenditures	37,000	$17,000	20,000	20,000				
	Retirements	(20,000)	(10,000)	(10,000)	(10,000)				
310-313	Construction of Wells—Expenditures[†]	200,000	20,000	180,000	40,000	40,000	$40,000	$20,000	
	Total Expenditures—Source-of-Supply Plant	$298,000	$37,000	$261,000	$101,000	$55,000	$45,000	$40,000	$20,000
	Total Retirements—Source-of-Supply Plant	($20,000)	($10,000)	($10,000)	($10,000)				
	Pumping Plant								
314	New Booster Pumping Station								
	(Structure and Parts)—Expenditures	$275,000	$10,000	$265,000	$85,000	$180,000			
315	Replacement of Pumps at Clear River Pumping Station								
	Expenditures	475,000		475,000		160,000	$315,000		
	Retirements	(375,000)		(375,000)		(175,000)	(200,000)		
	Total Expenditures—Pumping Plant	$750,000	$10,000	$740,000	$85,000	$340,000	$315,000		
	Total Retirements—Pumping Plant	($375,000)		($375,000)		($175,000)	($200,000)		

(Continued next page)

Table 14-1. Five-year capital expenditures* budget summary (continued)

The Willing Water Utility Five-Year Capital Expenditures Budget Summary
20B1 to 20B5

Project Number	Brief Description of Projects	Estimated Expenditures or Retirements*	Expenditures or Retirements as of Dec. 31, 20CY	Expenditures or Retirements Required to Complete	Budgeted Expenditures or Retirements				
					20B1	20B2	20B3	20B4	20B5
316–321	**Water Treatment Plant**†								
	Total Expenditures—Water Treatment Plant	$540,000		$540,000				$270,000	$270,000
	Total Retirements—Water Treatment Plant	($290,000)		($290,000)				($200,000)	($90,000)
	Transmission and Distribution Plant								
322	New Distribution Tank—Expenditures	$75,000		$75,000		$75,000			
323	Landscaping Around Standpipes—Expenditures	10,000		10,000	$10,000				
324–355	Extension and Replacement of Mains†								
	Expenditures	6,790,000	$190,000	6,600,000	1,130,000	$1,400,000	1,180,000	$1,440,000	1,450,000
	Retirements	(340,000)	(40,000)	(300,000)	(60,000)	(40,000)	(70,000)	(70,000)	(60,000)
356	Services‡								
	Expenditures	250,000		250,000	50,000	50,000	50,000	50,000	50,000
	Retirements	(10,000)		(10,000)	(2,000)	(2,000)	(2,000)	(2,000)	(2,000)
357	Meters‡								
	Expenditures	525,000		525,000	100,000	100,000	100,000	110,000	115,000
	Retirements	(5,000)		(5,000)	(1,000)	(1,000)	(1,000)	(1,000)	(1,000)
358	Meter Installations‡								
	Expenditures	105,000		105,000	20,000	20,000	20,000	20,000	25,000
	Retirements	(6,000)		(6,000)	(1,000)	(1,000)	(1,000)	(1,000)	(2,000)

(Continued next page)

Table 14-1. Five-year capital expenditures* budget summary (continued)

The Willing Water Utility Five-Year Capital Expenditures Budget Summary 20B1 to 20B5

Project Number	Brief Description of Projects	Estimated Expenditures or Retirements*	Expenditures or Retirements as of Dec. 31, 20CY	Expenditures or Retirements Required to Complete	Budgeted Expenditures or Retirements				
					20B1	20B2	20B3	20B4	20B5
359	Hydrants‡								
	Expenditures	420,000	20,000	400,000	80,000	80,000	80,000	80,000	80,000
	Retirements	(35,000)	(5,000)	(30,000)	(6,000)	(6,000)	(6,000)	(6,000)	(6,000)
	Total Expenditures—Transmission and Distribution Plant	$8,175,000	($210,000)	$7,965,000	$1,390,000	$1,650,000	$1,505,000	$1,700,000	$1,720,000
	Total Retirements—Transmission and Distribution Plant	($396,000)	($45,000)	($351,000)	($70,000)	($50,000)	($80,000)	($80,000)	($71,000)
360–384	**General Plant**†								
	Total Expenditures—General Plant	$1,050,000	$50,000	$1,000,000	$150,000	$200,000	$200,000	$250,000	$200,000
	Total Retirements—General Plant	($400,000)	($20,000)	($380,000)	($80,000)	($70,000)	($80,000)	($70,000)	($80,000)
	Total Expenditures—Water Utility Plant	$10,813,000	$307,000	$10,506,000	$1,726,000	$2,245,000	$2,065,000	$2,260,000	$2,210,000
	Plant Total Retirements—Water Utility Plant	($1,481,000)	($75,000)	($1.406,000)	($160,000)	($295,000)	($360,000)	($350,000)	($241,000)

*Expenditure figures include the cost of removal less salvage value of assets being retired as well as the cost of new assets. Retirement figures indicate the book cost of assets being retired.

†In order to conserve space these categories have not been classified by individual projects.

‡These categories of expenditures and retirements are considered as "blanket projects" as opposed to "major projects."

for each project, even though a project may affect the total in more than one primary plant account.

In some cases, the individual project budgets that support the summary of budgeted capital expenditures serve as work orders. Frequently, however, there is a substantial time lag between the time a proposed capital expenditure project is tentatively approved and included in the capital expenditures budget and the time work is to begin on the project. Prior to the time project work is to begin, various factors may develop that affect management's plans and that make it undesirable to start or to complete a project previously approved. As a result, work orders permit management to review previously approved projects and either give final authorization to begin work or to cancel projects. In the case of blanket projects, each individual item of work, such as a customer service or meter installation, also may be supported by a work order.

Sources of Funding

Part of the capital budgeting process is finding sufficient revenue to fund each approved project or pay for each capital item. The major sources of funding differ somewhat between governmental and private utilities. Governmental utilities generally fund equipment replacements out of a special account within the water fund. If the water utility was established or expanded through sale of a bond, equipment replacement funds may be mandated by bond covenants. In that case, the bond covenant may require water rates sufficient to cover not just routine expenditures but equipment replacement as well. In governmental water utilities, extensions of water services may be paid for by developers. These fees may be called *impact fees* or *system development fees* or *charges*. They are specifically for the purpose of defraying the capital costs generated by a new development or redevelopment project. Grants and loans from state and national government may cover some types of projects or equipment updating.

For larger projects or capital equipment or an accumulation of smaller ones, a bond may be sold. These would typically be revenue bonds repayable from the water fund revenues, but the general government may sell general obligation bonds because they are less expensive, backed by the full faith and credit of the governmental unit, and transfer the proceeds to the water utility, and get paid back from water utility revenues.

While some of the grants and loans from federal and state governments are available for both governmental and private water utilities, most are more geared for the public sector and nonprofits. Such grants and loans seek to achieve a defined public good, such as preservation of watersheds and wetlands, reduced energy usage, protection against bioterrorism, or the prevention of pollution. In some cases the goal is to create jobs or facilitate small businesses. The amount of money federal money available diminished fairly steadily after 2002, although specific programs such as those passed in 2009 (the American Recovery and Investment Act) to help counter the recession may come quickly and then disappear. The major federal agencies involved in grants and loans are the Environmental Protection Agency, the Department of Agriculture, the Economic Development Agency, and the Department of Housing and Urban Development.

For private water utilities, a major source of capital for improvements comes from the sale of stock. Like governmental water utilities, private water companies may sell bonds for capital purchases or projects. Retained earnings can fund capital items or projects, and some government grants and loans are available for privately owned water utilities. System development charges for new development are also possible for private utilities, as they are for governmentally owned ones, but the treatment for rate setting needs to be amenable to this form of financing, which is often not the case.

Capital Project Bidding

Two key issues face the managers planning major outlays for capital construction: the first is whether to perform the construction in house or contract out for it (or for some part of it), and second, if the decision is to contract out, which company to hire. The purchase of large pieces of equipment typically requires drawing up bid specifications and comparing products and prices.

Construction activities may be performed either by a utility itself or by outside contractors. Within a large water utility organization, specialized skills and services may be available that can be used for both operating and construction activities. The use of a utility's personnel resources to conduct construction activities may be more economical than construction by outside contractors if the special resources, such as engineering services, can be jointly applied to operating and capital expenditure activities. However, the performance of construction activities by the utility itself generally requires that special construction equipment be purchased, and that employees who are skilled in construction work be employed on a permanent basis. Construction equipment and personnel are expensive and, if such resources cannot be used fully throughout the year (either for construction purposes or for operating purposes during periods of reduced construction activity), then it may be uneconomical for a utility to construct plant assets. The use of outside contractors permits more flexibility because resources for carrying out construction activities are hired and paid for only when needed. Therefore, the appropriate procedure for conducting capital expenditure activities depends on whether it is more economical for the utility or for an outside contractor to construct the asset. The best solution to the problem of choosing between self-construction and construction by outsiders may be to employ the utility's own equipment and personnel resources to complete relatively small and/or routine construction projects (replacement or extension of distribution mains and service, and meter installations, for example), and to contract with outsiders to complete relatively large and/or nonroutine construction projects.

Consistent with the level of construction activity indicated by the capital expenditures budget, a determination must be made as to whether particular construction projects included in the budget are to be completed by an outside contractor or by the utility itself. The personnel and equipment resources of the utility should be allocated to those projects for which they are best adapted. Projects should be matched with the capabilities and skills of the equipment and personnel resources available to the utility.

The amount of equipment and personnel resources allocated to individual projects also must be sufficient to permit scheduled completion dates (or required completion deadlines) to be met. In some cases, construction work necessitated by a particular project may be partly performed by outside contractors and partly performed by the utility itself.

Effective planning requires that, for construction projects to be undertaken by outside contractors, the process of advertising and awarding bids (or by otherwise negotiating contracts) be initiated soon enough to permit the process to be completed prior to the scheduled date on which construction is to begin. Further, the purchase of construction materials and supplies, or the purchase of such utility plant assets as equipment (either through competitive bidding or by negotiating contracts), should be initiated and completed in time to permit the delivery of the materials and supplies, or the delivery of the utility plant assets, as needed to meet scheduled completion dates.

With regard to costs in excess of a specified amount, governmental utilities are frequently bound by laws that require competitive bidding for construction contracts, contracts for the purchase of construction materials and supplies, and contracts for the purchase of items of the utility plant. Normally, a contract will be awarded to the "lowest and best" bidder, but it should be kept in mind that the lowest bidder is not necessarily the best. The ability of the bidder to furnish goods and services promptly as needed, and the quality of goods and services furnished, as evidenced by past performance and current financial capability, are important factors in determining the best bid.

Recording of Capital Improvement Spending

Control Accounts

The NARUC classification of accounts segregates utility plant cost into general categories that serve as control or summary accounts. The categories are listed in the following sections:

Utility Plant in Service (101)

This account includes the original cost of the utility plant owned and used by the water utility. This account includes the cost of additions to, and betterments of, property leased from others that is used to provide water service to customers. The cost of property is subclassified in primary (detailed) accounts 301–399.

Utility Plant Leased to Others (102)

This account includes the original cost of the utility plant owned by the utility but leased to others as operating units or systems. The cost of property is subclassified into primary accounts.

Property Held for Future Use (103)

This account includes the original cost of property owned and held for future use in utility service under a definite plan for such use. The cost of property is subclassified into primary accounts.

Utility Plant Purchased or Sold (104)

This account contains the cost of the utility plant acquired as an operating unit or system by purchase, merger, consolidation, liquidation, or otherwise and is credited with the selling price of utility property transferred to others. The balance in this account is only temporary and is ultimately cleared by appropriate charges and credits to other accounts, including the other seven utility plant control accounts.

Construction Work in Progress (105)

This account includes the cost of a utility plant in the process of construction but not yet completed. The balance in this account is supported by work orders. (Work orders are discussed later in this chapter.)

Completed Construction Not Classified (106)

This account includes the cost of a utility plant that has been completed but not yet subclassified into primary (detailed) accounts. The balance in this account is supported by work orders for construction that has been completed.

Utility Plant Acquisition Adjustments (114)

This account contains the difference between

- The cost of the utility plant acquired as an operating unit or system by purchase, merger, consolidation, liquidation, or otherwise
- The original cost of such property, estimated if not known, less the amount credited by the utility at the time of acquisition to accumulated provisions for depreciation and amortization and to contributions in aid of construction with respect to such property

Other Utility Plant Adjustments (116)

This account includes the difference between the original cost, estimated if not known, and the amount at which property is recorded in other utility plant control accounts, to the extent that such difference is not properly includable in the "utility plant acquisition adjustments" account.

Construction Costs

Direct Construction Costs

The costs of assets constructed by outside contractors ordinarily may be determined on the basis of payments to the contractors. If, as is often true, a single contract covers the construction and acquisition of a number of different kinds of assets, then proper detail must be secured from the contractor to permit the determination and recording of costs by continuing property record (CPR) units or retirement units.

If assets are constructed partially or completely by the utility's own personnel, then labor and materials costs may be assigned to the project. The costs are assigned from labor time records and materials requisitions. Other items of cost, as discussed in the following section, are properly capitalizable but it is generally impossible or not clerically feasible to trace them directly to specific CPR units or to retirement units. Costs that cannot be so assigned are called "indirect" costs.

Indirect Construction Costs

Examples of indirect construction costs include salaries and wages of utility employees whose time is not assignable to specific construction projects, labor-related costs commonly called "fringe benefits," transportation costs, the cost of special machine service, shop service costs, engineering and supervision costs, general and administrative costs, and the cost of taxes and interest during construction. Some of these, particularly engineering and supervision costs, general and administrative costs, and the cost of taxes and interest during construction, are incurred for the benefit of the utility in its entirety and are only partially assignable to the construction activity. Such costs must be allocated between construction work and operating expense.

Indirect construction costs should be charged to individual projects, plant assets, and property units on the basis of amounts reasonably applicable to each. Each asset should bear an equitable proportion of indirect costs. Therefore, valid bases must be found for allocating the several kinds of indirect costs between construction work and operating expense and for allocating indirect construction costs among construction projects, plant assets, and property units.

Regarding indirect costs incurred by a utility in its entirety, two alternative methods are commonly used to determine the amounts that should be allocated to construction work. One method is called the "incremental cost" method. Under this method, only the costs specifically incurred for construction—costs that would not be incurred by the utility if construction were not undertaken—are chargeable to construction. Under an alternative method, called the "benefits-realized" method, costs incurred by the utility are allocated to construction work in proportion to the construction activities performed by various divisions (such as the administration and general division) of the utility organization.

Using the benefits-realized method, the indirect labor component of costs incurred by the utility in its entirety is allocated to construction work on the basis of studies made to determine the proportion of time spent by such personnel as administrators, supervisors, and engineers on construction work and on operations. Where expenditures made by the utility relate to things other than compensation for personal services, special studies are needed to determine that the expenditures have a beneficial relationship to construction and to determine a reasonable basis for capitalizing a portion of the expenditures.

The use of the benefits-realized method has the effect of reducing expenses and increasing net income during periods of heavy construction activity. The use of the incremental cost method avoids the effect of showing greater net income merely because of increased construction activity.

Administrative and General Costs

A portion of administrative and general activities usually is associated with construction work. That portion of the general officers' and administrators' pay, and other general expenses applicable to construction work, should be capitalized. The portions capitalized should have a provable relationship to construction work. As in the case of engineering and supervisory costs, the amount of administrative and general costs associated with construction work typically is determined by special studies. The portion of administrative and general expenses must then be allocated to construction projects, plant assets, and property units in an equitable and clerically feasible manner.

Interest During Construction

Interest costs during the period of construction of a utility plant asset are included as a cost of the asset by the utility industry. The recognition of interest as a cost of construction is based on the theory that the use of money to finance construction activities involves an opportunity cost. The cost of using money to finance investment in plant assets during the period of construction is equal to the income foregone by being unable to invest the money in some immediately productive asset. Therefore, interest during construction is properly considered as a cost of constructing the productive asset. As soon as the completed plant is placed in service, interest is treated as an expense to be matched against the revenues that presumably result from the use of the productive asset. The cost of the completed asset becomes a part of the rate base for private utilities.

Interest during construction is measured by the net cost (for the period of construction) of borrowed funds used for construction purposes and a reasonable cost for other funds when so used. Because a number of different sources of money are available to finance construction projects, the weighted average cost of capital is generally the preferable measure of an interest rate to use in determining the cost of money during construction for private utilities.

Transportation and Special Machine Service Costs

The labor costs associated with transporting equipment operators and special machine equipment operators generally can be identified with construction projects, plant assets, and property units through the use of labor time sheets; therefore, such costs are "direct construction" costs. Other costs of operating equipment (gasoline, lubricants, depreciation of equipment and garage, taxes on equipment, and other garage overhead expenses) and the costs of maintaining equipment (maintenance labor or maintenance materials and supplies) customarily are allocated to construction projects on the basis of a predetermined rate based on expected costs of operation and maintenance for each piece of equipment. After the cost of operating and maintaining transportation equipment and special machine equipment is allocated to construction projects, it must be distributed among plant assets and property units involved in the project. The cost must be allocated to plant accounts and property units on an equitable and clerically feasible basis.

Shop Service Cost

The cost of materials used or fabricated by a central shop may be charged to construction projects, plant assets, and property units on the basis of the cost of actual materials used plus an allowance for labor and overhead. The allowance is generally determined on the basis of a rate sufficient to absorb budgeted shop costs.

Engineering and Supervision Costs

A portion of engineering and supervision costs may be directly identified with construction projects, plant assets, and property units. However, if engineering and supervisory personnel are used jointly for construction and operating purposes, the associated costs must be appropriately allocated. Unless time sheets are kept by engineering and supervisory personnel, special studies will be required to determine the portion of costs allocable to construction work. After the portion of indirect costs of engineering and supervision is allocated to construction work, this portion must be distributed to individual projects, plant assets, and property units. This distribution must be made in an equitable and clerically feasible manner; for example, it may be in proportion to direct labor hours incurred with respect to the projects, plant assets, or property units.

Taxes During Construction

Taxes during construction, such as payroll taxes and sales taxes, need to be considered for private utilities. Payroll taxes should be included as part of the direct and indirect labor costs distributed to construction projects, plant assets, and property units. Sales taxes on construction materials and supplies should be included as part of the cost of materials and supplies distributed to construction projects, plant assets, and property units. The capitalization of property taxes generally is limited to substantial projects to which actual tax payments can be directly identified.

Accounting for Different Funding Sources

The Governmental Accounting Standards Board (GASB) issued a Discussion Memorandum (Oct. 15, 1993) on "Reporting Contributions, Subsidies, Tap Fees, and Similar Inflows to Enterprise and Internal Service Funds and to Entities Using Proprietary Fund Accounting." The user may want to verify the current status of this issue before using it as guidance.

Donated Utility Plant

The recommendations of NARUC and the National Council on Governmental Accounting (NCGA) vary somewhat with regard to accounting related to donated assets. NARUC states that plant assets contributed to a water utility, or constructed by a utility from contributions, are to be charged to utility plant accounts at the cost of construction. The costs can be estimated if not known. The accounts for accumulated depreciation and amortization should be credited for the estimated amount of depreciation and amortization expense applicable to the property at the time the property is donated to the utility. The difference between the amounts included in the utility plant accounts and the accumulated depreciation and amortization accounts is to be credited to account 271, "contributions in aid of construction." The remaining depreciated or unamortized balances associated with donated assets should then be depreciated or amortized, as appropriate, over the remaining estimated service lives of the donated properties.

NCGA recommends that a donated fixed asset be recorded in utility plant accounts at its estimated fair market value at the time received. The offsetting credit for the recorded value should be to an appropriately labeled contributed capital account within the equity capital (fund/equity) section of the balance sheet of the water utility (enterprise fund). NCGA also states that operating expenses associated with an enterprise fund should include depreciation on all depreciable fixed assets, including those donated to a utility (i.e., credits to accumulated depreciation on the contributed asset would be recorded as operating expenses that are closed to the contributed capital-equity account).

It should be noted that, under special circumstances, NCGA does permit depreciation charges associated with assets acquired through certain resources to be treated as a reduction of contributed capital as opposed to retained earnings, although the depreciation charges are recognized in the determination of net income. In turn, the income figure, unaffected by depreciation charges on capital assets so acquired, would be closed to retained earnings. These special circumstances arise when grant, entitlement, or shared revenue resources (as defined by NCGA) are restricted for the acquisition or construction of capital assets. As an alternative, NCGA permits the entire amount of net income to be closed to retained earnings, leaving the contributed equity balance unaffected.

Federal

Funding from the federal government typically comes in the form of a grant to construct a specific project. Governmental utilities are more likely to receive grants from the federal government than nonmunicipal utilities. When the utility applies for and receives a grant from the federal government, the requirements of the granting agency should be examined in detail. Federal governmental agencies require the utility to file periodic reports and have the grant funds audited. They may also require the transfer of the property acquired with the grant when the facility is no longer deemed useful.

State

Funding from the state government typically comes in the form of a grant or loan to construct a specific project. When the utility applies for and receives a grant from the state government, the requirements of the granting agency should be examined in detail. State governmental agencies generally require the utility to file periodic reports and have audits of the grant funds performed. Like the federal government, state government agencies may require the transfer of the property acquired with the grant when the facility is no longer deemed useful.

Bonds

The utility may at times pledge future earnings to fund additions to the water system. The pledge is done through the issuance of bonds. The bond and interest will be repaid over the life of the asset from the income generated by the asset acquired with the bond proceeds. The utility is not required to specifically identify the asset acquired when recording an asset acquired with bond proceeds. A utility using bond proceeds to generate funds for plant expansion will acquire cash and expend the cash for the assets.

Internally Generated Funds

Retained earnings are a source of funds the utility can use to acquire assets. The utility may build into its revenue requirements a factor for the replacement of assets. The revenue derived from rates will be reflected as net income to the utility. Net income will be transferred to retained earnings representing the internally generated funds. The utility using retained earnings to generate funds for plant expansion will acquire cash through operations and expend the cash for the assets.

Proceeds From the Sale of Assets

Sometimes a utility will dispose of an asset and use the funds provided from the disposal for the acquisition of additional assets. This method is infrequently used because a depreciated asset normally will not provide the funds necessary to acquire a new asset. The utility may find it advantageous to trade one asset for another. When this type of transaction is concluded, the utility will transfer the cost of the original asset to the cost of the new asset. Any additional payments will be additions to the cost.

Accounting for Retirement Units of Property

In order to maintain a proper record of plant assets, managers need to not only record expenditures for new or replacement items and capital projects, but also keep track of items being retired, with and without replacement. It is helpful in this regard to think about "retirement units" of property. In general, any item of property that is readily separable, and separately useful, from a larger assembly of which it forms a part should be treated as a retirement unit. A retirement unit usually consists of an assembly of items that perform a single function and are customarily installed or removed together. For example, a meter is a retirement unit. The cost of replacing any property item smaller than a retirement unit is accounted for, except for any substantial betterment involved, by charging such cost to maintenance expense.

List of Retirement Units of Property

NARUC and certain regulatory agencies provide lists showing the composition of retirement units for each kind of utility plant asset. Such lists furnish useful guides to the proper classification of expenditures. In the case of water utilities subject to the jurisdiction of a state public service commission, the commission customarily prescribes the list of retirement units to be used by the water utilities. The use of a prescribed list produces greater uniformity among utilities in accounting for replacements of property. If the list of retirement units is extensive and includes many small items, then maintenance expense will be less than if the list includes only relatively large items. Therefore, the cost of assets included in the utility plant accounts and the related depreciation expense depend on the size of the retirement units included in the list. When a prescribed list of retirement units is furnished by a public service commission, the list may be expanded by any water utility within the jurisdiction of the commission, but the list cannot be condensed. A prescribed list includes retirement units for each of the structures and improvements accounts and for each of the equipment accounts making up the primary or detailed utility plant accounts.

Minor Items of Property

Minor items of property include all parts or elements that make up a retirement unit of property. If a minor item of property is retired and not replaced, then the accounting treatment of costs involved is the same as when a retirement unit of property is retired—the cost of the minor item retired is credited to the utility plant account in which the cost is recorded, and the cost-less-net-salvage-value of this item is charged to accumulated provision for depreciation. If the cost of a minor item of property will be accounted for by its inclusion in the cost of the retirement unit of property of which it is a part, then no entry is made until the retirement unit itself is retired.

If minor items of property are replaced, then the cost of replacement is charged as maintenance expense to the activity in which the item of property is used. As noted previously, if the replacement of a minor item of property constitutes a betterment, then the replacement cost should be capitalized, the cost of the minor item retired should be credited to the appropriate plant account, and the cost-less-net-salvage-value of the replaced item should be charged to the accumulated depreciation account. However, even if the replacement of a minor item of property does constitute a betterment, then the cost of the replacement normally should not be capitalized unless the replacement exceeds an established minimum (such as $100). If the replacement involves a cost of less than the established minimum, then the expenditure is treated as maintenance expense.

Relationship Between Retirement Units and Continuing Property Records

A continuing property records (CPR) system involves the maintenance of a separate record for each unit of utility property (CPR unit). Generally, each CPR unit is composed of one or more retirement units. For a relatively large CPR unit, such as that representing structures (or major components thereof) and large items of equipment, the CPR unit may be composed of a number of retirement units. In the case of a smaller CPR unit, such as that representing a meter or hydrant, the CPR unit generally corresponds to a retirement unit.

For a further discussion of continuing property records, see National Association of Regulatory Utility Commissioners, Subcommittee on Valuation and Plant Costs of the Committee on Engineering (1975).

The National Committee on Governmental Accounting's *Governmental Accounting, Auditing, and Financial Reporting* (2005) defines a "betterment" as follows: "An addition made to, or change made in, a fixed asset which is expected to prolong its life or to increase its efficiency over and above that arising from maintenance (q.v.) and the cost of which is therefore added to the book value of the asset." NARUC, in *Uniform System of Accounts for Class A Water Utilities* defines a "betterment" as making "the property affected more useful, more efficient, of greater durability, or of greater capacity."

A list of retirement units is published by NARUC (see National Association of Regulatory Commissioners, Committee on Accounts and Statistics, 1962).

Comparing Budgeted and Actual Expenditures

Actual capital expenditures usually differ to some extent from budgeted capital expenditures. The accounting and reporting system should allow tracking on a project-by-project basis, so if there are major overages developing, managers can know about them in time to take appropriate action. It is the work order system that provides this information.

In addition to the capital expenditure budget, the work order system provides an accounting procedure to check the relationship between actual capital expenditures and the approved budget. The costs, accumulated through the use of a work order system, should be reported in detail sufficient to show the number and cost of the various CPR units involved in the capital expenditures project covered by the work order. A work order system operated in this manner permits management control of detailed capital expenditures for individual projects through comparison with authorizations.

In order to provide management with information concerning the costs associated with each project, or for each primary plant account and property unit involved in the project, a "work order record" is customarily maintained. In the case of an investment work order, costs included on the work order record include direct and indirect labor costs, the cost of contract work, the cost of materials and supplies, transportation expense, and all other indirect (or overhead) costs. In the case of a retirement work order, costs included on the work order record are the cost of property retired and the cost of removal and salvage value. By using work orders and work order records, the capital expenditures for, and retirements of, utility plant assets are identified, classified, and traced from the authorization stage, through the construction or retirement stage, to the continuing property records in support of the primary utility plant accounts. The cost of work in progress included on a work order record permits immediate reference to the corresponding work order estimate in order to determine the amount of variation between actual and budgeted expenditures for a particular project.

Minor variations from budgeted expenditures are to be expected. Significant variations should be investigated in order to determine necessary management action. In some cases, variations arise from faulty capital budgeting procedures. In other cases, managers or employees fail to follow appropriate procedures for conducting capital expenditure activities. Variations between budgeted and actual capital expenditures also may result from other causes, such as unanticipated changes in construction materials and supplies prices or labor wage rates. Any project that requires digging can discover unknown problems or situations, such as underground vaults or other utilities' wires or pipes that were not correctly mapped. Drainage can be unpredictable, weather can cause delays, or contractors can leave the job half done, either because of their own financial problems or in order to finish other work in other locations. Borrowing costs may not conform to expectations. Change orders may push up costs. Performance bonuses may result in projects performed on time and below predicted costs or they may be forfeited because of delays, resulting in lower costs than budgeted for.

If significant variations between budgeted and actual expenditures exist for individual projects, then management should be informed of the variations and the reasons for them, so that proper control action can be taken for the remainder of the project and for subsequent projects.

The amount of capital expenditures and the status of capital expenditure projects should be reported to management on a periodic basis, typically at monthly or quarterly intervals. Capital expenditure control reports usually consist of a listing of major projects and blanket projects. In cases in which total costs to complete a given project are expected to exceed budget authorization by a substantial amount, authorization to make additional expenditures should be required. In the case of a governmental utility subject to a legally binding capital expenditures budget, it may be necessary for utility management to obtain a supplemental appropriation in order to issue commitment documents and make expenditures beyond original authorizations.

Continuing Property Records

Proper accounting for utility plant assets includes the maintenance of a CPR system. As discussed earlier, a CPR system involves the maintenance of a separate record for each unit of utility property. A "unit of property" (or CPR unit) is defined as an item of property that can be readily identified and accounted for by itself. A single record may, however, be used for a group of small items, such as meters. The property record card for each unit of utility property should contain complete details on the unit, such as

- Any information that will identify the unit of property (for example, name of property item, brief description of the property item, and manufacturer's identification number)
- Location
- Administrative custody
- From whom acquired

- When acquired
- Where taxed (private utility)
- Information as to the cost of the asset, estimated service life, net salvage value, and any other factors that are useful for determining depreciation
- Recorded depreciation (if depreciation is charged by individual property units)
- Any date, such as that taken from an account number, that will tie the record in with the proper utility plant account

The CPR for each unit of property also must provide for recording changes in the cost of the property unit as a result of additions, replacements, and retirements. The recording of such changes is based on information contained in investment or construction work orders and retirement work orders. Completed work orders that have not been transferred to account 101, "utility plant in service," provide supporting data for account 106, "completed construction not classified"; and incomplete work orders provide supporting data for account 105, "construction work in progress." Account 106, "completed construction not classified," includes the total balances of work orders for the utility plant that have been completed and placed in service but for which work orders have not been entered in the CPRs as of the balance-sheet date. Account 105, "construction work in progress," includes the total balances of work orders for the utility plant in process of construction but not ready for service as of the balance-sheet date. Most public service commissions require that water utilities under their jurisdiction maintain adequate work order systems to record all changes in the water utility plant. Many public service commissions also prescribe the use of CPR systems for the larger water utilities under their jurisdiction.

In summary, investment or construction work orders serve as a basis for accumulating charges for construction work in progress. Ultimately, when the construction work is completed, the accumulated charges are transferred to the primary utility plant accounts. The continuing property records support the balances in the primary or detailed utility plant accounts. The primary utility plant accounts, in turn, support the balances in utility plant control accounts, principally account 101, "utility plant in service."

Normally, control account 106, "completed construction not classified," also would be supported by detailed accounts. However, the detailed accounts employed may differ from those presently recommended by NARUC, since such a difference is one reason for categorizing the assets as completed construction not classified. The "utility plant in process of reclassification" account represents a clearing account until audit and analysis permit the asset costs to be reclassified in a manner consistent with NARUC classifications.

It has been noted previously that additions to, and retirements of, the water utility plant customarily are made under the authority of work orders (in the case of the construction or retirement of plant) or by purchase requisitions (in the case of the purchase of plant). In turn, charges and credits to the plant accounts and to the continuing property records in support of the plant accounts are based on cost information shown

(1) on the work order records (in the case of the construction or retirement of plant) or (2) on invoices (in the case of the purchase of plant).

A CPR system can be an elaborate and detailed system for matching property units (CPR units) with their costs. The CPR system supports the plant accounts with a perpetual inventory of the property represented by the plant accounts and shows the portion of total plant cost associated with each individual unit of property or with each aggregate unit composed of similar small items of property.

Uses of a CPR System

In general, public service commissions require that water utilities under their jurisdiction maintain CPR systems. A CPR system is a tool of regulation and a way to compile a complete record of the original cost of property owned by the water utility. The CPR system is a useful tool not only for regulatory commissions' purposes but also for management purposes. Some of a CPR system's uses are as follows:

- Provides a record of plant costs for use in rate studies. Although the CPR system customarily shows the original cost of property units, the system also facilitates the computation of other kinds of property values. The reproduction or replacement costs of plant assets can be determined by applying price indexes to the historical cost or original cost of property units.
- As a record of the dates of property additions and retirements, provides historical information about the service lives of different property units. This facilitates service-life studies to determine appropriate depreciation rates.
- Provides cost data that may be useful to management in the preparation of capital expenditure budgets.
- Assists in determining the cost of property retired.
- Substantiates the costs included in the plant accounts. The cost of property as shown by the CPR system should be in balance with the cost of property shown by the plant accounts.
- Provides a useful tool for internal control of utility property. A physical inventory of utility property should agree with the inventory records generated by the CPR system.

Selecting Appropriate CPR Units

The development of a CPR system begins with selecting CPR units relating to which physical inventory records are maintained and which plant costs are allocated. The selection of CPR units also should be guided by reasonable limits of detailed property classification, since the cost of establishing and maintaining records increases with the degree of detail involved. The selection of appropriate CPR units should be guided by cost considerations as well as by anticipated usefulness of more detailed classification. Property records should be established and maintained in the degree of detail required to ensure a reasonably close relationship between recorded cost and the actual cost of utility property in use (NCGA 1968). NARUC defines a retirement unit for a main as two or more standard lengths of main, including fittings, or one continuous run of 24 ft or more.

In the case of land, each separate parcel of land constitutes a CPR unit. In the case of land rights, each land right having a useful life of more than one year constitutes a CPR unit. A CPR unit of depreciable property generally is composed of one or more retirement units.

In the case of structures and improvements and major items of equipment (such as those equipment items comprising source-of-supply plant, pumping plant, water treatment plant, transmission plant, and general plant), CPR units typically are relatively large in size. Each structure and improvement, or each major item of equipment, sometimes is treated as a CPR unit; however, a particular structure, improvement, or major equipment item may be composed of a number of retirement units. Distribution facilities are in large part composed of many small similar items of property (such as mains, services, meters, meter installations, and hydrants). Each item of property (for example, a given length of main, a service, a meter, a meter installation, or a hydrant) typically is chosen as a CPR unit. Each CPR unit is relatively small in size and generally corresponds to a retirement unit.

It was noted earlier that a major purpose or use of a CPR system is to permit tracing the cost of a particular property unit so that its cost can be eliminated from the plant accounts when that property unit is retired. However, a CPR system does not eliminate cost estimates in connection with the retirement of property items constituting less than a CPR unit or retirement unit. It would be impractical to establish and maintain cost records in detail sufficient to eliminate all cost estimates and to provide actual cost information for all property items retired.

Establishing a CPR System

For relatively large CPR units (such as those representing land, land rights, structures and improvements, or major components thereof), it is advisable to provide a separate cost record for each unit.

In the case of relatively small CPR units (such as those representing mains, services, meters, meter installations, and hydrants), a single cost record may be provided for groups of similar CPR units. For example, a single cost record may represent the aggregate cost of CPR units of the same size and the same year of installation. The average cost of similar units installed in each year can then be determined by dividing the aggregate cost by the number of CPR units represented by the aggregate cost. In the case of meters owned by the utility, it also is desirable to have a card showing the history of each meter, including its cost, date purchased, addresses at which used, and number of times repaired.

When a CPR system is first established, an inventory of property must be made in accordance with the selected CPR unite. This inventory can be prepared from existing utility records (such as maps and engineering reports) to the extent that such records exist. To the extent that records are unavailable or incomplete, a physical inventory of property units must be made.

After the inventory of property has been prepared, the cost of CPR units must be established. In the initial establishment of a CPR system, direct and indirect costs (original cost in the case of commission-regulated water utilities) associated with inventoried CPR units should, if possible, be based on accounting entries and supporting documents, such as work order authorizations and records, purchase requisitions and invoices, vouchers, and contracts. When accounting records are unavailable or incomplete, costs of inventoried property units must be estimated by referring to labor wage rates, material costs, and other historical information relevant to the period when property units were constructed or purchased.

Maintaining the CPR System

After the CPR system has been established, subsequent additions to, and retirements of, the utility plant must be reflected in the property records in terms both of costs and quantities. To the extent possible, physical inventory tests also should be conducted periodically to establish the existence of property reflected by the CPR system.

The direct and indirect costs associated with additions to the water utility plant are based on investment work order records and purchase invoices. These costs, which are transferred to property record cards, represent either the cost of individual CPR units (in the case of relatively large units) or the aggregate cost of CPR units (in the case of relatively small, similar units) installed during a given period of time.

The direct and indirect costs associated with retiring water utility plant assets are based on retirement work order records. The cost of retirements credited to property record cards represents either the cost originally assigned to the individual CPR units being retired (in the case of relatively large units) or the average cost of CPR units being retired (in the case of relatively small, similar units, where the original cost is represented by the aggregate cost of similar units installed during a given period of time).

If depreciation is accounted for by individual CPR units (which might be the case for relatively large property items) rather than by treating each plant account, functional group of accounts, or total depreciable property as a single account, then accumulated depreciation charges should also be reflected by the property record cards.

In summary, the elaborate procedures involved for allocating costs among property units in a CPR system permit the immediate determination of costs of property items being retired to the extent that the costs are recorded at the time of purchase or construction of property. In addition, the CPR system assists management in ensuring that recorded costs correspond closely to the actual cost of property in service. This is important from the standpoint of establishing an appropriate rate base value to use in determining water rates. Further, the CPR system facilitates the placing of insurance by identifying the items of property that are insurable and by identifying the costs associated with insurable property items. The recorded cost of individual items of property frequently serves as the starting point for determining insurable value. Insurable value will determine the amount of premium payments required to obtain full (or adequate) insurance coverage. Finally, the CPR system functions as an important tool of internal control by serving as a perpetual inventory record of utility property.

This page intentionally blank.

Chapter 15

Current and Other Assets

As discussed in chapter 10, the greatest portion of a water utility's total assets is its utility plant. Other classes of assets, however, are also important to a utility. Among the more important classes are current assets and restricted assets. The National Association of Regulatory Utility Commissioners (NARUC) defines *current and accrued assets* as:

> ...cash, those assets which are readily convertible into cash or are held for current use in operations or construction, current claims against others, payment of which is reasonably assured, and amounts accruing to the utility which are subject to current settlement, except such items for which accounts other than those designated as current and accrued assets are provided. There shall not be included in the group of accounts designated as current and accrued assets any item, the amount of collectability of which is not reasonably assured, unless an adequate provision for possible loss has been made therefor. Items of current character but of doubtful value may be written down and for record purposes carried in these accounts at nominal value.

Asset items classified by NARUC as current and accrued assets include the following four broad categories: (1) cash and cash equivalents; (2) notes and accounts receivable; (3) materials and supplies; and (4) prepaid expenses and other receivables. A complete list of current and accrued assets is provided in appendix A.

Restricted assets are comprised of cash and investments that have been segregated in special funds for insurance, savings, relief, hospital, and other purposes. Special funds are not classified under current and accrued assets according to NARUC but instead are shown under the balance-sheet asset category, "other property and investments." This chapter is concerned with the planning and control of major kinds of current assets and restricted assets.

Liquid Assets

Cash

Current assets that are cash or cash equivalents are called "liquid assets." Liquid assets include cash, temporary cash investments, and accounts receivable (primarily those from customers). In general, inventories of materials and supplies are not considered to be liquid assets.

Nature of Cash

Cash includes demand deposits in banks, monies, checks (and other similar credit instruments that function as money) held by the utility for deposit, and petty cash (or working funds). Bank demand deposits generally comprise the greatest portion of cash. In order to be classified as cash, deposits with banks or other institutions must be available for use for general purposes. The deposits must be free and their use must not be restricted either by contract or special trust agreement. The fact that water utility management may intend to use cash for the discharge of a particular obligation is not material if there is no legal compulsion to use the particular cash for that obligation. However, special deposits with fiscal agents or others for the payment of interest and dividends (in the case of private water utilities), and for other special purposes are not considered to be cash.

Sources of Cash

The sources of cash available to a water utility are many and varied. Most of the sources are described elsewhere in this book and are only briefly summarized here. The two major sources of cash for a water utility are (1) cash received from the sale of water service to customers and (2) cash received from creditors and investors in return for evidence of debt or ownership.

Other important sources of cash may include cash received from the rent of utility and nonutility plant assets leased to others, interest or dividends on securities owned, sale of property and investments, customer deposits, and advances and contributions for construction from customers, subdividers, and governmental authorities.

Uses of Cash

The disposition of cash falls into the following four major categories:

1. Operating—expense payments incurred in the conduct of utility and nonutility operations, primarily operation and maintenance expenses and taxes.
2. Financing—interest payments and repayment of principal amounts to creditors (and dividend payments to stockholders in the case of private water utilities).
3. Capital expenditures.
4. Repayment of customers' meter deposits and repayment of advances for construction.

In general, the cash generated from the sale of water service and from the conduct of other miscellaneous utility and nonutility operations is the source for payment of expenses incurred in the conduct of utility and nonutility operations. It is also the source for payment of interest and dividends. During periods when cash from operations is generated at a rate less than that required to pay obligations, short-term borrowings may be required to supplement cash resources.

To the extent retirement of long-term debt is not financed by new security issues, cash generated from sale of water service is used to repay long-term debt obligations. For example, in the case of revenue bonds issued by a governmental water utility, a portion of cash generated from operations typically is transferred periodically to asset accounts restricted for revenue bond debt service. The restricted funds may then be used to pay interest and to repay debt principal, though reserve accounts can be set up in many different ways, based on the structure as defined in the official statement. Debt service on general obligation bonds of governmental water utilities typically is payable from utility revenues. If operating revenues are insufficient, then a general property tax levy may be required to meet debt service requirements.

Cash generated from the sale of water service (in excess of cash required to pay operation and maintenance expenses, taxes, interest, dividends, and to repay debt principal) can be used to finance current capital expenditures. Cash received from creditors and investors, and advances and contributions in aid to construction, provide the other major sources for financing capital expenditures. In some cases, particularly in the case of governmental water utilities, cash proceeds from a securities issue are segregated in a restricted asset account (or construction fund) to be used solely for capital expenditures.

In some jurisdictions, cash received as customer deposits must be segregated in a restricted asset account. The restricted assets sometimes serve as the source for repayment of deposits to customers. If cash received from customer deposits is not segregated, then cash generated from the sale of water service normally serves as the source for repayment of the deposits. Repayment of advances from customers or others for construction typically is also made from cash generated from the sale of water service.

If, during a given period of time, the cash accumulated by a water utility exceeds cash needs, then the excess can be used to purchase investments, such as short-term government securities. This permits the temporary use of idle cash to purchase earning assets with little risk of loss of principal when the investments are sold. Temporary investments are liquidated as required to meet obligations.

Although special deposits with fiscal agents or others for the payment of interest or dividends and for other special purposes are considered current assets by NARUC, the Governmental Accounting Standards Board (GASB) considers such deposits restricted assets. GASB recommends use of the term "restricted assets" to describe cash and investments that have been segregated for use for specific purposes. NARUC uses the term "special deposits."

Controlling Cash

Cash is perhaps the easiest asset to lose through theft; therefore, strong internal controls should be established and maintained. Proper internal control requires that persons handling cash should not account for cash, and vice versa. The work of every employee who deals with cash should be continuously reviewed by other employees.

In the case of cash receipts, internal controls require that a receipt is prepared at the time the utility receives cash. The receipt document then passes through accounting channels while the cash itself passes through cashier channels for ultimate bank deposits. Persons receiving cash should not maintain accounting records. In addition, employees who receive cash should not prepare customer bills.

Cashiers should be required each day to turn over to the head cashier the amount of cash collected through payments made in person by customers or received from other sources. The reports of individual cashiers summarizing cash receipts, together with the receipt stubs, should be reconciled by the head cashier with the amount of cash received from each cashier. Copies of the cashiers' reports, together with the receipt stubs, should be turned over to the accounting personnel.

Remittances received by mail should be handled by employees under effective supervision, and each remittance should be accompanied by an invoice. Remittances by mail should be turned over daily to the head cashier, and a report summarizing remittances by mail, together with invoices as verified by the head cashier, should be turned over to accounting personnel. Each day's cash receipts should be deposited intact in a bank and a copy of the deposit slip should be reconciled with the daily cashiers' reports and the daily mail receipts report by an employee having no other connection with the accounting records or the handling of cash. Figure 15-1 presents a summary diagram of the flow of cash received by a water utility and of the accounting for cash receipts so as to obtain effective internal control over the receipts.

All cash disbursements, except for minor expenditures made through the petty cash fund or working fund and certain other payments made by wire transfer, should be made by check. Vouchers should be issued for goods and services received only after comparison between what was ordered and what was actually received. Cash disbursements should be authorized by the treasurer of the utility or his or her properly designated representative. All checks should be signed by an authorized person responsible for examination of the voucher and other documents supporting the disbursement. Check signers should not be the same individuals as those responsible who prepare the checks.

Disbursements from the petty cash fund (or working fund) should be supported by receipts or other support. Petty cash on hand should be defined as some nominal sum of money such as $50 or $100, depending on the size and needs of the utility. At the time it is reimbursed, the petty cash fund should be examined by someone other than the person in charge of the fund to verify that the amount of the reimbursement check (properly vouchered) corresponds to the amount by which the petty cash fund is depleted. Figure 15-2 presents a summary diagram of the flow of cash disbursed by a water utility and of the accounting for cash disbursements so as to obtain effective control over the disbursements.

For proper internal control, it is also necessary that the bank statement cash balance be reconciled monthly with the cash balance according to the general ledger. This reconciliation should be performed by an employee having no other connection with the accounting records or cash handling. In addition to maintaining adequate internal control over cash in order to prevent theft, it is important that management

Figure 15-1. Accounting for cash receipts

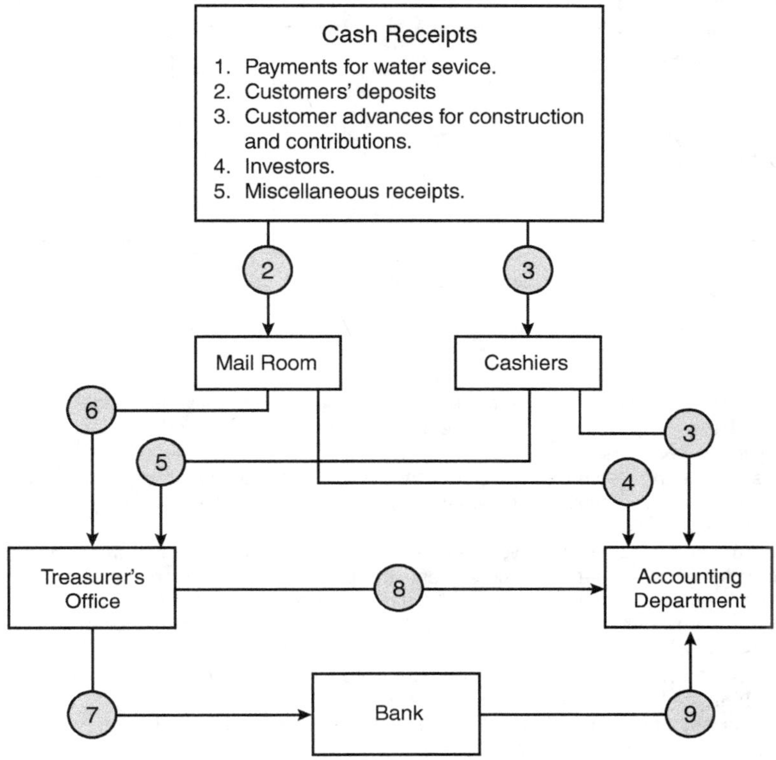

1. Payments from customers or other sources are made in person. Cashiers record receipts or customer account numbers or other sources of payment, and the amounts received.
2. Payments are received by mail. Mail clerks prepare a mail remittance list showing customer account numbers or other sources of payment, and the amounts received.
3. A copy of the list of receipts, together with receipt stubs, is routed to the Accounting Department where it is used as the basis for recording the receipt transactions as an increase in cash and a decrease in accounts receivable or an increase in liabilities or equities.
4. A copy of the mail remittance list, together with receipt stubs, is routed to the Accounting Department where it is used as the basis for recording the receipt transactions as an increase in cash and a decrease in accounts payable or an increase in liabilities or equities.
5. Cash received by cashiers, together with a list of the cash receipts, is forwarded to the Treasurer's Orrice.
6. The mail remittances, along with a copy of the remittance list, are forwarded to the Treasurer's Office.
7. The Treasurer's Office deposits cash receipts intact in the bank on a daily basis.
8. A copy of the bank deposit slip is sent to the Accounting Department. It is compared with the list of receipts from cashiers and the mail remittance list to see that all cash receipts were deposited in the bank.
9. At month-end, the bank sends a bank statement showing the opening cash balance, the daily bank depositis, the checks drawn against the account, and the closing cash balance. The Accoutning Department prepares a reconciliation of the bank balance of cash with the book balance of cash.

Figure 15-2. Accounting for disbursements

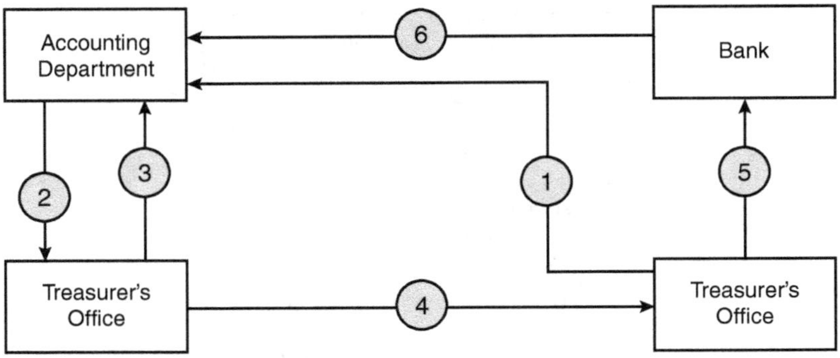

1. The Accounting Department receives invoices and bills from payees (vendors, contractors, employees, etc.) that are approved for payment. Included among the payees is "petty cash."
2. The Accounting Department prepares checks to be signed and forwards them, together with vouchers and supporting documents (invoices and bills approved for payment), to the Treasurer's Office.
3. The Treasurer examines the vouchers and supporting documents, and the checks to be signed. If satisfied that the disbursements are proper, he or she signs the checks. The supporting documents are stamped "paid" and are returned to the Accounting Department where they are used as the basis for recording the disbursement transaction.
4. The signed checks are not returned to the Accounting Department, but are sent from the Treasurer's Office directly to the payees.
5. The payees present the checks to the bank for payment and the bank balance is reduced by the amount of the checks.
6. At month-end, the bank sends a bank statement, together with the canceled checks, to the water utility. The Accounting Department or auditing department reconciles the bank balance with the book balance of cash.

monitor cash balances in order to ensure sufficient cash is available to meet maturing obligations. The treasurer customarily receives a daily cash report that summarizes cash receipts and disbursements and the cash balance. The report is similar to that shown in Table 15-1.

The daily cash report permits management to observe the utility's cash position and to compare the actual cash position with the position forecast by the budget. If the actual cash position differs substantially from the forecast position, a revision of the forecast may be required. In addition, reports of actual cash positions may indicate that financing plans should be altered, both from the standpoint of seeking additional sources of cash and from the standpoint of making revisions to planned borrowing and debt repayment schedules.

Cash Flow Statements

Information concerning the sources and uses of cash funds is frequently presented in the form of cash flow statements. An example is illustrated in Table 15-1. Preparing

Table 15-1. Statement of cash flows

The Willing Water Company Statements of Cash Flows For the Years Ended December 31, 2011, and 2012		
	2011	**2012**
Cash flows from operating activities:		
Cash received from customers	$ 16,729,699	$ 13,882,136
Cash paid to suppliers and employees	(11,579,752)	(8,173,973)
Federal and State income taxes	(1,319,438)	(826,245)
Interest received	66,009	71,407
Interest paid	(751,345)	(660,972)
Net cash provided (used) by operating activities	3,145,173	4,292,353
Cash flows from investing activities:		
Purchases of utility plant	(3,202,996)	(2,877,268)
Proceeds from notes and receivable	—	30,091
Related party receivables	326,309	(276,097)
Net cash provided (used) by investing activities	(2,876,687)	(3,123,274)
Cash flows from financing activities:		
Proceeds from issuance of long-term debt	291,335	905,401 6
Payment on long-term debt	(237,635)	(272,898)
Related party payables	100,534	—
Proceeds from contribution in aid of construction and advances	125,931	310,962
Dividends paid	(1,750,000)	(961,000)
Net cash provided (used) by financing activities	(1,469,835)	(17,530)
Increase (decrease) in cash and cash equivalents	(1,201,349)	1,151,549
Cash at beginning of year	1,581,669	430,120
Cash at end of year	$ 380,320	$ 1,581,669
Reconciliation of net income to net cash provided by operating activities:		
Net income	$ 2,207,273	$ 1,792,724
Adjustments to reconcile net income to net cash provided by operating activities:		
Depreciation	3,500,891	3,142,840
Amortization	(1,507,580)	(1,250,667)
Deferred taxes, net	243,737	(121,195)
(Increase) decrease in:		
Accounts receivable	(325,711)	30,570
Materials and supplies	(11,577)	(35,513)
Deferred debits	(494,437)	98,888
Unbilled revenues	(251,717)	86,558
Prepaid expenses, bonds, and deposits	(1,493)	5,614
Income tax receivable	(116,701)	413,074
Increase (decrease) in:		
Accounts payable	85,339	(136,805)
Accrued expenses	(228,043)	264,211
Accrued interest	18,147	(476)
Operating reserve	23,713	—
Customer deposits	3,332	2,530
Net cash provided (used) by operating activities	$ 3,145,173	$ 4,292,353

the statement requires that cash receipts from operations and cash disbursements for operations be calculated.

Preparing a statement of cash flows requires compiling information contained in other statements, such as the balance sheet and income statement. The statement reconciles net income to net cash provided by operating activities. For example, depreciation expense must be added back to net income because this expense (reduction in net income) does involve a disbursement of cash. Other expense items, such as operation and maintenance expenses, taxes, interest, and the purchase and construction of assets during the accounting period, may not include all cash disbursements; therefore, changes during the accounting period in the balances of current asset accounts other than cash and in current liability accounts must be considered in order to determine actual cash disbursements.

For example, an increase in current liabilities means cash disbursements are less than the related expenses and the purchase and construction of assets during the period; therefore, an increase in current liabilities represents a source of cash. Similarly, an increase in current noncash assets represents a use of cash. Operating revenues from the income statement and the sale of plant assets and investments also do not fully reflect cash sources to the extent there is a change in receivables during the accounting period. Therefore, an increase in receivables represents a use of cash.

Determining Appropriate Cash Balances

Perfect synchronization between cash received from operations and cash disbursements is impossible. Cash may be received more rapidly than needed to discharge obligations, resulting in cash growth; or cash received from operations may be inadequate and borrowing may be required in order to pay current obligations. Cash held in checking accounts and cash on-hand can sometimes be noninterest bearing, or may pay low interest rates. To the extent cash balances are excessive, the utility is not maximizing the usefulness of its resources.

The amount of cash to be retained in bank accounts depends in part on the amount to be held as minimum balances to compensate banks for services rendered, lines of credit or other credit agreements, and bank loans. In addition to minimum balances, cash in banks must be sufficient to permit a utility to conduct normal activities (both operating and capital expenditure activities). The amount held in banks for normal activities depends on the seasonal requirements of a utility for cash needed for transactions. A utility also may wish to maintain cash to meet contingencies. The amount of cash held as a safety factor to meet contingencies depends on the subjective feelings of utility management toward risk. Contingencies should be interpreted as minor unforeseen requirements for cash. The amount of cash required to conduct normal utility activities and to meet contingencies, plus minimum balances required by banks, determines the appropriate amount of cash to be retained.

It should be noted that lines of credit and other credit agreements with banks may serve to reduce the appropriate amount of cash to be retained in bank accounts by reducing the amount of cash needed as a safety factor to meet contingencies. However, the use of lines of credit or other credit agreements will increase the appropriate amount of cash to be retained in bank accounts to the extent that additional compensating balances are required by banks under the terms of the credit arrangement. Lines of credit or other credit agreements are not for the purpose of meeting long-run cash needs; rather, they serve as a quick source of money to meet cash deficiencies that arise in the normal course of utility operations. Additionally, a utility should evaluate the costliness of establishing and drawing on a line of credit or other credit agreement.

Forecasting Cash Balances

Although it is important that a water utility earn an adequate return, it is also important that the utility maintain an adequate cash position in order to discharge obligations as they mature. It is essential to sound financial planning and to the maintenance of an adequate cash position that cash forecasts be prepared. Cash flow forecasts permit water utility management to anticipate future cash deficiencies and to augment cash balances by short-term borrowing or by issuing long-term securities. Likewise, cash flow forecasts permit management to formulate debt repayment plans and to plan the investment of excessive cash balances.

Cash flow forecasts may be made for a year, a quarter, a month, or even a week. A one-year cash flow forecast may be developed by months (or by quarters) and updated each month (or quarter) by dropping the elapsed month (or quarter) and adding the next month (or quarter). If a one-year cash flow forecast is made by quarters, the earliest quarter forecast should be made for each of the three months in that quarter. Table 15-2 presents an example of a one-year forecast of cash receipts and disbursements by quarters, with the earliest quarter forecast by months. The forecast anticipates the need for short-term and long-term borrowing in order to meet cash deficiencies and to maintain a minimum cash balance. In general, the longer the period covered by a cash flow forecast and the more distant in time the period covered, the less reliable are the estimates. Therefore, periodic revisions in cash flow estimates are required in order for the estimates to serve as useful financial planning guides.

Cash flow forecasts are based in part on past experience and in part on anticipated changes in the activities of a water utility during the budget period. Forecast monthly or quarterly cash receipts from the sale of water service are based on budgeted revenues, adjusted for differences between the revenue estimates as determined on the accrual basis and revenues as determined on the cash basis. This adjustment may be made by applying a ratio, based on past experience, of cash receipts to revenues. Forecasting other sources of cash, such as the rental of utility property, interest and dividends on securities owned, customer deposits, and advances and contributions for construction, can be based on past experience adjusted for anticipated changes during the period. Cash receipts from sales of utility property and investments generally are more difficult to estimate. To the extent possible, such estimates must be based on management's plans to dispose of property and investments and on prospective market prices for such property and investments.

Table 15-2. Cash flow forecast

The City Water Department Cash Flow Forecast for the Year 20XX

	First Quarter—20XX			Second Quarter 20XX	Third Quarter 20XY	Fourth Quarter 20XZ
	January	**February**	**March**			
Estimated Cash Balance, Beginning of Period	$250,000	$174,000	$69,000	$142,000	$96,000	$75,000
Estimated Cash Provided By:						
Sale of water service	$500,000	$500,000	$570,000	$1,630,000	$1,720,000	$1,790,000
Rent of property	3,000	3,000	3,000	9,000	9,000	9,000
Interest on investments	1,000	2,000	3,000	12,000	15,000	10,000
Sale of plant assets and other property	12,000	5,000	18,000	25,000	30,000	10,000
Advances and contributions in aid of construction (net of repayment of customer advances)	10,000	12,000	14,000	50,000	60,000	60,000
Customer meter deposits (net of repayments)	1,000	1,000	1,000	3,000	3,000	3,000
Use of restricted assets—revenue bond proceeds				380,000	420,000	200,000
Short-term borrowings				300,000		
Issuance of bonds			1,972,000			
Other	5,000	5,000	5,000	15,000	15,000	15,000
Estimated Total Cash Provided During Period	$532,000	$528,000	$2,586,000	$2,424,000	$2,272,000	$2,097,000
Estimated Total Cash Available During Period	$782,000	$702,000	$2,655,000	$2,566,000	$2,368,000	$2,172,000

(Continued next page)

Table 15-2. Cash flow forecast (continued)

The City Water Department Cash Flow Forecast for the Year 20XX

	First Quarter—20XX			Second Quarter 20XX	Third Quarter 20XY	Fourth Quarter 20XZ
	January	**February**	**March**			
Estimated Cash Disbursements:						
Salaries and wages	$80,000	$80,000	$75,000	$250,000	$255,000	$235,000
Materials and supplies	160,000	165,000	150,000	670,000	540,000	450,000
Payments to outside contractors for construction	200,000	250,000	150,000	930,000	870,000	530,000
Purchase plant assets and other property	75,000	60,000	65,000	225,000	210,000	100,000
Interest (payments from other than restricted assets)	15,000	10,000	25,000	50,000	75,000	60,000
Taxes	8,000	10,000	20,000	75,000	32,000	98,000
Repayment of short-term borrowings	15,000	5,000	10,000	20,000	60,000	310,000
Transfers to restricted assets—bond debt service	40,000	40,000	35,000	200,000	195,000	190,000
Transfers to restricted assets—customer meter deposits	1,000	1,000	1,000	3,000	3,000	3,000
Transfers to restricted assets—proceeds from sale of bonds			1,972,000			
Other	14,000	12,000	10,000	47,000	53,000	32,000
Estimated Total Cash Disbursements During Period	$608,000	$633,000	$2,513,000	$2,470,000	$2,293,000	$2,008,000
Estimated Cash Balance, End of Period	$174,000	$ 69,000	$ 142,000	$ 96,000	$ 75,000	$ 164,000

Forecasts of monthly or quarterly cash disbursements for operations are based on the operating budget, adjusted for any material differences between expense estimates as determined on the accrual basis and expenses as determined on the cash basis. For example, cash disbursements for wages and salaries in any given month or quarter may vary depending on the number of pay periods falling within the time frame. Since monthly or quarterly labor expense included in the operating budget reflects expenses incurred (but not necessarily paid), an adjustment is necessary to convert labor expenses to a cash basis.

In addition, monthly or quarterly materials and supplies expense included in the operating budget ordinarily differs from cash outlays for operating materials and supplies. Particular material and supply items used are usually included in expenses at the average unit costs of the material and supply items on hand during the accounting period. Therefore, to the extent that materials and supplies are on hand at the beginning of the budget period, the cost of such items will influence the expense estimates included in the operating budget. However, cash disbursements for operating materials and supplies depend on actual outlays during the budget period, regardless of whether or not such materials and supplies are actually used during the period. Therefore, it may prove helpful in estimating cash outlays for operating materials and supplies to base such estimates on a separate materials and supplies budget (discussed later in this chapter) rather than in the estimate of materials and supplies expense included in the operating budget. The materials and supplies budget is based on requirements for materials as reflected in the operating budget.

Cash outlays for taxes also often differ from tax expense. Monthly or quarterly cash outlays for taxes depend on the scheduled tax payment dates falling within each period. The operating budget reflects tax expenses and is not affected by dates when the taxes are actually paid.

Cash Management

Monthly or quarterly cash outlays for interest payments, repayment of debt principal, and dividend payments (in the case of private water utilities or governmental utilities required to pay a dividend) must also be anticipated. Interest payment dates for short-term borrowings depend on the terms of existing borrowing agreements. Dividends on capital stock typically are paid quarterly. Monthly or quarterly cash disbursements for repayment of debt principal depend on existing repayment schedules as determined by debt agreements. Repayments of principal amounts of serial bond issues typically are made semiannually or annually. Cash disbursements for repayment of term bond issues also must be included in the cash budget if such issues mature during the budget period. Cash disbursements for repayment of debt principal (or for both the payment of interest and the repayment of debt principal) may be based on a schedule of payments to asset accounts (for example, special funds) restricted for bond debt service.

Monthly or quarterly cash outlays for capital investment projects (both additions and retirements) are an important component of estimated monthly or quarterly cash disbursements. The capital expenditures budget, together with the construction work schedule and the schedule for purchasing plant assets during the budget period, serves as the basis for forecasting these disbursements. To the extent the capital expenditures budget reflects accrued costs, as opposed to actual payments, the budget must be adjusted to a cash basis. In the case of contracts with outsiders, progress payment dates and final payment dates as provided by existing or proposed contracts determine when cash outlays will occur. In addition, monthly or quarterly outlays for the payroll of construction workers must be estimated. The cost of construction materials and supplies as included in the capital expenditures budget may differ substantially from actual outlays for such items. (See the preceding discussion in this section concerning cash outlays for operating materials and supplies.) Therefore, in estimating cash outlays for construction materials and supplies, it may prove helpful to base the estimates on a separate materials and supplies budget (discussed later in this chapter).

To the extent capital investment projects are paid for from assets (for example, special funds) restricted for construction or replacement of the utility plant, disbursements from general cash for capital investment are reduced. Therefore, total disbursements for capital investment, as shown in the cash budget, may be reduced by the amounts to be paid from restricted assets. As an alternative, the assets that are restricted for construction or replacement of the utility plant and that are to be expended during a budget period may be considered separately as a source of cash rather than subtracted from total cash disbursements for capital investments. Similarly, scheduled payments to restricted asset accounts during a budget period (for future expenditure for construction or replacement) must also be included among cash disbursements.

Past experience, adjusted for anticipated changes during the budget period, serves as the base for estimating repayments of customer deposits and advances for construction. Estimated cash outflows resulting from repayment of customer deposits and advances for construction should be offset against estimated cash inflows from customer deposits and advances and contributions. Accordingly, estimated net cash inflow (outflow) from customer deposits and advances for construction should then be included as a source (use) of cash.

After cash sources and uses (including interest and repayment of principal amounts on existing debt) are estimated for each month or quarter of a budget period, the resulting net cash balance for each month or quarter will indicate the need for, and the timing of, additional financing through borrowings (and/or through the issuance of stock, in the case of private water utilities). The cash forecast included in Table 15-2 includes anticipated borrowings during the budget period. A monthly or quarterly cash forecast, including the cash flows resulting from additional financing during a budget period, also permits management to plan for temporary investment of excessive cash balances that are forecast to develop during the budget period.

Other Liquid Assets

Temporary investments represent a short-term use of cash that temporarily exceeds cash needs. These excess amounts of cash might develop from such sources as seasonal or other periodic excesses of cash inflows from the sale of water service over cash outflows for operating expenses, or cash received through contributions or from investors (other than amounts transferred to restricted asset accounts) that is temporarily held pending more permanent investment in plant assets. Cash also may be accumulated from a number of sources in anticipation of future outlays for general utility purposes, such as payment of taxes, interest (if not paid from restricted assets), and dividends (in the case of private utilities or governmental utilities required to pay dividends). Unless invested temporarily, pending future cash needs for ordinary utility purposes or pending a more permanent investment decision, the excess cash would lie idle in a checking account rather than contributing to net income.

Temporary investments ordinarily consist of readily marketable securities. Governmental water utilities usually are limited by statute or charter as to the types of securities in which cash can be invested. Such investments may include bank certificates of deposit, or federal, state, and municipal securities. Private water utilities may invest in certificates of deposit, stocks, bonds, or other debt instruments. In some cases, the utility's board of directors may limit the type of securities eligible for investment. In all cases, the general manager or other members of top management should approve specific investments in temporary securities. An attempt should be made to invest in securities that will bring a reasonable return, but safety of principal should receive primary consideration. Certificates of deposit, government securities, and other debt instruments customarily offer a small risk of loss (or gain) of principal and offer a relatively safe investment; they provide interest income for whatever period they are held. Even among debt instruments there are variations in risk. For example, short-term government securities are less risky than long-term government securities, since the price of short-term securities is expected to change less during the period of investment than the price of long-term securities. In addition to differences in risk resulting from differences in maturities, risk among debt instruments differs depending on the issuing body. For example, investments in government securities generally are considered to involve less risk for a given maturity than investment in corporate debt instruments. Of course, income from investment in high-grade debt instruments may be less than if investment were made in such securities as stocks or low-grade debt instruments.

General guidelines concerning the type of securities that can be purchased and the composition of the securities portfolio should be provided by the board of directors, city council, state legislature, or other policy-making group. The guidelines should not, however, render management incapable of taking advantage of market conditions that permit improved returns from temporary securities consistent with reasonable risk. Within the limits set by law and by the board of directors, city council, or other policy-making group, it is reasonable for a water utility to invest in longer-term securities or non-US government securities and to bear the accompanying risk if management believes the increase in income over short-term US government securities is such that the risk is outweighed by the expected return. Water utility management may also have a policy of buying securities that mature on a date close to the time when cash from the liquidation of securities is expected to be needed. However, utility management may desire to invest in securities that mature after the time cash is needed, but that can be readily converted into cash when needed.

To maintain effective internal control, detailed records regarding owned securities should be maintained and should include information regarding description, purchase price, maturity date, call date, amortized cost, market value, unrealized gains and losses, interest rate, and income of the securities. These records should be reconciled at least monthly to investment statements provided by external parties. The employee performing the reconciliation should not have authority to trade securities.

Receivables

Receivables expected to be paid to the utility within a year are customarily classified as current assets. Included within the classification "receivables" are receivables from associated companies (in the case of private organizations), customer accounts receivable, receivables from officers and employees, and amounts due from other municipal departments (in the case of governmental water utilities). Typically, accounts receivable from customers comprise the major portion of receivables (unless customers are billed in advance, as is done in many flat-rate territories).

Types of Receivables

Customer

Receivables, together with cash and temporary investment, represent purchasing power in suspense. As such, the utility is primarily interested in the realizable value of the receivables. Therefore, the utility must provide for possible losses from uncollectible receivables. The appropriate amount to be included in the "accumulated provision for uncollectibles" account depends on the utility's credit and collection policies, the existing economic conditions of the utility's service area, and the meter reading and billing periods used by the utility. The total investment in customer accounts receivable also depends on the length of the meter reading and billing period—the longer the period, the greater the investment in accounts receivable.

Employee

Receivables due from employees may come in many forms. Examples are travel advances and, less commonly, loans to an employee. As with other receivables, employee receivables must be classified as current or long term depending on the term in which the payment of the debt will be made. Most employee receivables will be classified as current.

Employer-provided travel advances have income tax implications to the employee and employment tax consequences to the employer. Under current Internal Revenue Code regulations, there must be a reasonable timing relationship from the time the employee receives the advance to the dates of travel and to the substantiation of travel costs (determining a reasonable period of time depends on individual facts and circumstances). Additionally, the size of the advance must bear a relationship to the estimated travel costs.

When an employee does not substantiate his or her expenses or return excess advances promptly, the employer must include the advance in the employee's wages subject to income and employment taxes. The payroll adjustment must be made by the first payroll period following the time the "reasonable period" has passed.

Associated Companies

A corporate water utility may have several affiliated companies that receive centralized services. The affiliated companies may either be those that the utility owns or a company that owns the utility and other companies. In either case, the utility may provide service to these companies.

Receivables from affiliated companies must be segregated from other receivables, whether or not the receivable is current or long term. The segregation is required to allow consolidation of the balance sheets and income statements of affiliated companies. Without the segregation, the receivables must be analyzed individually to determine those of affiliated companies.

Other Municipal Departments

A governmental-owned water utility may have other municipal departments that receive its services. As long as charges and fees equal or approximate those that an independent external entity would have paid, they should be classified as interfund services provided and used. These revenues should ***not*** be segregated for elimination upon consolidation, but rather, should be treated as revenues just as if the transaction had involved an external party instead of another municipal entity. Otherwise, the utility's cost data are distorted.

Classifications of Receivables

Short Term and Long Term

Accounting for receivables presents two types of problems to the utility. The first is the classification of the receivable on the balance sheet. The second problem area is the valuation of the receivable. The utility's receivables are classified similarly to payables. A receivable must be classified by the time period in which payment for the amount due is expected. If the payment is expected to be paid within one year or within the current operating cycle, the receivable is classified as current. Most of the utility's receivables will relate to the furnishing of water to the customers. These receivables will be trade receivables. All other types of receivables are nontrade or special receivables. If the receivable is not expected to be paid within one year or within the current operating cycle, the receivable is classified as a long-term receivable.

Valuation

Utilities will normally not have receivables valuation problems that other organizations have because the utility can withhold service when warranted. Utilities with a turn-off policy find that most receivables will be paid before services are disconnected.

Customers filing bankruptcy and those accounts that are disconnected will be accounted for as uncollectible receivables. The utility's historical record of uncollectibles will determine the method used in recognizing the bad debt expense. Utilities with immaterial amounts of bad debt expense can use a direct write-off method. The direct write-off method does not allow the utility to match the bad debt expense to the period in which the revenue has been recorded. The allowance method for recognizing bad debt expense is preferred. In this method, the utility will recognize an estimated bad debt expense in the period when the revenue is recorded. Examples of the allowance method are the percentage of sales or percentage of outstanding receivables.

The utility should use an acceptable method of recognizing bad debt expense on nontrade receivables. Nontrade receivables have a higher probability to become a bad debt than the trade accounts because of the inability of the utility to curtail service when the receivable has not been paid.

Customer Accounting

The utility has a choice of two methods of customer accounting—the invoice method and the open-account billing method.

If the utility bills on an invoice basis, each payment received should identify the invoice where the payment should be applied. The utility should prepare a policy for application of payments that do not have the invoice identified. Normally the oldest outstanding invoice will have the cash applied to it. Using the invoice method may require the separation of a payment among several invoices.

Utilities billing on an open-account basis will increase the amount due for each customer at each billing. The customer's payment will reduce the amount due by the amount of the payment. With an open-account billing method, the customer's account could have a credit balance if overpayments have been made to the account or payments have been credited to an incorrect account.

The invoice method of billing requires more detailed information when applying payments than the open-account method.

A history of the customer's account should be maintained from the application for the service to the cut-off of the tap at the main. Some utilities require payments for all services performed, from processing the application for service, installation of the tap, through disconnection of service. Each of the transactions will be recorded on the customer's account history.

Customers with no meter will be billed based on anticipated requirements the customer will place on the utility. The number of water-using devices and the area that is irrigated will be factored together in determining the amount to be billed. Some utilities bill these customers in advance, while others bill in arrears. The utility should periodically inspect each account billed under the flat-rate method to determine that factors for the basis of billing have not changed, for example through the addition of a swimming pool.

Metered customers require more labor in preparing the billing. Each customer's meter must be read at a recurring period. Some utilities may read the meter monthly, others bimonthly or another regular period. Larger utilities may have automated the meter reading process through inquiry through telephone lines or hand-held computers. Once consumption has been determined by comparing the previous reading to the current reading, the customer's bill can be calculated.

The bills should contain statements concerning the due date of the payment from the customer for the service provided. The utility can estimate the cash flow based on a historical record of billings during a similar period in previous years. The depositing and recording of the cash received should be separated. The separation of these duties will aid the internal control of cash receipts.

Materials and Supplies

Water utility inventories are not the type accounted for in a manufacturing concern. Items in the water utility's inventory may remain in the stock account for many years before the item is issued. Regardless of the historical manner in which the utility maintains its inventory, the inventory is recorded as a current asset.

The materials and supplies inventory of a water utility is comprised of many items, including fuel stocks, chemicals for the treatment of water, materials and supplies used in the operation of utility plant facilities, maintenance materials and supplies, construction materials and supplies, and materials and supplies held primarily for merchandising, jobbing, and contract work. In general, all material and supply items, regardless of their purpose, are considered as current assets. The NARUC classification of accounts (see appendix A) provides a number of current asset accounts to be used to record the cost of materials and supplies. These accounts provide for the cost of supervision, labor, and other expenses incurred in purchasing, storing, handling, and distributing material and supply items, as well as the invoice price of the items.

Particular material and supply items may be held in stock for a relatively short or relatively long period of time depending on the nature of, and frequency of need for, the item. For example, fuel stocks and chemical stocks may be maintained in amounts sufficient for operating requirements for an extended period of time. The turnover of some operating material and supply items may be quite rapid because the items are continually used in operation and maintenance activities. The turnover of other operating items may be extremely slow because such items are held to meet emergency requirements.

The costs of materials and supplies purchased by a water utility are charged to the appropriate materials and supplies account and the items placed in stores until required for use by the utility. The cost of material and supply items is charged to expense accounts or investment work orders when the items are issued from stores for a specific purpose. Typically, the cost of material and supply items is charged to expense accounts or investment work orders and credited to inventory accounts on the basis of actual cost, average cost, first-in/first-out, or such other method of inventory accounting in conformance with accepted accounting standards consistently applied.

Cost Basis

Actual Cost

Ideally an inventory would be valued at the historical cost for each item in the stock account. Valuation using this type of accounting would be through a specific identification methodology. When using this valuation method, the utility records the cost of each item as it was acquired and charges the issuance of the item with the acquisition cost.

The costs included in the acquisition of the materials for stock are similar to those found in chapter 10. The cost of transportation and other incidental costs required to acquire the item should be included as a cost of the stock item.

Specific identification is the theoretically preferred method of valuing the inventory, although it may be impractical. If the utility maintained a small inventory of expensive items, the cost to maintain this valuation method might be justified. But when the utility maintains stock ranging from nuts and bolts to large butterfly valves, using the specific identification valuation method may be cost-prohibitive.

Utilities that use the specific identification valuation method risk accounting manipulation when more than one item of a group is held in stock. The inventory manager may influence net income by issuing a lower-priced or higher-priced item from stock. The utility may also find it difficult to identify costs of a specific item when the costs involve transportation, storage, trade or cash discounts. When it becomes difficult to identify costs of specific items, the utility will find it more practical to allocate the costs. When allocation begins, the theoretical basis diminishes as the value of the item in stock is now not specific.

Average Cost

The average cost method or the more frequently used weighted average cost method of valuing stock allows the utility to maintain the valuation without the enormous record-keeping requirements of the specific identification method.

When using the weighted average cost method, the utility recalculates the costs at the end of a specific period, perhaps as frequently as every day. With high-use items, such as gasoline, the utility should consider the calculation of the average cost daily. This will allow the utility to issue the item from stock and value the item at the current value.

Theoretically, the use of a weighted average cost would not be preferred. The use of this method is founded on a practical, not a theoretical basis. Advocates of this method argue that it is impossible to measure the specific identification of an item of inventory and, logically, it follows that the average weighted cost is more practical and representative of the value of the inventory.

First In/First Out

Another acceptable method of inventory valuation under generally accepted accounting principles is first in/first out or FIFO. This method assumes the first products purchased are also the first products used. The remaining inventory represents the utility's more recent purchases.

The inventory system required for a FIFO inventory tracks all receipts into the inventory account and applies the issues against the receipts. FIFO requires a more sophisticated system than used in a weighted average cost system.

The FIFO system more accurately represents the specific identification method of valuing the inventory than the average weighted cost valuation method. FIFO also has the advantage of reducing the ability of management to manipulate net income with the issues from stock.

The inventory value under FIFO approximates the current replacement cost of the stock. However, FIFO does not allow current costs to be matched against current revenue as the costs of issues are the oldest stock cost.

Conformity With Generally Accepted Accounting Principles

Generally accepted accounting principles have identified other acceptable valuation methods. Other methods available to utilities include standard costs, last in/first out (LIFO), and dollar value LIFO.

The LIFO method assumes that the cost to acquire the inventory in the current period should be the cost that is assigned to items issued from stock. The valuation of inventory under LIFO requires that the stock on hand be valued at a base-year layer. The quantity on hand in the base year must be maintained or the utility will be required to adjust the base year to the appropriate period in which the quantity was on hand. The issues from stock are made at the most recent cost.

A variation of the LIFO is dollar value LIFO. With dollar value LIFO, the utility adjusts the base-year value of the inventory based on an appropriate price index. The use of the dollar value LIFO method allows the utility to record the value of the inventory at a cost that more closely represents the current cost of acquiring the inventory.

Planning for Inventory Levels

Planning Investment in Materials and Supplies

Investment in material and supply inventories for a water utility is substantial and requires careful planning. Such planning takes the form of a materials and supplies budget, which is a plan for the purchase of materials and supplies during the budget period. This budget is developed after considering the material and supply requirements from the operating and capital expenditures budgets, the existing inventories of material and supply items, and the desired inventory level at the end of the budget period. The greater the construction work performed by the utility itself (as opposed to work by outside contractors), the greater will be the materials and supplies budget.

The materials and supplies budget should show material and supply requirements in terms of dollars, as well as a detailed listing of material and supply items required for stock. A time schedule for the purchase of such items during the budget period should be prepared. This will permit management to plan the purchase of material and supply items so as to avoid the cost of maintaining higher-than-necessary levels of inventories (resulting from premature purchases) while at the same time ensuring adequate levels of material and supply items are on hand to meet operating and construction requirements.

The materials and supplies budget in terms of dollars, together with the time schedule of purchases, facilitates the determination of cash disbursements resulting from the purchase of materials and supplies and provides information for the development of the cash budget (as discussed earlier in this chapter). The listing of material and supply items included in the budget, together with the proposed time schedule of purchases, permits stores personnel to plan their operations during the budget period.

The operation and maintenance budget and the capital expenditures budget are the foundation for the preparation of the materials and supplies budget. The operating and construction requirements for material and supply items are adjusted for items already on hand and for planned reductions or increases in existing levels of inventory items during the budget period. Inventories should be maintained at levels that minimize cost. In the language of operations researchers, a proper inventory level for a particular item is one that minimizes the cost of carrying a given inventory level plus the cost of not carrying enough inventory. The cost of carrying inventory includes the risk of obsolescence or deterioration while in stock, interest on investment, handling and storage cost, property taxes and property insurance, and clerical costs. The cost of not carrying enough inventory includes the costs associated with an interruption of services supplied by the utility (loss of revenues, loss of customer goodwill, and the extra cost of making emergency purchases). In determining the amount of purchases during the budget period, utility management also should consider the benefits of quantity discounts, transportation conditions, and possibilities of changes in market prices of material and supply items.

Delivery Time

Manufacturers attempt to have their additions to stock delivered just in time for the items to be issued, thus allowing the company a minimal amount of inventory on hand at any one point in time. Utilities have a different requirement for inventory, as the inventory is required to be at a level that will allow the utility to meet emergency requirements.

Utilities review usage and delivery times to determine the order point for the items in stock. Most water utilities will have a policy that the inventory for certain stock items used in emergency repairs will never have a quantity of zero.

With this policy, the purchasing agent sets order points for each item in stock. When the order point is reached, the agent requests quotations from vendors able to supply the item. The vendor that can supply the item at the most favorable price and delivery terms is selected for the purchase. The agent reviews the delivery status of the item periodically to determine that the vendor will meet the promised terms. If the vendor does not deliver as promised, the purchasing agent contacts the vendor to determine the delivery date. If the delivery date is not acceptable, the agent may cancel the order and reorder with a vendor capable of meeting the required delivery schedule.

Quantity Discounts

The utility should consider quantity discounts for all purchases. The amount purchased may satisfy the utility's needs for a specific time period, but a larger purchase may afford an economy of scale.

Type of Material and Identification

Items carried in inventory must be properly classified and identified so they can be accounted for and located when needed. A large water utility may, for example, have 20,000 separate items in its inventory. Clearly, proper classification and identification of inventory items are a requisite to efficient operation of the store's activity. As an example, pipe must be classified by type and diameter. In addition, a unit of issue must be chosen (feet of pipe, for example) and a stock number assigned to each item.

Record Keeping

Inventory requires additional record keeping that materials and supplies purchased for direct use do not require. Inventory requires that usage patterns, location of the material, economic order quantities, and other pieces of information be retained on the inventory stock. Each receipt and issue of inventory stock must be recorded. The inventory is maintained in a perpetual inventory system, which allows the access and determination of the status of each stock item as needed.

Physical Storage

The inventory stock must be kept in a secure location. As issues and receipts of the stock must be maintained, the stock can only be placed into the storage location or removed from the location by authorized personnel.

Purchasing Procedures

Although the size of a water utility determines the complexity of its purchasing organization, the purchasing activity should be centralized. In some municipalities, a separate working capital fund handles purchasing, storing, and issuing. Centralized purchasing permits the realization of quantity discounts from combined purchases (as opposed to losing such discounts as a result of each segment of the organization making its own purchases); it allows the elimination of overstocking or duplications of materials and supplies inherent in a system of decentralized purchasing; and it permits the use of personnel who are skilled or specially trained in purchasing activities.

The two major decisions required in placing a purchase order for a particular item are (1) when to place an order and (2) the size of the order. When to place an order depends on the lead time (the time interval between placing an order and receiving delivery) and the rate of usage of an item. For example, if the lead time is 20 days and the average rate of use of an item is four units per day, a purchase request should be initiated when the inventory level for the item reaches 80 units (the "order point" for that item). A safety factor is normally included to allow for fluctuations in usage of an item. This increases the order point for the item.

The size of the order depends on such factors as the quantity of an item used per unit of time, the incremental cost of placing an order, the cost of carrying one unit of an item in stock per unit of time, the cost of being out of stock one unit, and quantity discounts. The optimum size of order or economic order quantity (EOQ) is the quantity that minimizes the cost-enumerated above. A number of mathematical techniques and formulas have been developed to determine the EOQ for an item of inventory.

A decrease in the order point and/or a decrease in the order size decreases the carrying cost of inventory and increases the cost of being out of stock. An increase in the order point and/or an increase in the order size increases the carrying cost of inventory and decreases the cost of being out of stock.

Physical Receiving

When materials are received in the storeroom, they should be inspected, counted, and recorded by the storekeeper. A copy of the purchase order should be on hand so that the storekeeper can verify that the goods received are in compliance with the specifications. A receiving report should then be prepared by the storekeeper for comparison with the vendor's invoice and with title purchase order, to ascertain the prices, quantities, and terms are in agreement. Any irregularities between amounts ordered, amounts received, or amounts billed by vendors should be resolved before payments are made to vendors. Figure 15-3 presents a diagram that summarizes the flow of information and documents related to the purchasing and receiving of materials and supplies. This diagram also reflects the segregation of duties necessary for effective internal control.

Requisitions of Materials

When the level of a particular material or supply item approaches the order point, a purchase requisition should be prepared by stores personnel and forwarded to the purchasing department. The ordering procedure depends on the amount to be ordered and the requirements of law. For contracts with outsiders for construction, governmental water utilities typically are required by law to obtain competitive bids for purchases in excess of a stated amount. Even if not required by law, it may be desirable for a utility to request formal bids before placing an order. Before selecting vendors, the purchasing department should obtain information regarding prices, payment terms, reliability of vendors with respect to meeting delivery dates, and quality of products.

In addition to selecting vendors, the purchasing department is also responsible for obtaining proper authorization to make purchases. The approved materials and supplies budget may serve as authorization. If the budget is a legally binding document for governmental water utilities, then the purchasing department must ensure limits on committing funds are not exceeded. In cases where budgeted amounts are inadequate, additional authorization to commit funds must be obtained.

Physical Inventories

It is necessary for several reasons to supplement the maintenance of the perpetual inventory records with an actual physical count of the materials and supplies on hand. A

Figure 15-3. Flow of information and documents related to the purchasing and receiving of materials and supplies

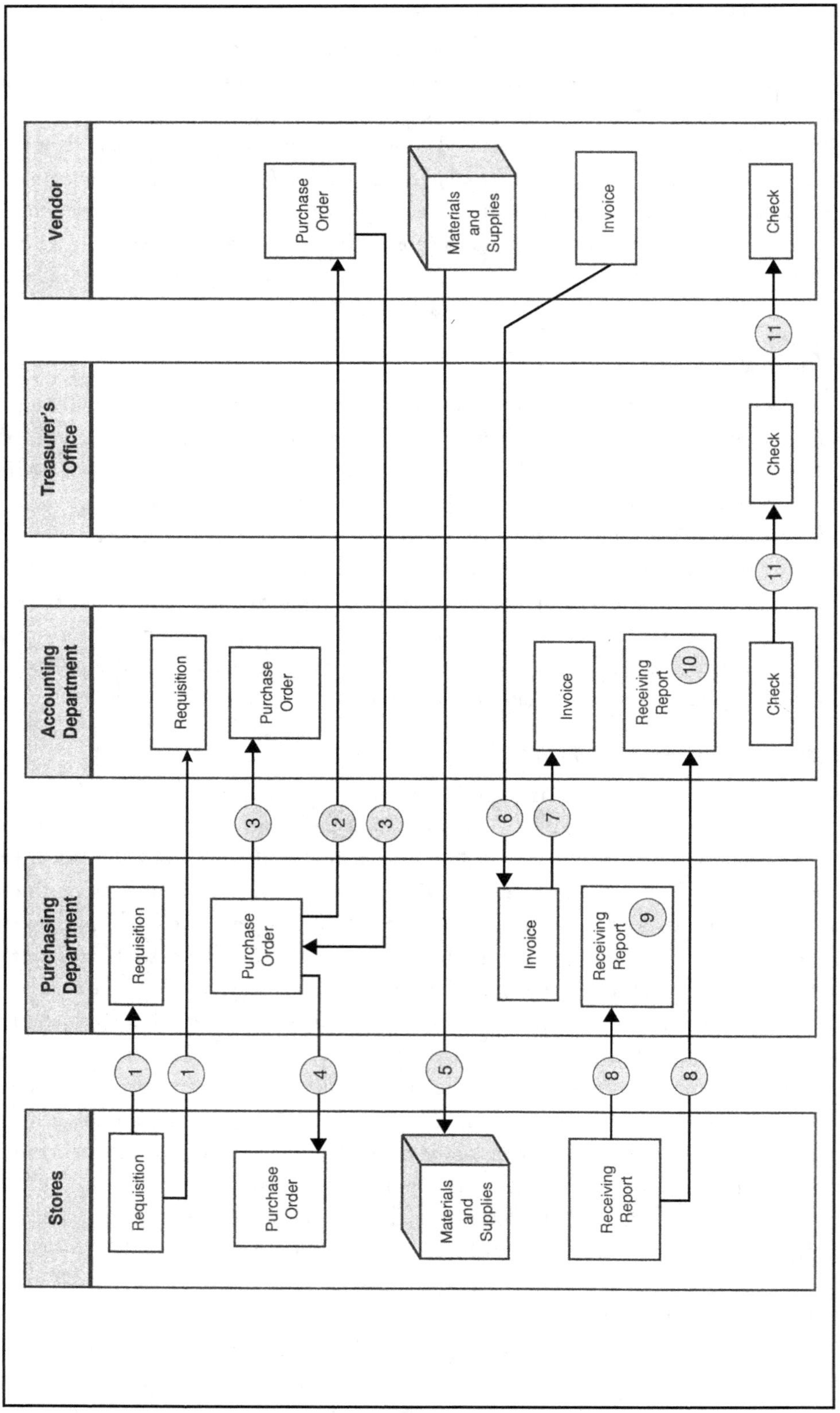

(Continued next page)

Figure 15-3 Flow of information and documents related to the purchasing and receiving of materials and supplies (continued)

1. The purchase requisition is prepared by stores personnel indicating the item and the quantity to be purchased (EOQ). Copies are forwarded to the purchasing department and accounting department.
2. A purchase order is prepared by the purchasing department indicating the desired items and quantities to be purchased, and the desired time and place of delivery. Typically, the order is placed with a supplier on the basis of competitive bidding.
3. Receipt of purchase order is acknowledged by vendor. A copy of the acknowledged purchase order is forwarded to the accounting department for the purpose discussed in item 10 below.
4. A copy of the purchase order also is sent to stores as notification of the status of the order and expected delivery date.
5. Materials and supplies shipped by vendor and received by stores.
6. Invoice (showing description and quantity of items shipped, date shipped, carrier, prices the utility is being billed, and payment terms) is forwarded from vendor to purchasing department for the purpose discussed in item 9 below.
7. Copy of invoice forwarded from purchasing department to accounting department.
8. On receipt of the purchased goods from suppliers, stores personnel count, weight, or otherwise measure the quantity of goods received; the quality of the goods also is determined. A receiving report is prepared by stores personnel indicating the quantity, conditions, and description of all items received. Copies of the receiving report are forwarded to the purchasing department and to the accounting department.
9. The purchasing department compares the receiving report with the sales invoice and purchase order to determine any discrepancies that require settlement with vendors.
10. The accounting department also compares the receiving report with the purchase order and the sales invoice. If the three documents agree (if the utility is being billed for the quantities actually received and at the agreed prices), then the invoice can be approved for payment. The accounting department then records the acquisition of the materials and supplies and the related liability to the supplier.
11. A check, properly vouchered and supported by the purchase order, invoice, and receiving report, is prepared by the accounting department and forwarded for signature to the treasurer's office. The signed check is then mailed to the vendor.

physical count verifies the inventory records and substantiates the figures in the utility's financial reports. It is also necessary to take the physical inventory regularly in order to adjust the records because of any errors that may have occurred in the preparation or recording of the material documents. All materials and supplies in stores should be physically inventoried at least once a year. The physical inventory can be conducted by counting all stores items at the end of a fiscal or calendar period, at a time of minimum activity, or when minimum quantities of stores items are on hand. Further, the physical count can be made on a piecemeal basis by inventorying only certain items at one time, since separate records are available for each category of materials and supplies. The responsibility for the physical inventories should be vested in a different individual, or department, from the one responsible for maintaining the storerooms and inventory records. This segregation of responsibility helps ensure inventory shortages are discovered instead of being covered up (by falsifying inventory counts) by those persons responsible for the maintenance of stocks.

Any material differences between the inventory records and the physical count should be investigated to determine whether they were caused by shrinkage, breakage, counting errors, recording errors, or theft. After this is completed, and the proper steps taken to correct the situation, the inventory records should be adjusted to the figures disclosed by the physical count.

Status Reports of Material on Hand

To facilitate the operation of the stores control system, and to obtain benefits from the system, periodic reports showing the status of materials and supplies should be prepared weekly, monthly, or as otherwise needed. Reports on materials and supplies should show, for the period covered by the reports, information regarding the activity of each major type of material and supply item. For each type of item, activity information includes the balance at the beginning of the period, quantities received and issued during the period, the balance at the end of the period, and amount of the item ordered but not yet received.

In addition, the status report should note the order point and maximum inventory level for each type of material and supply. The maximum inventory level typically should be equal to the order point quantity plus the economic order quantity (as discussed earlier in this chapter). For example, if the order point is 200 units for an item and the EOQ is 800 units, the maximum inventory level should be set at 1,000 units. Normally, the maximum inventory level for a particular item will not be reached, since units comprising the order point will be issued during the time interval between placing an order and receiving delivery.

If, for a particular item, the inventory on hand is less than the order point and no action has been taken to reorder, an explanation should be sought to explain the lack of reordering. Likewise, if units of a particular item on hand plus amounts ordered but not yet received exceed the maximum inventory level, management should seek an explanation. In summary, status reports on materials and supplies permit management and personnel of the purchasing department to observe the status of inventory levels and to initiate corrective action when necessary to increase or reduce inventory levels of particular items of materials and supplies.

Reconciliation of Inventory Records to General Control Account

The inventory records maintained on a perpetual basis represent the actual stock on hand at any particular date. Accounting for the receipts and issues through the general ledger may not correspond to the stock records. Timing differences between the methods that record the receipts and issues will cause differences between the general ledger and the stock records.

Reconciliation of the general ledger and the stock records requires review of receipts and issues. Receipts in stock records may be recorded when the material is placed on the stock floor while the receipts on the accounting records may be delayed until the invoice for the item has been paid. Timing differences in issues may not be as obvious as those with receipts. The issue may be posted a day later than the actual issue. Adjustments may also be required in the stock records for price variances that are not known at the time of the receipt. These variances will include freight and price changes.

Restricted Assets

Planning and Controlling Restricted Assets

As discussed earlier in this chapter, restricted assets consist of money and investments that have been segregated and that are to be used for specific purposes, such as debt service and replacement or construction of plant assets. For private utilities, the restriction of assets may be voluntary or in compliance with the provisions of a contract. A balance in a restricted asset account is established through the transfer of cash from the general cash account or through the direct transfer of cash to the restricted asset account at the time the cash is originally received by the utility (proceeds from the sale of bonds, for example). When the money in restricted asset accounts is to be held for extended periods of time, it is commonly invested in interest-bearing securities administered by the utility or a trustee. These securities should not be classified as temporary investments (since temporary investments are current assets, the proceeds from which, on liquidation, are available for general utility purposes).

A distinction can be made between restricted assets classified as current assets and restricted assets classified as noncurrent assets. Special deposits are made with fiscal agents or others for the purpose of meeting liabilities (interest payments and repayment of debt principal, for example, and dividend payments in the case of private water utilities) maturing within a relatively short period of time. The deposits represent a segregation of cash for a specific purpose and are appropriately considered as restricted assets. The NARUC classification of accounts considers special deposits as current assets (see appendix A). Other restricted assets, termed "special funds" by NARUC, are classified as noncurrent assets. Conversely, in the case of governmental water utilities, GFOA recommends that special deposits with fiscal agents be included among the restricted asset accounts as noncurrent assets.

Assets Restricted for Bond Debt Service

In the case of term bonds issued by water utilities, the bond indenture frequently calls for the accumulation of restricted assets (commonly called a redemption reserve account) during the life of the bonds to provide for redemption of the bonds at maturity. The restricted assets may be administered by a trustee to whom the utility periodically transfers cash generated from operations for investment by the trustee, or may be administered by the utility itself. If the restricted assets are administered by a trustee, the income from investments, less trustee's fees, is retained by the trustee for reinvestment, and the amount is reported periodically to the water utility for inclusion in net income.

The amount of the periodic contribution to asset accounts restricted for the retirement of term bonds may be calculated by compound interest methods. The procedures for determining periodic contributions are similar to those discussed in chapter 9 in connection with the compound interest method and sinking fund method of determining depreciation charges. Table 15-3 presents an example of a schedule of periodic contributions to a restricted asset account (or sinking fund) to provide for the retirement of a term bond issue, assuming that the restricted cash can be invested to earn a net return of 4 percent per year. In Table 15-3, at the end of the twentieth year, the restricted assets represented by securities are converted into cash that is used to pay off the bondholders. Any deficiency must be made up from other sources, whereas any excess in the restricted asset account over $100,000 would be handled as prescribed by law or at the discretion of management. If the average return actually realized for several years is substantially different from original estimates on which periodic contributions are calculated, it would be advisable to recompute periodic contributions.

Sometimes the trustee or other administrator of restricted cash has the power to buy the utility's own bonds as restricted assets. In such cases, the following two alternative treatments are possible: (1) the bonds are canceled, or (2) the bonds are held "alive" as restricted assets.

If the bonds are canceled, then the carrying value of the bonds is eliminated from the books. However, because of the dependence on interest income accumulation to make up part of the cash necessary to redeem bonds at maturity, the use of restricted cash to purchase and cancel a portion of the bond issue before maturity may impair the ability of the restricted cash to redeem the remaining bonds at maturity. Therefore, contributions to the restricted asset account may be increased to cover the loss of interest income accruing to the restricted asset account. There is no net loss to the utility because of the offsetting saving of interest expense on the canceled bonds.

If the bonds are held "alive" among restricted assets, they are accounted for in the same manner as any other investment and the utility pays the regular interest to the trustee or other administrator. However, this investment does create a balance-sheet and income statement problem since the repurchased bonds are shown both as assets and liabilities, and interest expense and interest income earned by restricted assets are overstated. This situation should be disclosed in a note to the financial statements.

Table 15-3. Accumulation of restricted assets (sinking fund) to provide for the retirement of 20-year term bond issue

	(1)	(2)	(3)	(4)
Year	Restricted Asset Account Balance Beginning of Year	Income Earned on Restricted Assets Each Year	Annual Contribution at End of Each Year *	Restricted Asset Account Balance End of Year
1	$0	$0	$3,358.18	$3,358.18
2	3,358.18	134.33	3,358.18	6,850.69
3	6,850.69	274.03	3,358.18	10,482.90
4	10,482.90	419.32	3,358.18	14,260.40
5	14,260.40	570.42	3,358.18	18,189.00
6	18,189.00	727.56	3,358.18	22,274.74
7	22,274.74	890.99	3,358.18	26,523.91
8	26,523.91	1,060.96	3,358.18	30,943.05
9	30,943.05	1,237.72	3,358.18	35,538.95
10	35,538.95	1,421.56	3,358.18	40,318.69
11	40,318.69	1,612.75	3,358.18	45,289.62
12	45,289.62	1,811.58	3,358.18	50,459.38
13	50,459.38	2,018.38	3,358.18	55,835.94
14	55,835.94	2,233.44	3,358.18	61,427.56
15	61,427.56	2,457.10	3,358.18	67,242.84
16	67,242.84	2,689.71	3,358.18	73,290.73
17	73,290.73	2,931.63	3,358.18	79,580.54
18	79,580.54	3,183.22	3,358.18	86,121.94
19	86,121.94	3,444.88	3,358.18	92,925.00
20	92,925.00	3,717.00	3,358.00†	100,000.00
Totals		$32,836.58	$67,163.42	

*Amount of an annuity of 1 at 4 percent for 20 years equals 29.778 (arrived at using annuity tables which employ the formula

$$\frac{(1+i)^n - 1}{i}$$

where n represents the number of years and i the rate of interest). $100.000 (amount of bonds to be retired ÷ 29.778 (amount of an annuity of 1) equal $3,358.18, which is the amount that must be contributed annually to the restricted asset account (sinking fund) for a period of 20 years in order to accumulate an amount equal to $100.000.

†An adjustment of $0.18 due to rounding errors, required to bring restricted assets to $100,000.

In the case of serial bonds (or in the case of term bonds that are callable and that are to be redeemed), restricted asset accounts also may be employed. Indenture agreements associated with serial bonds (or callable term bonds that are to be regularly redeemed) issued by private water utilities may provide for periodic contributions to restricted asset accounts sufficient to meet the periodic payments for serial bonds as they mature or to meet the periodic payments for term bonds to be called. In the case of callable bonds, the indenture agreement typically provides that the utility may deliver either cash or redeemed bonds to the trustee. If cash is delivered, then the cash must be used by the trustee to redeem the bonds that are callable. The balance in a restricted asset account associated with serial bonds or term bonds that are to be regularly retired will be relatively small at any given time.

In the case of revenue bonds issued by governmental water utilities, the bond indenture typically provides for several restricted asset accounts to be created to protect bondholders against late or inadequate payment of interest and repayment of debt principal as the serial bonds mature. Three typical restricted asset accounts associated with a revenue bond issue are "assets restricted for bond debt service," "assets restricted for reserve use," and "assets restricted for contingencies." These three accounts, together with amounts transferred from the three accounts to fiscal agents for the purpose of making periodic interest and principal payments, are known as the "asset group of accounts restricted for bond debt service."

With regard to the "assets restricted for bond debt service" account (usually called an "interest and sinking fund"), a typical provision is that there be contributed to this account a monthly amount equal to one-sixth of the next maturing semiannual interest payment plus one-twelfth of the next annual repayment of debt principal. Amounts are then transferred from this account to fiscal agents as required to make debt service payments.

The purpose of the "assets restricted for reserve use" account is to provide for the payment of matured bonds and interest in the event of a deficiency in the "assets restricted for debt service" account. The balance in this account is usually accumulated over the first 60 months following the issuance of a series of revenue bonds. The amount to be accumulated is specified (an amount equal to the average or maximum annual debt service, for example) by the bond indenture. Under normal circumstances, the cash accumulated in this account is invested in interest-bearing securities and will not be used until the final retirement of the bond issue.

The purpose of the "assets restricted for contingencies" account is to provide cash for meeting unforeseen operating expenditures of an emergency nature or replacement of plant assets. The balance to be accumulated in this account over a prescribed number of months following a bond issue is specified in the bond indenture. Table 15-4 presents an example of a statement that summarizes the annual changes that take place in an asset group of accounts restricted for revenue bond debt service.

As in the case of temporary investments, governmental water utilities generally are limited by statute or charter as to the types of securities in which cash restricted for debt service can be invested. Such investments include certificates of deposit and federal, state, and municipal securities. Private water utilities are subject to no such legal restrictions regarding the investment of restricted cash. However, the trustee administering the restricted assets must exercise reasonable care in investing restricted cash. In some instances, the board of directors may specify the types of securities that can be purchased. Within the limits set by law or directives of policy-making groups, an

Table 15-4. Statement of changes in the group of assets restricted for revenue bond debt service

The Municipal Water Utility Statement of Changes in the Group of Assets Restricted for Bond Debt Service for the Year Ended December 31, 20XX

	Cash With Fiscal Agents	Assets Restricted for Debt Service	Assets Restricted for Reserve Use	Assets Restricted for Contingencies	Total Restricted Assets
Total Cash and Investments Jan. 1, 20XX	$240,000	$6,000	$168,000	$22,500	$436,500
Cash Balance, Jan. 1, 20XX	240,000	6,000	8,000	2,500	256,500
Cash Receipts					
Transfers from general cash (see Figure 19.2)		230,000	50,000	6,000	286,000
Income from restricted investments			5,600	700	6,300
Intergroup transfer of cash restricted for revenue bond debt service	226,500				
Total Cash Available	466,500	236,000	63,600	9,200	775,300
Cash Disbursements					
Principal payments	108,000				108,000
Interest payments	216,000				216,000
Fiscal agents' fees	500				500
Purchase of investments		—	59,000	9,000	68,000
Intergroup transfer of cash restricted for revenue bond debt service		226,500			226,500
Total Disbursements	324,500	226,500	59,000	9,000	619,000
Cash Balance, Dec. 31, 20XX	$142,000	$ 9,500	$ 4,600	$ 200	$156,300
Investment Balance, Jan. 31, 20XX			160,000	20,000	180,000
Additions			59,000	9,000	68,000
Deductions					
Investment Balance, Dec. 31, 20XX			$219,000	$29,000	$248,000
Total Cash and Investments Dec. 31, 20XX	$142,000	$9,500	$223,600	$29,200	$404,300

attempt should be made to invest restricted cash in securities that will bring the greatest return consistent with the maintenance of a reasonably low degree of risk of loss of principal. In general, securities should be selected so they will mature as required to meet disbursements that must be made from restricted assets.

Particularly in the case of governmental water utilities, there may be several restricted asset accounts or groups. For the purposes of investment, it may be desirable for the utility to pool cash belonging to the various accounts. In this case, earnings on investments must be prorated among each of the accounts on the basis of the amount of cash contributed by each.

Capital Expenditures

In the case of governmental water utilities, the proceeds of both general obligation bonds and revenue bonds issued for or by the water utility usually are segregated in a restricted asset account. This segregation is made to ensure the cash proceeds are spent only on authorized capital expenditure projects and are not commingled with general utility cash. Cash is disbursed from the restricted asset account as required to meet liabilities incurred with regard to authorized capital expenditure projects. Eventually, the balance in the restricted asset account is depleted to zero or to an amount near zero, as all authorized expenditures from the bond proceeds are completed. If the proceeds exceed the total of all authorized expenditures, the balance is returned to general utility cash or is disposed of in accordance with the terms of the bond indenture or other applicable statutory provisions. The restricted cash should be invested in interest-bearing securities until needed to meet authorized expenditures. Generally, investments should be made in highly marketable securities that can be liquidated as needed without material loss of principal.

Private water utilities may also desire to segregate proceeds from security issues in restricted asset accounts. In addition, water utilities may desire to restrict a portion of cash generated from operations in order to provide for future replacement of plant assets. Typically, the cash so restricted is invested in securities until needed for replacement of plant assets.

Other Purposes

In the case of governmental water utilities, proceeds from customer deposits typically are placed in a restricted asset account. The restricted proceeds may be invested in authorized securities with the income from such investments being used to pay required interest to customers on their deposits or to increase general utility cash. Disbursements are made from the restricted asset account as required to reimburse customers for their deposits. Private water utilities ordinarily do not place proceeds from customers' deposits in a restricted asset account; rather, the proceeds are placed in general utility cash, and repayment of deposits is made from general cash.

Assets (cash and investments) may be restricted for many other purposes. Included among other types of restricted assets are those established for the redemption of preferred stock (in the case of private water utilities) as a result of contractual agreement or management policy, and those established for self-insurance.

Some governmental utilities maintain their own retirement systems and establish a separate fund (as used in the governmental accounting sense) to account for the transactions associated with the retirement systems. Payments made by the utility to the retirement fund are classified as pension expense to the utility, and no related restricted asset accounts are required to be maintained within the fund.

Relationship to Various Liability Accounts

The restricted asset accounts discussed in this section are often associated with appropriations of retained earnings or with liabilities to be paid from restricted assets. See chapter 12 for additional discussion.

Deferred Charges

Deferred charges are debit entries that cannot be classified as a current asset, long-term investment, property plant and equipment, or an intangible asset.

Deferred charges are prepaid expenses that will not be amortized during the current period. Examples include receivables that cannot be classified as current because of the payment terms associated with the receivable, or premiums on bonds issued that will be amortized over the life of the bonds to increase the effective interest rate. Some accountants classify intangible assets as a deferred charge. Utilities that have their rates prescribed by a rate-making body may be allowed to capitalize items as a deferred charge that will be recovered in rates over subsequent periods.

Typically, deferred charges arise from prepayment. The classic example is bond discounts that are a reduction in the cash received for the issuance of bonds. The bonds are issued at a face amount with a stated interest rate. To accomplish this requirement, the purchaser pays a lower amount than the face amount and receives the full amount at the maturity. In effect, the purchaser receives a higher rate of interest than the amount stated on the bond. The seller of the bond pays a higher rate of interest because of the lower cash received at the sale.

Disposition

The utility will dispose of the deferred charge over a period of time that reflects the cause of the charge. If the charge is a long-term receivable, the receivable is transferred into current assets in the period in which the payment is expected. Most other deferred charges are amortized into the utility's expense during the periods that the utility has received some benefit from the charge.

Rate-Making Treatment

Not all deferred charges of a utility arise from transactions that are a result of normal activities. Utilities whose rates are set by a rate-making body are allowed to defer charges into periods in which they will have revenue resulting from the charge.

Financial Accounting Standards Board Statement Number 71 (SFAS 71) allows regulated enterprises to defer and amortize costs that are likely to be recovered in rates in a future period. For a utility to apply SFAS 71, the utility must meet the following criteria:

- The utilities rates must be regulated by an independent third party or a governing board authorized by law
- The approved rates are designed to cover explicit costs of the utility
- The rates are likely to be collected by the utility

To defer the explicit cost, the utility must demonstrate that the intent of the regulatory body is to provide recovery of the cost through rates that will produce sufficient revenue to cover the cost deferred. The utility will then amortize the deferral in the years the regulatory body has provided rates to cover the deferred cost.

Chapter 16

Liabilities and Other Credits

The "liabilities and other credits" side of the balance sheet presents the sources from which the utility's assets are financed. These sources reflect both external financing (liabilities, contributions, and, in the case of private utilities, common and preferred stock) and internal financing (through retained earnings). This chapter discusses the following major categories of liabilities and other credits:

- Current and accrued liabilities
- Long-term liabilities
- Capital paid in by stockholders (applicable to private water utilities)
- Retained earnings
- Customer advances for construction and contributions

Differences Between Private and Governmental Utilities

Utilities typically record three types of credits other than owners' equity (referred to as net assets for governmental water utilities). These credits are current liabilities, long-term liabilities, and deferred credits. Contributions in aid of construction are discussed in chapter 13.

Generally, both governmental and private utilities have similar current liabilities. Both types of organizations have accounts payable, payroll payable, notes payable, and similar type obligations to others. Dividends payable are only seen on the balance sheet of the private utility, unless a governmental utility is required to pay a dividend to its owner. Income taxes payable are only recorded on the balance sheet of the private utility (see chapter 6 for a discussion of tax issues).

Long-term liabilities also appear the same on the balance sheet of the governmental and private utility. Long-term notes payable and bonds payable are the items typically seen in the long-term liabilities.

Accounts identified as deferred credits are those accounts that represent a balance carried into future periods to amortize against income in those periods. Examples of deferred credits are deferred income taxes and unamortized premiums on bonds.

Deferred income taxes are only found in an private utility, since governmental utilities are exempt from income taxes.

Current and Long-Term Differences

As in the case of assets, the historical cost standard should be employed to record liabilities. In general, current liabilities represent liabilities that are definite in amount and that are due either as of the date of the balance sheet, within a year from the date of the balance sheet, or on demand by creditors. Accrued current liabilities are those not yet payable but that mature within one year and that are being provided for or accumulated over the period to date of maturity The National Association of Regulatory Utility Commissioners (NARUC), however, makes some exceptions to these definitions, as indicated by the following description of current and accrued liabilities:

> ...current and accrued liabilities are those obligations which have either matured or which become due within one year from the date thereof; except, however, bonds, receivers' certificates and similar obligations which shall be classified as long-term debt until date of maturity; accrued taxes, such as income taxes, which shall be classified as accrued liabilities even though payable more than one year from date; compensation awards, which shall be classified as accrued liabilities regardless of date due; and minor amounts payable in installments which may be classified as current liabilities. If a liability is due more than one year from date of issuance or assumption by the utility, it shall be credited to a long-term debt account appropriate to the transaction, except, however, the current liabilities previously mentioned.

In this definition, NARUC recommends that bonds payable be classified as current liabilities only if the bonds have matured and have not yet been retired. Conversely, the Governmental Accounting Standards Board (GASB) recommends that debt obligations be classified as current liabilities if matured or if due within a year from the date of the balance sheet. The latter view is consistent with generally accepted accounting principles.

Definitions of Key Liabilities

Liabilities come in many varieties. They can be classified as current or long term. Following are liabilities and their definitions, which may be reported on the utility's balance sheet.

Accounts Payable

Accounts payable refers to the utility's recurring trade obligations. The liability is incurred when the title to the goods passes. Specific attention should be paid to goods in transit at the end of a period. In most instances, the liability is recorded when the goods or services have been received.

Notes Payable

Notes payable are liabilities that identify obligations of the utility that contain a definite payment schedule. Obligations identified by notes payable are usually trade notes, short-term loan notes, or current-year maturities of long-term debt. The note payable may contain obligations that are current liabilities and long-term liabilities. Occasionally, notes payable may be secured with specific assets. When assets are secured, the note should be reported consistent with the collateral pledged to the note. The reporting can be accomplished in a footnote or as a pledged asset.

Short-Term Obligations

Short-term obligations expected to be refinanced may be classified as a long-term obligation. To be classified as such, the utility must show that it intends to refinance the obligation and demonstrate that it has the ability to consummate the refinancing.

Declared Dividends Payable

Declared but unpaid dividends payable are liabilities. If the intent is to pay the liability within the current period, the dividend payable is classified as a current liability. Dividends that have not been declared or preferred stock dividends in arrears are not to be recorded as a liability. Dividends payable are only found on the balance sheet of an private utility unless a governmental utility is required to pay a dividend to its owner.

Advances and Returnable Deposits

Advances and returnable deposits representing the obligation of the utility to provide service in the future are a liability to the utility. The utility may require that a customer make a deposit for future services when the customer's credit history is unknown. The deposit agreement must be reviewed to determine if the deposit is to be classified as current or long-term liability. The time period between the date of the deposit and the end of the relationship requiring the deposit determines the classification.

Water Service Billed

Water service billed in advance is a liability of the utility. Revenue is recorded and the liability reduced as the period of time of the advance billing expires. Typically, water service billed in advance is used when customers do not have meters.

Taxes Payable

The utility collects taxes from employees and customers for third-party governments. Sales taxes are collected on the sale or transfer of personal property by the utility to the customer. Various governmental bodies collect a percentage of the value of the item transferred. Governmental bodies require the collection of taxes from employee wages.

Accrued Liabilities

Utilities often have liabilities that were unrecorded at the end of an accounting period. These liabilities become known after the accounting period is over but before the financial records have been finalized. A journal entry to record these items as accrued liabilities is necessary. Examples of accrued liabilities include:

- A utility with a December year-end receives an invoice in January for services provided through December. This item should be recorded as an accounts payable.
- A utility's last full pay period of the year ends on December 28, but its year end is December 31. An entry for salaries and wages payable should be made for payroll costs through the end of the year.

Salary and Wages Payable

Payroll-related liabilities consist of all amounts owed to the utility's employees. The liabilities include the wages and salaries owed at the end of an accounting period, including compensated absences payable. Liabilities also recognize the rights that an employee may have earned but are not currently payable to the employee. To be recognized as a liability these rights must meet four conditions:

- The employee's obligation relating to the employee's rights to receive compensation for future absences is attributable to the services the employee has already rendered
- The obligation relates to a right that vests or that is expected to vest
- The payment of the compensation is probable
- The amount can reasonably be estimated

Net Pension Obligation/Net Other Postemployment Benefits Obligation

Both investor- and governmental utilities may offer a defined benefit pension or other postemployment benefits, such as health care, to their employees. Unlike defined contribution pension plans, with defined benefit pensions the employer assumes investment risk and specifies the amount of benefits to be provided at a future date. If market rates of return decline, employers have to increase their contributions, or unfunded liabilities increase.

A major change occurred in the reporting of "Other Postemployment Benefits" when GASB adopted standard 45, which treats retiree health benefits more like pensions. Governments had treated retiree health benefits on a pay-as-you-go basis, with little information on the size of future obligations. GASB 45 makes the assumption that those costs are known or knowable and should be recorded, and that unfunded portions of the future obligations should be reported just as they are in pensions. Recording costs for defined postemployment benefit plans is no longer on a pay-as-you-go system. Rather, employers must accrue certain aspects of underfunded plans as liabilities.

Income Taxes Payable

Income taxes payable are recognized by private utilities. Utilities that recognize a liability for income taxes record a liability proportional to the net income of the utility, except that the income on which tax rates are applied may differ from the income reported on the income statement because of timing difference. Tax laws may allow the recognition of expenses in a different manner than is allowed under generally accepted accounting principles.

Pollution Remediation Obligations

Governmental-owned water utilities are required to record a liability for estimated outlays for pollution remediation if pollution is known and any of the following criteria exist:

- The pollution poses an imminent danger to the public or to the environment and the utility has little or no discretion to avoid fixing the problem
- The utility has violated a pollution prevention–related permit or license
- A regulator has identified (or likely will identify) the water utility as responsible (or potentially responsible) for cleaning up pollution or for paying all or some of the cleanup costs
- The utility is named (or likely will be named) in a lawsuit to compel it to address the pollution
- The utility begins or legally obligates itself to begin cleanup or postcleanup activities

Expenses and related liabilities are estimated using an "expected cash flows" measurement technique. Governmental utilities must also disclose information about pollution obligations associated with cleanup efforts in the financial statements footnotes.

Bonds Payable

Bonds payable represent the promise to pay that the utility has made under a contract known as an indenture. The contract describes the utility's promise to pay a sum of money on the maturity date and the promise to pay interest at a specified rate on face value of the bond. Bonds have numerous types of features that can be included in the issue.

Leases Payable

Leases payable are the obligations a utility has incurred while obtaining the right to use a property owned by another. The lease document specifies the term of the lease and the periodic payments that are due. Leases come in two varieties, operating or capital. To be classified as a capital lease, the lease at inception must meet one of the following four criteria:

- The lease transfers ownership of the property to the lessee by the end of the lease term
- The lease contains a bargain purchase option

- The term of the lease at inception is at least 75 percent of the estimated economic life of the property being leased
- The present value of the minimum lease payments at the beginning of the lease term equals or exceeds 90 percent of the fair value of the leased property at the inception of the lease

If the lease does not meet any of these criteria, then the lease is an operating lease. Property acquired under a capital lease is identified separately, as is the obligation on the balance sheet.

Definitions of Other Credits

Deferred Credits

Deferred credits are credit balances normally carried forward into future periods to be matched against the income in those periods. Other credits may represent other obligations into which the utility has entered. These obligations represent items the utility currently has an obligation for but may not have an obligation for in the future when an action has occurred. Examples include customer advances for construction and obligations for deferred compensation.

Customer Advances for Construction

Deposits customers have made to facilitate the construction of assets that serve the customer in the future are deferred credits. The credit (if not refundable) is converted into contributions when the construction of the asset has been completed. The utility may have an obligation to refund the advance if the construction is not completed.

Deferred Compensation Plans

Previously, governmental utilities that offered employees participation in a deferred compensation plan under section 457 of the Internal Revenue Code were required to retain property ownership and record a related obligation to the employee. However, Section 1404 of the Small Business Job Protection Act of 1996 added section 457(g). This new section requires that governmental 457 plans hold plan assets and related income in trust or alternatively in custodial accounts or annuity contracts for the exclusive benefit of plan participants and their beneficiaries. As a result, plan assets and related liabilities are typically no longer recorded for 457 plans, provided that withheld employee monies are remitted to a third-party administrator. An exception would be if an employer held 457 plan assets on behalf of employees or if significant oversight of investment manager activities was retained. Therefore, the key regarding whether or not to record plan assets is whether or not the employer is considered to be *holding* the plan's assets.

Bond Premiums

When bonds are sold at a premium, the utility receives more cash than the face value of the bonds. The additional amount is the bond premium on the bond. The premium is amortized over the life of the bond as a reduction of interest expense. The amortization can be done in either of two methods, straight-line or effective interest method. The bond premium should be amortized using the effective interest method unless the straight-line method is not materially different.

Chart of Accounts

NARUC's 1996 edition of the *Uniform System of Accounts for Class A Water Utilities* lists accounts 221 through 224 to be used for long-term debt. Accounts 231 through 241 are to be used for current and accrued liabilities. Deferred credits are recorded in accounts 251 through 265. Accounts 271 and 272 identify contributions in aid of construction. Accumulated deferred income taxes, for nongovernmental utilities, are accounted for using accounts 281 through 283.

Suggested long-term debt accounts are:

- *Bonds (221).* This account is used to record the face value of bonds issued but not yet repaid, refinanced, or cancelled, including bonds issued by other entities that the utility has assumed. Separate subdivisions for each class and series of bonds should be maintained.
- *Reacquired Bonds (222).* This account is used to record bonds issued and reacquired by the utility that have not yet been repaid, refinanced, or cancelled.
- *Advances From Associated Companies (223).* This account is used to record the face value of notes payable to and any advances from associated companies.
- *Other Long-Term Debt (224).* This account is used to record all long-term debt not accounted for in NARUC accounts 221 through 223. Examples of debt that would be recorded in this account include receivers' certificates and assessments for public improvements. Separate subaccounts for each class of obligation should be maintained.

Suggested current and accrued liability accounts are:

- *Accounts Payable (231).* This account is used to record all amounts payable due within one year that are not accounted for in other NARUC accounts.
- *Notes Payable (232).* This account is used to record the face value of all indebtedness payable within one year (or on demand), except for indebtedness to associated companies.
- *Accounts Payable to Associated Companies (233).* This account is used to record the face value of amounts payable to associated companies due within one year that are not accounted for in other NARUC accounts.
- *Notes Payable to Associated Companies (234).* This account is used to record amounts due to associated companies payable within one year, excluding advances from associated companies (see account 223).
- *Customer Deposits (235).* This account is used to record amounts deposited by the customers as security for the payment of bills.
- *Accrued Taxes (236).* This account is used to record estimated net taxes payable.

- *Accrued Interest (237).* This account is used to record unpaid interest due on all debt. Supporting records shall be maintained that show each obligation's interest due.
- *Accrued Dividends (238).* This account is used to record dividends declared but not yet paid.
- *Matured Long-Term Debt (239).* This account is used to record matured long-term debt that has not been paid, unless there is an agreement for payment extension. Additionally, bonds called for redemption that have not yet been presented are recorded in this account.
- *Matured Interest (240).* This account is used to record matured interest on the utility's long-term debt unless the interest is rolled into the principal obligation.
- *Miscellaneous Current and Accrued Liabilities (241).* This account is used to record any other current liability that cannot be recorded in another NARUC account.

Suggested deferred credit accounts are:

- *Unamortized Premium on Debt (251).* This account is used to record all not-yet-amortized credit balances on long-term debt premiums, discounts, and expenses.
- *Advances for Construction (252).* This account is used to record advances made by customers for construction activity that will be partially or wholly refunded in the future.
- *Other Deferred Credits (253).* This account is used to record all deferrals not accounted for in other NARUC accounts. Examples include certain deferred gains and certain advance billings. Additionally, subaccount 253.1 is used to record regulatory liabilities and subaccount 253.2 is used to record other deferred liabilities.
- *Accumulated Deferred Investment Tax Credits (255).* This account is used to record investment tax credits that will be amortized in future periods.

Controlling and Monitoring Current and Accrued Liabilities

Effective internal control of current and accrued liabilities requires that proposed commitments associated with incurring a liability be reviewed before they are approved and become actual liabilities. Proposed commitments should not exceed the limits of the operating budget, capital expenditure budget, or the materials and supplies budget, unless additional authorization to commit funds is obtained through top management or policy-making groups. Procedures associated with the purchase of materials and supplies are discussed in chapter 12. In the case of personnel services, procedures also must be adopted to ensure proper control over commitments associated with wages and salaries. Often, control over employee hiring and firing is centralized in an employee services department, which is responsible for ensuring that personnel budgets are adhered to. Employee selection, discharge, transfers, and wage rates should be subject to review and approval by top management. This review and approval help ensure that proposed wage and salary commitments are properly considered before they become actual liabilities and that personnel requirements are being met adequately and efficiently.

Effective internal control of current and accrued liabilities requires that all obligations are properly recorded, that procedures for cash disbursement are followed, and that due dates for the payment of obligations are met. A systematic routine for recording liabilities is basic to a sound disbursements procedure. Procedures related to recording and discharging obligations arising from the purchase of materials and supplies have been described previously. Similar procedures are also required regarding the purchase of labor services.

Detailed records pertaining to other current obligations, such as those related to bank borrowings, taxes, customer meter deposits, interest, construction contracts, dividends, and matured or maturing long-term debt also must be maintained. The detailed or supporting records permit the identification of a utility's current obligations with specific individuals or other entities. Identification of liabilities is necessary to properly pay obligations to the proper entities. All disbursements associated with current obligations should be vouchered and properly authorized for payment.

To ensure obligations are paid on or before their due dates, schedules of due dates that identify payment of taxes, interest, and other contractual obligations should be maintained. This allows scheduling of disbursements and helps ensure legal penalties and other costs associated with late payment are avoided. In the case of accounts payable, files of vendors' invoices should be maintained by purchase discount dates to facilitate payment within the discount period.

Types of Financial Reports

Corporate water utilities report changes in shareholders' equity, including capital stock accounts, each year. The report that is used, which is a statement of shareholders' equity, identifies the beginning balance of the capital stock account and all additions, re-acquisitions, and restructuring thereof.

Corporations, proprietorships, partnerships, and governmental utilities report the changes in the appropriated and unappropriated retained earnings each year (referred to as net assets for governmental water utilities). The report of changes includes the beginning balances, additions from net income (referred to as change in net assets for governmental water utilities), transfers to and from appropriated retained earnings, and prior period changes, if any.

The footnotes of the utility's financial statements contain a paragraph detailing any capital leases. All capital leases of a material nature are detailed in the footnote, including a description of the lease, the amount of assets recorded under capital leases, total minimum future sublease rentals and contingent rentals incurred, and amortization of undisplayed leased assets (or a statement noting that lease amortization is included in depreciation expense). Additionally, the minimum future lease payments for each of the next five years, and for at least each five-year increment thereafter, presenting a deduction for the amount of imputed interest to reduce the net minimum future lease payments to their present value shall be disclosed.

Long-term debt is also detailed in the footnotes. The type of long-term debt is disclosed, with the range of interest rates and the average interest rate. The maturities in the current year and the next four years are stated. Maturities greater than five years are summarized into five-year increments.

See appendixes B and C for example presentations of current and noncurrent liabilities in financial reports.

Chapter 17

Equity, Capital, and Financial Ratios

This chapter discusses the following major categories of equity in the utility: (1) retained earnings, (2) capital paid in by stockholders (applicable to private water utilities), and (3) customer advances for construction and contributions. Information about equity and changes in the amount of equity is often used in the creation of ratios that measure the financial health of the utility.

Differences Between Private and Governmental Utilities

Equity for private utilities represents the residual interest in the enterprise's assets, after liabilities have been subtracted, arising from investments by owners and the retention of earnings over time. In the balance sheet, owners' equity is usually displayed in two broad categories: paid-in or contributed capital and retained earnings. Paid-in or contributed capital represents the amount provided by stockholders in the original purchase of shares of stock or resulting from subsequent transactions with owners, such as treasury stock transactions. Retained earnings represent the amount of previous income of the utility that has not been distributed to owners as dividends or transferred to paid-in or contributed capital.

Equity for governmental water utilities is called fund net assets. Fund net assets are categorized as 1) invested in capital assets, net of related debt, 2) restricted, and 3) unrestricted.

A private utility may be organized as a corporation, partnership, or sole proprietorship. The utility organized as a partnership or sole proprietorship is unusual and will not be discussed.

The corporate equity will be recognized by the owner's equity, legal or stated capital, and retained earnings. Legal (or stated) capital is usually defined by state law. It refers to the amount of capital that must be retained by the utility for the protection of its creditors. Owner's equity describes the amount the owners of the corporation have contributed reduced by the legal capital. Retained earnings recount the net income of the corporation reduced by the dividends paid to the owners of the corporation.

Public utility commissions may require contributions be made to the utility from those seeking to acquire service from the utility. The contributions may be in the form of cash, which enables the utility to acquire the assets required to service the customer, or specific assets. For private utilities, these contributions are recorded as capital invested in the organization but do not indicate an ownership position to those who have made the contributions. Governmental water utilities may also require contributions from those seeking to acquire service from the utility; however, they are not presented as a separate component of fund net assets.

Retained Earnings-Fund Net Assets

The retained earnings of a private water utility can be characterized as the portion of the ownership interest in the utility's assets that is not represented by paid-in or contributed capital. Retained earnings represent the net incremental assets resulting from water utility operations. Common items that affect the retained earnings balance are:

- Income or loss from the normal and incidental operating activities of the water utility
- Extraordinary gains and losses of the utility
- Prior-period adjustments, such as corrections of errors of prior periods concerning the first two items
- Recapitalizations
- Dividends to stockholders (in the case of private water utilities)

In order to distribute retained earnings, sufficient unrestricted retained earnings and cash or cash equivalents must be available. However, the utility may still be unable to distribute retained earnings because such earnings have been appropriated or restricted and are unavailable for distribution.

Statement of Changes in Retained Earnings-Fund Net Assets

For private utilities, a statement of changes in retained earnings is customarily prepared at the end of each accounting period. This statement presents an analysis of the changes that have taken place during the accounting period in both appropriated and unappropriated retained earnings balance. For governmental water utilities, the change in fund net assets is incorporated in the operating statement entitled Statement of Revenues, Expenditures and Changes in Fund Net Assets.

Appropriated Retained Earnings/Restricted Net Assets

Operating reserves are generally created by charges to operating expenses whereas appropriations of retained earnings by private utilities and are usually are usually created by direct charges to unappropriated retained earnings. The purpose for reserving or appropriating a portion of retained earnings is to ensure that assets will be available to pay designated obligations when due.

The appropriation of retained earnings may be required by law or contract or may be an expression of utility policy. In some states, for example, the law requires that retained earnings of a private water utility may be restricted in an amount equal to the legal capital (par or stated value, or amounts paid in on no-par stock) associated with reacquired capital stock (treasury stock). This requirement, in effect, substitutes retained earnings for legal capital of the reacquired stock. Bond indentures may require that an annual appropriation of retained earnings be made so that the sum of the appropriations will, over the life of the bonds, equal the bond indebtedness at the time the bonds mature. Creditors supplying relatively short-term funds may require that no distribution of retained earnings be made during the time the short-term debt is outstanding. This implies a restriction of the entire retained earnings balance. Restrictions of retained earnings may also be an expression of a utility policy that requires appropriations to provide working capital.

The appropriation of retained earnings for specific purposes does not ensure that assets of the utility will be available in a form that can be used by the utility for specific purposes giving rise to the appropriations. To ensure the availability of assets for a specific purpose, assets (cash and investments) must be either segregated or restricted for the specific purpose.

For governmental water utilities, fund net assets are restricted either by an investment in capital assets or for some other purpose. A common restriction is the unspent portion of bonds issued to build infrastructure and/or acquire capital assets. A portion of the proceeds may already be spent on capital assets or construction. Any remaining proceeds are held to pay future construction-related costs (restricted) and thus not available to finance general operations.

Contributed Assets

Sources

Customer advances for construction and contributions arise from several sources. Governmental water authorities may be established by capital contributions from the governmental unit of which the utility is a part. The amount of cash or value of services and property so contributed should be credited to an appropriately labeled contributions equity account (see account 272 in appendix A) for reporting as a "transfer in" on the utility's operating statement. To the extent that the establishment of governmental water utility is financed by a governmental water utility is financed by contributions from persons or organizations outside the utility, the amounts so obtained should be included in the appropriate contributions accounts (see accounts 273–275 in appendix A) and reported as contributions on the utility's operating statement. The establishment of private water utilities usually is financed by bond and stock issues.

Once a water utility is established, a portion of the financing of plant expansion frequently is provided by advances and/or contributions from customers, subdividers or developers, and governmental agencies. Contributions from governmental units may also be provided for plant replacement, particularly in cases where utility plant assets must be relocated because of highway construction or urban renewal projects. Such contributions should be recorded and reported as either operating or nonoperating contributions on the utility's operating statement.

The NARUC classification of accounts provides deferred credit account 252, "customer advances for construction," to which is credited amounts advanced by or on behalf of customers for construction and that is to be refunded either entirely or in part. On completion of the project, if a person is refunded the entire amount to which they are entitled according to the agreement or rule under which the advance was made, then any amounts originally advanced but no longer refundable because of the expiration of the agreement normally are transferred to an appropriately labeled contribution account. As shown in appendix A, the NARUC classification of accounts provides account 271, "contributions in aid of construction," for private or governmental water utilities to use for this purpose. With regard to account 271, NARUC states that the balance in this account includes credits for donations or contributions in cash, services, or property from states, municipalities, or other governmental agencies, individuals, and others for construction purposes. NARUC classifies contributions in aid of construction as a major and distinct category in the balance sheet. Typically, for rate-determination purposes, the balance in the account is deducted from the cost of the utility plant or the related asset is otherwise treated as a zero cost rate base element.

The GASB also provides specific recommendations concerning accounting and reporting for governmental grant, entitlement, and shared revenue resources. Resources received for operations and/or for either operations or capital acquisitions or construction are to be reported as contributions. The GASB requires such contributions to be reported as either operating or nonoperating depending on their character and source. The fact that capital contributions are reported on a utility's operating statement does not mean that they result in an increase in "net assets invested in capital assets (net of related debt)." Each must be evaluated to determine the correct classification within fund net assets. As shown in appendix A, four accounts —"contributions from municipality" (account 272), "contributions from customers" (account 273), "contributions from developers" (account 274), and "other contributions" (account 275)—are provided for governmental water utilities to record contributions in aid of construction.

Service Extension Policies

A large portion of advances or contributions made by or on behalf of customers for construction frequently arises in connection with the extension of distribution facilities to provide water service to new customers. The reasons for requiring customer advances or contributions for this purpose are (1) to protect existing customers served by the system by ensuring that the existing customers do not bear, in a discriminating manner, the specific costs of extending service to new customers; and (2) to ensure that an adequate return will be realized on the incremental plant investment required to service prospective customers.

The cost of providing service to new customers varies depending on the distance the proposed customers are located from existing distribution mains and on requirements for any special construction to provide the quality and quantity of water service needed by the customers. In addition, with rising construction costs, the construction expenditures required to add new customers frequently exceed the expenditures that were made with respect to existing customers. As a result, customer advances or contributions may be required in order to equalize investment per customer in relation to revenue per customer. Further, customer advances or contributions must be sufficient to permit the water utility to earn an adequate return on its investment in the new facilities. To this end, customer advances and contributions may be considered as sharing the cost of plant construction. In lieu of requiring advances or contributions, some utilities recover the cost of construction by means of special rate agreements. (Governmental water utilities frequently charge customers located beyond city limits higher rates for water service than those inside city limits in order to compensate for the added cost of serving out-of-city customers.)

The water main extension policies employed by water utilities vary widely. For water utilities subject to public service commission jurisdiction, extension policies generally are a result of commission rule or are subject to the approval of the commission. Customarily, amounts paid by or on behalf of customers for construction are in the form of advances, with a provision for refunds against the advances. Refund provisions typically reflect a desire to return that portion of the advance that is in excess of the contribution necessary to permit the utility to make an adequate return on the incremental plant investment that is financed by the utility. It is extremely difficult to devise extension policies that result in a water utility retaining only that portion of an advance, as a contribution, that is necessary for the realization of an adequate return on investment and that avoids all discrimination among customers.

In some cases, an advance of the entire estimated construction cost is required by the utility. In other cases, the excess of estimated construction cost above a fixed limit is required to be advanced. The fixed limit typically is based on the construction costs associated with a minimum size and length of main. Advances made by customers, groups of customers, subdividers, or developers typically are not interest-bearing. Frequently, different policies regarding the portion of cost to be advanced are applicable to customers and subdividers.

Any excess of the advance over actual construction cost is refunded in a lump sum. Additional refunds frequently are based on established schedules that permit refunds according to the number of customers using the extension or the amount of revenue derived from customers using the extension.

It is imperative that detailed records be maintained concerning advances and contributions from customers, subdividers, and other persons. Such records include information concerning the names and addresses of those providing advances and contributions, the amounts advanced or contributed by each, and the terms of the extension agreements. These detailed records serve not only as supporting documents for the "customer advances for construction" account and for the contributions accounts but also as evidence supporting refunds of advances or portions of advances. When a person is refunded the entire amount to which he or she is entitled, as evidenced by the detailed records, any remaining balance of advances is transferred to the appropriate contributions account.

Frequently, the customer is charged for the cost of the service line, either from the meter to the curb or from the meter to the distribution main. The cost of the meter, in some instances, also is paid by the customer. Amounts paid by customers for service and meter installations should be considered as contributions for construction.

Customer advances and contributions for main extensions, service and meter installations, and other plant construction should not be considered as a reduction of the cost of plant construction (unless a utility is required to do so by a public service commission). The construction should be recorded in the plant accounts at its full cost, with the advances or contributions for construction included on the liability side of the balance sheet.

Requirements From Governing Authorities

Two major sources influence how equity is recorded and reported: one is the bond rating agency, and the second is NARUC.

Bond Rating Agencies

When a governmental water utility sells a bond, that bond comes with a covenant, a set of legally enforceable requirements, that reassures the investors that money from the utility will not be spent on other matters outside the utility, that equipment will be replaced on time, and that their loan will be repaid. The covenant may specify a coverage ratio, that is, net revenue must be greater than the debt service by a stated margin. The higher the perceived risk, the greater the margin.

If the bond is a revenue bond, it will be backed by revenue from the utility; if it is a general obligation bond, it may formally be backed by a city or county and its tax-raising powers, but actually repaid from the revenues of the water utility. The source of revenue pledged to repay the bond is one of the specifications of the covenant. The requirements of the covenant are agreed to by the governing body. Enforcement may be through bondholders' lawsuits and market discipline, that is, failure to adhere to the requirements will result in increased costs of borrowing.

Before a bond is sold, regardless of whether by an private or a governmental water utility, it is normally rated by a rating agency, which reviews the finances and prior history of the utility, the purposes of the bond, and the level of risk entailed. The rating given by the rating agency often determines the cost to the utility—higher perceived risk results in higher borrowing costs. Because an issuer may offer different bonds over time and because bonds are sold and typically resold, ratings may need to be renewed from time to time. Managers may need to make arrangements for this to be done and to have all the relevant financial information, especially audited financial reports including information on equity, available to rating agencies. The key is to demonstrate compliance with all the bond covenant requirements, for the present bond and any prior ones.

The NARUC Chart of Accounts

Equity accounts will be found in the accounts 201 through 218 (appendix A), depending on the type of organization of the utility. A corporate utility will use accounts 210 through 213 to identify common and preferred stock. Proprietorships and partnerships identify the proprietary capital in account 218. Corporations, proprietorships, and partnerships use accounts 214 and 215 to identify appropriated and unappropriated retained earnings. Governmental utilities may also use these NARUC accounts; however, as explained above, GASB now refers to the equity section as "fund net assets" with three distinct subcategories.

Specifications of suggested equity accounts are as follows:

- *Common Stock Issued (201).* The par or stated value of the capital stock actually issued.
- *Common Stock Subscribed (202).* The legally enforceable subscriptions to capital stock.
- *Common Stock Liability for Conversion (203).* The par or stated value of the capital stock that the utility has agreed to exchange for securities of other companies.
- *Preferred Stock Issued (204).* The par or stated value of the preferred stock actually issued.
- *Preferred Stock Subscribed (205).* The legally enforceable subscriptions to preferred stock of the utility.
- *Preferred Stock Liability for Conversion (206).* The par or stated value of the preferred stock that the utility has agreed to exchange for securities of other companies.
- *Premium on Capital Stock (207).* The excess of the actual value received over the par or stated value for capital stock issued. The account will be subdivided for all issues of capital stock.
- *Reduction in Par or Stated Value of Capital Stock (209).* Credits resulting from the reduction of the par or stated value of the capital stock.
- *Gain on Resale or Cancellation of Reacquired Capital Stock (210).* The credits resulting from the resale or cancellation of reacquired capital stock.
- *Other Paid-in Capital (211).* The balance for credits of paid-in capital for items not properly includable in other accounts.
- *Discount on Capital Stock (212).* With a separate subdivision for each class of capital stock, all discounts related to the original issue and sale of the capital stock will be recorded.
- *Capital Stock Expense (213).* With a separate subdivision for each class and series of capital stock, all expenses incurred in the issuance of the stock.
- *Appropriate Retained Earnings (214).* Retained earnings that have been set aside for specific purposes. Subaccounts will be required for each appropriation.

- *Unappropriated Retained Earnings (215).* The balance of net income less any transfer to or from retained earnings.
- *Reacquired Capital Stock (216).* In a subaccount for each class and services of capital stock, the cost of capital stock reacquired.
- *Proprietary Capital (218).* For proprietorships and partnerships, the investment of the proprietor or partners in an unincorporated utility. Each year, income or loss will be entered into this account. Separate subaccounts will be in a partnership for each partner.

Tools for Evaluating Utility Financial Position and Operations

Utilities may be in various states of financial condition. Financial analysts and credit agencies use a variety of techniques to determine the utility's financial condition. The analysts compare performance over time, tracking trends. They frequently use percentage changes, performance ratios, and changes in ratios over time. The change in the ratios allows the determination of the utility's progress, improvement, or deterioration.

Percentage Analysis

Financial statements are presented with comparative statements for the current year and at least one prior year. The comparative statement allows the reader to determine the variation in the accounts from one year to the next. The differences from year to year may be expressed as percentages. The percentage analysis can also be used to determine changes in the composition of the accounts over the period presented. For example, what percent of labor costs are due to benefits, and how is this percentage changing over time?

Comparing Estimates to Actuals

Management reporting uses a variety of comparative statements in which the actual experience is compared to the budgeted amounts. This provides management the ability to determine factors that have changed since the budget was developed. Unusual nonrecurring items should be reported separately to avoid distortion.

Ratio Analysis

Ratio analysis is the selection of two amounts from the financial statements and dividing one into the other. The analysis allows the reader to determine additional factors than can be obtained from individual amounts. The ratios typically used involve the following three types:

- Those that indicate the current position
- Those that indicate the equity position
- Those that indicate the income or operating position

Ratios used in analyzing the current position refer to the relationship of the current asset to current liabilities. These ratios indicate the overall solvency of the utility or the movement of the utility's current assets. Examples of the ratios used to determine the overall solvency of the utility are the current ratio (net current assets divided by current liabilities), the quick ratio (cash and short-term investments divided by current liabilities), and working capital to total assets. Ratios relating to the movement of current assets can be in the receivable, inventory, or working capital asset types.

Equity ratios are used to determine the financial condition and the amount of leverage of the utility. The equity ratio can be seen from different viewpoints. From a creditor's view, a high proportion of equity to debt is preferred. The equity holder will prefer a high proportion of debt to equity. The types of equity ratios that an analyst may use are

- Total debt to equity
- Owner's equity to total assets
- Creditor's equity to total assets
- Owner's equity to total liabilities
- Net income to owner's equity
- Sales to owner's equity
- Fixed assets to fixed liabilities
- Fixed assets to owner's equity
- Sales to total equity
- Sales to fixed assets
- Book value per share of common stock

Investors may find the ratios relating to income or operation of more interest than the equity or current position ratios. Income ratios will give an indication of the utility's profitability. Creditors may not grant loans to a utility that does not indicate a profitable position even though adequate collateral is available. Management will also be concerned with the utility's income ratios, as they may indicate the trend that income is falling. Examples of income or operating ratios are

- Net income to net sales
- Net income to owner's equity
- Investment turnover
- Net income per share of common stock
- Earnings rate on market value per share
- Price-earnings ratio
- Return on investment

This page intentionally blank.

Part 5

Financial Management Functions

This page intentionally blank.

Chapter 18

Financing

This chapter focuses on the financing of water utility operations and how the accounting system helps support the funding process.

Financing Water Utility Operations

The three primary funding sources for governmental-and-operated water utilities are

- Revenues from rates and other fees and charges
- Proceeds from issuance of debt
- Receipts from contributions in aid of construction

Occasionally, ad valorem taxes are also used by local governments for repayment of general obligation debt used to finance water facilities, although this source is becoming rarer. The use of proceeds from the sale of common or preferred stock (a source widely used by private utilities) is unavailable to governmental utilities.

A more comprehensive discussion of these financing sources is contained in the Manual of Water Supply Practices series published by the American Water Works Association. The values in this series include the following:

- Manual Ml, *Principles of Water Rates, Fees, and Charges,* discusses the development of rates, including the development of revenue requirements, cost allocation, and rate design.
- Manual M29, *Fundamentals of Water Utility Capital Financing,* discusses the various means to finance plant investment and the numerous financial instruments involved.

These manuals should be consulted for detailed presentations on financing sources. The focus here will be on how the accounting system supports the various financing mediums. The following discussion on accounting requirements is not intended to encompass all circumstances but rather to indicate how accounting requirements may differ as financial policy and local economic conditions vary.

Rate Financing

Rates, fees, and other charges usually are the major sources of funding the repayment of principal and interest costs of debt issues. In addition, some portion of plant investment is usually financed directly through rates, without borrowing. Rates must be set sufficiently high to generate enough revenue to cover these purposes.

Almost all local government utilities use either the cash or the utility method of calculating revenue requirements. Most governments use the cash basis method, which consists of determining the annual operating and maintenance expenses, debt service repayments, and capital outlay funded from revenues. The cash method is highly adaptable to the standard accounting and budgeting functions of most local governments that focus on the annual cash resources needed to provide service during the year.

Another typical budgeting and accounting need is to segregate (and account for) capital costs that are growth-related and those that are not growth-related, so that the utility will have a basis for developing capacity fees, system development charges, availability fees, or whatever nomenclature is used for fees established to recoup at least some portion of the costs of building capacity to serve new customers.

The utility method of calculating revenue requirements, however, requires substantially different accounting information not customarily maintained in many local government accounting organizations. The different revenue requirement components include

- Development of a rate base—generally original cost of plant investment less accumulated depreciation
- Calculation of depreciation and amortization expense on plant investment
- Determination of the cost of capital to apply as a rate of return on capital invested in plant

These different revenue requirement components call for much more emphasis on accounting for plant investment and depreciation, and how the plant was financed. Guidance for the added accounting needs can be obtained from private utility regulatory bodies that exclusively prescribe the utility method. Their long-standing, record-keeping practices can be very useful in developing the appropriate accounting practices for using the utility method in a governmental environment. While each state establishes its own accounting practices, the National Association of Regulatory Utility Commissioners (NARUC) has created a standard chart of accounts and other accounting guidelines that are widely adopted by the various state utility regulatory authorities. Even these guidelines, however, must be modified to meet the utility's goals, the local economic conditions in each community, and the governmental environment.

When a government utility offers both retail service to its citizens and wholesale service outside its corporate boundaries, record-keeping practices are likely to be affected. Those utilities that also provide wholesale service, for example, are more likely to use the utility method of determining revenue requirements (at least for determining the cost of service to their wholesale customers). Thus more emphasis should be given to such activities as plant accounting, depreciation studies, and the financing of plant facilities. Further, the utility's distribution system may be constructed in such a manner that one portion of it is used only by the retail customers, another portion is used in common by both wholesale and retail customers, and another portion may be used only by the wholesale customers. Under these circumstances, continuing property records need to be kept in sufficient detail to provide the information needed for allocation of distribution system costs to water service functions and customer classes. Such an allocation is frequently performed using the diameter of mains as an allocation basis. If the diameter of mains is used as the allocation basis, then the continuing property records should provide cost by main size as well as the related data on plant financing.

Many government water utilities also offer wastewater service, which adds considerable complexity to the accounting process. There is generally a need to keep the costs of water service separate from those of wastewater. This separation of service costs frequently is derived from a policy to have each of the services be self-supporting. How the separation of costs is accomplished varies considerably and can have significant impacts on the cost and complexity of the accounting process. The two major bases are:

- Budget and account for all costs separately (e.g., 100 percent of all distribution system costs would be recorded as water costs; general management costs may be split one-half to water and one-half to wastewater or on some other defined basis)
- Budget and account for all costs together, and when cost-of-service studies are necessary, a separate cost allocation study is performed to separate water costs from wastewater costs

Many utilities use a combination of the two accounting bases to maintain a balance between service-cost separation and the cost to account for an increased level of detailed data.

To figure the amount of revenue that needs to be earmarked for system maintenance (the amounts for debt service are straightforward), the accounting system needs to be able to identify and track maintenance costs for each historical period, to identify trends and needs. The ability to identify and track maintenance costs for specific portions of a utility's infrastructure is necessary to support sound decision-making for "repair or replace" determinations and the relative life-cycle costs of various types of utility assets and appurtenances.

Besides historical accounting requirements for debt already issued, accounting records can also be used to help forecast the need for debt issues and other financing. Continuing property records, for instance, should contain data on the date of asset acquisition and the asset's useful life so that replacement of these assets can be anticipated. If a particular type of asset (e.g., a distribution main) usually needs replacement in 50 years, then all distribution mains with acquisition dates about 50 years ago may need replacement. While it is recognized that few assets follow a precise useful-life pattern, the availability of historical asset data is very useful in forecasting an order of magnitude of financing needs for replacing assets. If the continuing property records also have the ability to use indices to indicate replacement cost, then the calculation of potential financing needs can be more easily performed.

Debt Issuance

Two primary types of accounting data requirements are related to the issuance of debt, especially revenue-supported bond issues. The first is the preparation of annual financial statements attested to by independent accountants. Almost all debt issues have a covenant requiring the preparation of annual financial statements within a stated time frame after the end of the utility's fiscal year. Chapter 8 contains considerable detail on how these annual financial reports are prepared.

The second type of accounting requirement is also related to the bond covenants, but the individual covenants may vary considerably from utility to utility. Typical covenant requirements include

- Maintenance of cash reserves at specified levels for principal and interest, major repairs, or other purposes
- Maintenance of revenue bond coverage at prescribed level(s) for various stated purposes
- Definition of how net revenues available for coverage are to be calculated
- Prescription of insurance coverage requirements
- Use of proceeds from disposition of major assets used to provide service
- Other matters that may be particular to any specific utility
- Verification of meeting bond covenants are typically included in annual financial reports or bond certification statements, which may be required to be prepared on a routine basis in accordance with the bond covenants

Management should also be alert to any accounting definitions in long-term contracts, which from a legal standpoint, may be different for coverage calculation purposes than for financial statement presentation purposes. Therefore, for calculating revenue bond coverage, such payments should be treated as operation and maintenance expenses in arriving at net revenue available for debt service. For financial statement purposes, the outstanding debt and annual payments thereon would be classified as debt and payments thereon.

Contributed Capital

Accounting for contributed capital is needed for rate-making, financial statement, and financial planning purposes. The financial statement and financial planning requirements can be met at a fairly high level of detail. For financial statement purposes, there is a need to classify contributed capital as a separate source of funding on the statement of cash flows and on the balance sheet. Additional detail, such as the source of the contribution (e.g., federal grant or customer or developer contribution), can also be disclosed.

Financial planning requirements for contributed capital information relates primarily to the need to finance the replacement of those assets originally funded through contributions. Thus, the timely recording of all contributed assets in much the same detail as those funded from other sources is important.

For rate-making purposes, accounting for contributed assets must get quite detailed. The level of detail should be the same as that used to categorize plant investment (e.g., water supply, treatment, etc.). Probably the best way to accomplish this level of detail is to indicate the funding source(s) on the fixed-asset records at the time the asset is completed and put in plant-in-service. Information on the funding source(s) of assets by plant category, especially as to contributed assets, will permit the calculation of plant investment funded by debt and revenues for use in cost allocation under the cash basis method and the calculation of net plant investment for rate base determination under the utility method. Further, the amount of depreciation expense on contributed assets can also be determined for rate purposes and for financial statement purposes when depreciation expenses on contributed assets are charged to contributed capital accounts instead of retained earnings.

This page intentionally blank.

Chapter 19

Audits

For most water utilities, annual audits are a fact of life, often mandated by state law, charter bylaws, or funding agreements. Boards and management can affect audits' outcome and cost favorably by establishing and documenting controls and keeping records, then by planning for the specific needs of any audit. Audit standards that regulate independent, outside auditors are continually changing, but management and boards need to recognize that water utilities often share specific risks and coordinate their cooperation with auditors.

Financial Audits

A financial audit is an external review of an organization's books and financial reports. The goal is to certify that the information provided in these internally prepared reports is an accurate representation of the financial condition of the utility. The credibility of the audit certification depends on the independence of the audit team, its level of expertise, and the reputation of the audit firm.

Financial audits vary in complexity, cost, and reporting depending on the standards mandated for their auditors to follow. The basic "certified" audit is usually planned and performed following generally accepted auditing standards (GAAS). Beyond that, legal requirements may require the audit to follow Government audit standards (GAS), formerly called generally accepted government audit standards (GAGAS) or Yellow Book standards. Finally, the most complex and costly financial audit is one which complies with Single Audit Act (SAA) audit standards, which are required when an entity has expended federal grant or loans of $500,000 or more in its audit period. Generally, the progression of standards and audit cost correlates to the extent of compliance testing, audit documentation and auditor qualifications required. One should not underestimate the extent and internal cost of an organization's cooperation and preparation of documents for an audit.

Roles and Responsibilities

A number of actors have major roles in the financial audit process, beginning with the board and its audit committee and including internal and external (independent) auditors.

Boards and Audit Committees

Boards are responsible for selecting the audit firm and drawing up the contract delineating the scope of the audit. On the one hand, they must ensure the experience and independence of the auditors; on the other, they must ensure that records are complete, timely, and freely available to auditors. A utility can keep the costs of an audit modest by providing the auditors quick access to well-designed and well-maintained records.

Boards and management are responsible for the internal controls that produce reliable records for the auditor; they are also responsible to provide the independent auditor with access to those records. Access to records may be compromised if auditors are hired too late to observe significant beginning inventories, or if data reports at year-end are not preserved so that subsidiary balance reports agree with control account balances. Electronic records may be written-over or documents may be discarded or destroyed prematurely. Management or boards may mistakenly withhold sensitive information from auditors relating to legal issues. They may overlook the need to confide and obtain competent legal opinions for open litigations needed for the audit. In such cases, an audit report may include a "qualification" disclosing a limitation in its opinion. Standards generally require current-year auditors to obtain written authorization from management to contact the auditors from the immediately prior year. Withholding such permission may be regarded as a serious limitation on the audit and affect final reports. Such limitations may have serious effects; managers should take whatever steps are necessary to avoid such outcomes.

Audit committees typically include at least three board members who understand operations, personnel, accounting, audit, and legal issues for water utilities. Audit committees should be the principal selectors of independent auditors. Delegating the choice, discussion with, or retention of auditors to management may jeopardize the objectivity of the audit.

Changes in independent auditor standards now require outside auditors to communicate problems that they encounter before, during, and after their audit field work. Audit committees should arrange in writing for the form, timing, and method of receiving those communications according to legal policy, in the engagement letter, which is an annual contract between the independent auditors and the entity. Even before the engagement letter, boards should direct management to obtain from their auditors thorough lists of dates and times for documents and records, and hours and costs for personnel assistance and outside consultants that must be arranged. Before it is signed, the audit committee needs to understand what the auditors consider to be the level of materiality contained in the utility's statements, and management's need to prepare records and financial statements that satisfy GAAP for water utilities. *Materiality* refers to the auditors' definition of what is an important enough problem to report.

The committee may decide it wants outside auditors to expand their audit testing or to perform specific audit procedures beyond the level chosen by its independent auditors' judgment. For example, the committee may direct auditors to test for "lapping" (misappropriation of cash receipts), a test that when performed is done at unpredictable intervals. Managers inside the organization are responsible for the preparation of the financial statements, including the required footnote disclosures, while outside independent auditors prepare the audit statement. Preparation of the statements by the auditors may jeopardize the independence of the auditor, and threaten the value of his or her report.

The final step in many audits is the issuance of the auditor's report. Audit standards require that the some member of the board must sign a representation letter before the auditor's report is released. It is crucial that the board and management consider the contents of that letter in advance so that any problems in its assertions can be avoided at that final moment for signing.

Role of the Independent Auditor

The independent auditor may be required to satisfy additional training and firm requirements besides the minimum licensure required by a state board of accountancy. This is particularly true for *Yellow Book* and SAA audits. Before starting an audit, it is also common for audit firms to inquire of their audit staff whether they have any personal, family, or financial involvements that would appear to impair their independence in relation to the water utility. Impairment may even be caused by unpaid prior year audit invoices! It is every independent auditor's legal obligation to never knowingly be associated by report with any false or intentionally misleading financial statements. The audit committee and management should bear in mind that auditors are required now to exercise extreme professional skepticism, despite any personal feelings.

Role of the Internal Auditor

Some water utilities use hired consultants or maintain internal auditors as regular employees. Internal auditors may perform customer or employee fraud audits, contract and vendor audits, performance and contract compliance audits, and even assist independent auditors during financial audits. However, their independence will never be equal to that of the outside auditor because they serve management. Within that limitation, their independence is chiefly determined by their organizational level of reporting and their administrative status. If they report directly and regularly to the audit committee and may not be fired without its approval, that is very different than when they are embedded down in an organization below a finance director. Except in rare circumstances, the internal auditor is generally not obliged to report outside the organization, and such disclosure may be prohibited by organization policy.

Changing Auditors

Some water utilities may feel obliged to change independent auditors every few years in order to ensure the independence of the auditor. This concern about getting too comfortable with an auditor should be traded off against the cost-effectiveness of an auditor who is thoroughly familiar with the functions and accounting systems of the water utility. The decision to change outside auditors should be done by the utility's board, based on objective factors of satisfaction or need to improve audit service.

Operational, Management and Other Audits

Water utilities are subject to audits by other agencies for such reasons as payroll, workers' compensation, health and safety, and bond-rating, as well as other state and federal requirements. They may "host" audit teams whose task is to investigate costs of joint ventures. Specialists in machinery, energy, investment, or even entomology may be valuable contributors to an audit team.

A management audit focuses on such issues as vulnerabilities to fraud, weaknesses in the control environment, appropriate communications channels, or timeliness and inclusiveness of reports. The audit team looks not for actual present problems so much as problems that might occur because of the way the utility is run, and makes recommendations for preventing those problems.

A utility may wish to carry out a performance audit, which may be done by internal or external auditors. Such audits compare the goals of a utility, including legal requirements, with its actual performance. Such audits rely heavily on information provided by the accounting system.

Summary

Regardless of the type of audit, audit committees can make audits run smoother, obtain better results, and even save money through their planning and preparations for the audits. While the basic required financial audit is performed by an outside, independent auditor, other types of audits may be performed by consultants or internal auditors, for the benefit of management and sometimes the public as well. Some contracts, loans, and grants (i.e., federal grants and loans that necessitate SAA audits) may create immediate needs to add new or upgrade existing accounting procedures; even so, actual audits may take longer and cost more than anticipated. Outside auditors are obligated to communicate more and earlier in the audit process that in the past. It is crucial, at the highest level, for water utility managers to consider their special risks, to implement controls, and to develop plans and communications early with auditors and not to wait until year-end.

Chapter 20

Internal Controls

The Committee of Sponsoring Organizations (COSO) of the Treadway Commission defines internal control as "a process, effected by an entity's board of directors, management and other personnel, designed to provide reasonable assurance regarding the achievement of objectives in the following categories: effectiveness and efficiency of operations; reliability of financial reporting; and, compliance with applicable laws and regulations." These objectives are critical to utility managers to ensure the trust of ratepayers, regulators, and elected officials. The key benefit of effective internal control is the enhanced ability for management to make representations about utility performance to stakeholders. This chapter will focus on the reliability of financial reporting.

Water utilities in the United States have many characteristics similar to smaller public companies: fewer lines of business, geographic concentration, fewer levels of management with wider spans of control, fewer personnel with wider ranges of duties, and limited resources in line and staff positions. Some of the challenges are also similar: obtaining sufficient resources to pursue internal control activities, recruiting individuals with financial reporting experience, providing management attention to accounting practices, and ensuring control of information technology. Water utility managers interested in enhancing performance through improved internal controls can adopt best practices used by smaller public companies.

Financial Reporting Objectives

Effective controls over financial reporting are a clear statement of reporting objectives. Reporting objectives pertain to the preparation of reliable reports that may relate to financial or nonfinancial reporting and to internal or external reporting. Internal reporting objectives are driven by internal requirements in response to a variety of potential needs such as the utility's strategic direction, operating plans, and performance metrics at various levels. External reporting objectives are driven primarily by regulations and/or standards established by accounting bodies and other standard-setting organizations. COSO states this principle as "management specifies financial reporting objectives with sufficient clarity and criteria to enable identification of risks to reliable financial reporting." Financial reporting objectives should include these attributes: complies with generally accepted accounting principles; it reflects all utility activities; it is supported by relevant financial statement assertions (existence, completeness, rights and obligations, valuation or allocation, presentation, and disclosure); and it considers materiality. Here is an example of a statement of objectives for overall financial reporting:

> Financial statements are prepared in compliance with generally accepted accounting principles; accurately reflect underlying transactions and events in a manner that presents the financial position, results of operations, and cash flows within a range of acceptable limits; and are supported by informative disclosures and relevant assertions.

An example of the objective for the revenue recognition process reads as follows:

> Collect revenues from customer accounts that are billed according to the service rules and regulations and are based upon accurate metered consumption. Design and execute internal controls that prevent or detect errors in customer accounts to an acceptable level.

In addition to revenue recognition, objectives can also be established for:

- Expense recognition
- Capitalization of expenses
- Estimation of expenses
- Maintaining adequate documentation to support assertions (existence, completeness, rights and obligations, valuation or allocation, presentation, and disclosure)
- Accounts receivable aging
- Accounts payable aging
- Compliance with changes in accounting standards
- Security of assets
- Control of changes to automated processes
- Disaster recovery and business continuity
- Prevention of fraud or sabotage

These objectives should be articulated by senior management in specific and concise terms and should be supported by measurable performance standards.

Internal Control Components

The COSO Internal Control–Integrated Framework is widely acknowledged and accepted as a standard internal control framework for use by business in the United States. The COSO framework consists of five interrelated components:

1. *Control Environment:* The control environment sets the tone of management's intentions for internal control within the utility by influencing how work gets accomplished. It includes the integrity, ethical values and competence of the utility management and staff, the way management assigns authority and responsibility, and the attention and direction provided by the governing body.

2. *Risk Assessment:* Risks are occurrences that may adversely affect a utility's ability to achieve its' objectives and successfully execute its' strategies. Risk assessment is the identification and evaluation of risks and the planning on how to best control those risks at an acceptable level.
3. *Control Activities:* Control activities are the policies and procedures used by a utility to ensure that management's plans are carried out. These include requirements for approvals, authorizations, verifications, reconciliations, and segregation of duties.
4. *Information and Communication:* Information must be recorded and communicated in a form and that enables utility personnel to carry out their responsibilities. Communication includes financial information as well as other operating information flowing down, across, and up the organization. Communication also enables all personnel to understand their internal control responsibilities and importance to the achievement of the utility's objectives.
5. *Monitoring:* Internal control systems need to be monitored over time to ensure that the controls upon which management relies remain intact and effective in achieving the control objectives. The frequency and methods used to evaluate the internal control systems will depend upon the assessment of reporting risks and how much change has occurred in the reporting process.

The internal controls system will vary from utility to utility based on size, complexity, and management philosophy. Although all utilities need to maintain control over their financial reporting, one utility's approach will often look very different from another's.

Control Environment

The control environment component is the foundation upon which all other components of internal control are based and sets the tone of an organization. Because of its importance to effective internal control over financial reporting, management must evaluate the control environment at the utility. COSO has identified seven principles related to the control environment component:

1. *Integrity and Ethical Values:* Senior management should develop a clearly utility articulated statement of ethical values that is understood at all levels of the organization. Processes should be in place to monitor adherence to principles of sound integrity and ethical values. Deviations from sound integrity and ethical values should be identified in a timely manner and appropriately addressed and remedied at appropriate levels within the utility.
2. *Board of Directors:* The board should define and communicate authorities retained at the board level and those delegated to management. The audit committee should actively evaluate and monitor risks of management override of internal control and consider risks affecting the reliability of financial reporting. The audit committee should provide oversight to the effectiveness of internal control over financial reporting and financial statement preparations.

3. *Management's Philosophy and Operating Style:* Management should set the "tone at the top" emphasizing reliable financial reporting. Management's attitude should support a disciplined, objective process in selecting accounting principles and developing accounting estimates. Management should establish and clearly articulate financial reporting objectives, including the role of internal control over financial reporting.
4. *Organization Structure:* Management should establish appropriate lines of financial reporting for each functional area and business unit in the organization. Management should maintain an organizational structure that facilitates effective reporting and other communications about internal control over financial reporting.
5. *Financial Reporting Competencies:* Management should identify the competencies that support reliable financial reporting. The utility should employ or otherwise retain individuals who possess the required competencies related to financial reporting. Needed competencies should be regularly evaluated and maintained.
6. *Authority and Responsibility:* Assignment of responsibility and delegation of authority should be clearly defined for all employees, including the board of directors, management, and front-line employees. The assignment or authority and responsibility should include appropriate limitations and accountability by individuals.
7. *Human Resources:* Management should establish human resource practices that demonstrate its commitment to integrity, ethical behavior, and competence. Employee recruitment and retention for key financial reporting positions should be guided by principles of integrity and by necessary competencies associated with the positions.

As part of evaluating the control environment, management should assess whether:

- The utility management's philosophy and operating style promote effective internal control over financial reporting
- Sound integrity and ethical values, particularly of top management, are developed and understood
- The governing board or audit committee understands and exercises responsibility over financial reporting and internal control

Risk Assessment

In order to adequately meet these financial reporting objectives, management must also consider the financial reporting risks. COSO states this principle as "the company identifies and analyzes risks to the achievement of financial reporting objectives as a basis for determining how the risks should be managed." Management's risk identification process should include the identification of: relevant financial statement assertions for each significant account and disclosure; business utility processes and departments that support financial statement accounts and disclosures; and information technology (IT) systems supporting key processes relevant to financial reporting objectives.

Risk assessments can be performed in different ways, using a single method or a combination of methods, according to management's discretion. A criteria-based assessment can be performed using a high, medium, and low risk ranking:

- *High:* direct and significant link to the financial statements.
- *Medium:* indirect and significant link to the financial statements.
- *Low:* loosely connected to the financial statements, takes several steps, and low probability.

Risk assessments can also be performed using a severity, occurrence, and detective rating:

- *Severity:* what is the absolute worst that could happen?
- *Occurrence:* what is the probability that this could happen?
- *Detective:* if it happened, would it be discovered easily?

Used in combination, these two methods can provide management with a clear insight into the distribution of risks by process or account.

Utility management should evaluate the qualitative and quantitative risk factors related to significant financial statement line-items and disclosures. Risk factors relevant to the identification of these items are:

- Size and composition of the account
- Susceptibility of misstatement resulting from errors or fraud
- Volume of activity, complexity, and homogeneity of the individual transactions processed through the account or reflected in the disclosure
- Nature of the account or disclosure
- Accounting and reporting complexities associated with the account or disclosure
- Exposures to losses in the account
- Possibility of significant contingent liabilities arising from the activities reflected in the account or disclosure
- Existence of related party transactions in the account
- Changes from the prior period in account or disclosure characteristics

Control Activities

Control activities are performed at various levels of a company to reduce risks to achievement of financial reporting objectives. Pre-event controls are controls intended to prevent potential risks from occurring. Post-event controls are controls intended to detect and correct errors that have already occurred. Pre-event and post-event controls can exist at the entity level as well as the account or process level.

Entity-level controls vary in nature and precision. Some entity-level controls have an important, but indirect, effect on the likelihood that a misstatement will be detected or prevented on a timely basis. Some entity-level controls monitor the effectiveness of other controls. Such controls might be designed to identify possible breakdowns in lower-level controls, but not at a level of precision that would, by itself, sufficiently address the assessed risk that misstatements to a relevant assertion will be prevented or detected on a timely basis. Other entity-level controls might be designed to operate at a level of precision that would adequately prevent or detect on a timely basis misstatements to one or more relevant assertions. Entity-level controls include:

- Controls related to the control environment
- Control over management override
- The utility's risk identification and assessment process
- Controls to monitor the results of operations
- Controls to monitor other controls, including the activities of the internal audit function, the audit committee, and self-assessment programs
- Policies that address significant business control and risk management practices
- Period-end financial reporting process

Identifying Deficiencies in the Design of Controls

A material weakness in internal control is a deficiency, or a combination of deficiencies, that results in a reasonable possibility that a serious misstatement of the utility's financial statements will not be prevented or detected on a timely basis. A significant deficiency is a deficiency, or a combination of deficiencies, in internal control over financial reporting that is less severe than a material weakness, yet important enough to merit attention by those responsible for oversight of the utility's financial reporting.

The severity of a deficiency depends upon whether there is a reasonable possibility that the utility's controls will fail to prevent or detect a misstatement of an account balance or disclosure and the magnitude of the potential misstatement resulting from the deficiency. The severity of a deficiency does not depend upon whether a misstatement actually has occurred. Factors that affect the magnitude of a misstatement that might result from a deficiency in controls include the financial statement amounts exposed to the deficiency and the volume of activity or class of transactions exposed to the deficiency.

The following are examples of circumstances that suggest control deficiencies, significant deficiencies, or material weaknesses:

- Lack of sufficient expertise in selecting and implementing accounting principles
- Ineffective oversight of the utility's financial reporting and internal control by those charged by governance
- Restatement of previously issued financial statements to reflect the correction of a material misstatement
- Identification by the auditor of a material misstatement in the financial statements that was not initially identified by the utility's internal control

- An ineffective internal audit function, risk assessment function, or regulatory compliance function
- Identification of fraud of any magnitude on the part of senior management
- Inadequate documentation of the components of internal control
- Absent or inadequate segregation of duties (record keeping, asset custodianship, and transaction authority) within a significant account or process
- Employees or management who lack the qualifications and training to fulfill their assigned functions
- The absence of an internal process to report deficiencies in internal control to management on a timely basis
- Failure by management or those charged with governance to assess the effect of a significant deficiency previously communicated to them and either correct it or conclude that it will not be corrected
- Failure by management or those charged with governance to assess the effect of a significant deficiency previously communicated to them and either correct it or conclude that it will not be corrected

These examples can be used as a checklist for utility managers and governing boards interested in beginning an assessment of internal control.

Controlling Fraud Risk

Management should evaluate whether the utility's controls sufficiently address the risks of material misstatement resulting from fraud, including management override of internal controls. Management should consider the most common types of fraud and the known means to prevent and detect them. Controls that might address fraud risks are:

- Controls over significant, unusual transactions, particularly those that result in late or unusual journal entries
- Controls over journal entries and adjustments made in the period-end financial reporting process
- Controls over related party transactions
- Controls related to significant management estimates
- Controls that mitigate incentives for, and pressures on, management to falsify or inappropriately manage financial results

Controlling Accounting Estimates

Management should design appropriate controls to provide reasonable assurance with respect to accounting estimates, including:

- All required estimates are made in preparing the financial statements.
- The people involved have the requisite expertise and understand the accounting objectives.

- The financial and nonfinancial data used in making estimates are complete and accurate.
- The assumptions used in making estimates are reasonable and free from bias.
- An appropriate methodology is used in preparing the estimates.
- If specialists are used in preparing an estimate, there is appropriate oversight of the specialist and the terms of the engagement.
- The final estimates produced are reasonable, free from bias, and fairly presented in the financial statements and management discussion and analysis (MD&A).
- Senior management over-ride is precluded.

Controlling Information Technology Applications for Financial Reporting

The control objectives for information and related technology (COBIT) is widely acknowledged and accepted as a standard information technology governance framework for use by business in the United States. COBIT identifies seven information control criteria:

- *Effectiveness:* deals with information being relevant and pertinent as well as delivered in a timely, correct, consistent, and usable manner.
- *Efficiency:* concerns the provision of information through the optimal use of resources.
- *Confidentiality:* concerns the protection of sensitive information from unauthorized disclosure.
- *Integrity:* relates to the accuracy and completeness of information.
- *Availability:* relates to information being available when required.
- *Compliance:* deals with complying with laws, regulations, and contractual arrangements.
- *Reliability:* relates to the provision of appropriate information to operate the entity and fulfill its fiduciary and governance responsibilities.

COBIT defines IT activities in a generic process model with four domains:

- *Plan and Organize:* concerns the way IT can best contribute to the business objectives.
- *Acquire and Implement:* concerns the way IT solutions need to be identified, developed, or acquired.
- *Deliver and Support:* concerns the service delivery, management of security, and continuity of support.
- *Monitor and Evaluate:* concerns the assessment of IT processes for quality and compliance with control requirements.

The IT Governance Institute recommends a six-step road map documenting and improving information technology controls:

1. *Plan and Scope IT Controls*
   - Review overall project documentation and identify application controls.
   - Identify in-scope applications.
   - Identify in-scope infrastructure and databases.
2. *Assess IT Risk*
   - Assess the likelihood and impact of IT systems causing financial statement error or permitting or facilitating fraud.
3. *Document Controls*
   - Document application controls (automated or configured controls and hybrid controls).
   - Document IT general controls (access, program development and change, and computer operations).
4. *Evaluate Control Design and Operating Effectiveness*
   - Determine that all key controls are documented.
   - Test controls to confirm their operating effectiveness.
5. *Prioritize and Remediate Deficiencies*
   - Evaluate deficiencies by assessing their impact and likelihood of causing financial statement error or fraud.
   - Consider whether compensating controls exist and can be relied upon.
6. *Build Sustainability*
   - Consider automating controls to improve their reliability and reduce testing effort.
   - Rationalize to eliminate redundant and duplicate controls.

Examining and Complying with Externally Imposed Internal Controls

It is a utility's responsibility to know what laws and regulations affect their operations. Because of the regulated environment in which utilities operate, there are frequent occasions when internal controls affecting financial reporting are imposed from outside. This is particularly true when the utility exists within a larger entity (such as a water department within a municipal government) or is regulated by an entity outside of its organization (such as an private utility regulated by a state public utility commission). Utility management should identify these externally imposed internal controls and ensure that these are included in the documentation and evaluation. It is not sufficient to rely upon the external auditors to provide updates on internal control issues affecting the utility.

Information and Communication

Information systems identify, capture, process, and distribute information supporting achievement of financial reporting objectives. COSO has identified four principles related to the information and communication component:

1. *Financial Reporting Information:* Relevant, quality information should be identified, captured, used at all levels of the utility, and distributed in a form and time frame that supports the achievement of financial reporting objectives.
2. *Internal Control Information:* Internal information needed to facilitate the functioning of other internal control components should be identified, captured, used, and distributed in a form and time frame that enables personnel to carry out their internal control responsibilities.
3. *Internal Communication:* Communications should enable and support understanding and execution of internal control objectives, processes, and individual responsibilities at all levels of the utility.
4. *External Communication:* Matters affecting the achievement of financial reporting objectives should be communicated with relevant external stakeholders.

Information flows in smaller utilities are likely to be less formal than in large ones, but their role is as significant. Effective internal communication between top management and employees may be facilitated in smaller utilities, because there are fewer levels and numbers of personnel and greater visibility and availability of the utility director. Internal communications can take place through the frequent meetings and day-to-day activities in which management participates.

Monitoring

In the publication *Guidance on Monitoring Internal Control Systems*, COSO states, "The process of effective monitoring requires thoughtful planning and the evaluation of persuasive and reliable information to support conclusions regarding the effectiveness of the internal control system." It should be designed to provide evidence that the internal control system remains effective, both in its current operation and in its ability to respond to changes in relevant risks; and that control weaknesses are analyzed, and appropriate follow-up actions are taken that address root causes. This is accomplished through ongoing monitoring activities, separate evaluations, or a combination of the two.

Those responsible for monitoring need a reasonable basis for concluding that the information they are using is persuasive and reliable. Reliable information is accurate, verifiable, and comes from an objective source. Persuasive information must be produced and used in a time frame that makes it possible to prevent or detect and correct control weaknesses before they become significant to the organization. Evaluators must gather sufficient information to support a reasonable conclusion about control effectiveness. Sufficiency can refer to the number of instances of that control selected for evaluation. Sufficiency can also refer to qualitative assessments of adequacy, particularly when monitoring controls that do not lend themselves to sampling.

Monitoring should be built into the utility's operating activities and provide objective consideration. Evaluators should understand the components being evaluated and how they relate to activities supporting the reliability of financial reporting. Management may vary the scope and frequency of separate evaluations depending on the significance of risks being controlled, the importance of the controls in mitigating those risks, and the effectiveness of ongoing monitoring. Management may also consider past effectiveness of control activities in managing risks and the extent of ongoing monitoring within the associated processes. For smaller utilities, managers may also rely upon their firsthand knowledge of the business process controls.

A More In-Depth Look at Fraud

Fraud can be considered as an intentional act that results in a material misstatement of the financial statements or in a misappropriation of assets. Fraud typically occurs when one or more of these conditions are present:

- Incentive—the reason to commit fraud
- Opportunity—the circumstances that allow fraud (i.e. weak controls)
- Rationalization—the perpetrator's morals or character that allow for dishonest behavior

There are typical "red flags" to watch for in efforts to detect financial statement or asset misappropriation fraud.

Detection of Fraud: Financial Statement Fraud "Red Flags"

- Management dominated by a single person.
- Commitment by management to unattainable financial goals
- Rapid growth or unusually high profitability compared to like companies
- Very complex transactions (especially close to year-end)
- Significant related party transactions with entities not audited
- Management dismisses auditor concerns as not material
- Auditors scope is limited in performing the audit and meeting with audit committee
- Significant volume of sales to entity the ownership of which is not known

Detection of Asset Misappropriation Fraud

- Employee leads a lifestyle not suited to his or her income level
- Employee seldom or never takes a vacation
- Employee has very close relationships with certain vendors or customers
- Employee has control over too many accounting functions
- There are significant discrepancies in inventory and consistent inventory shrinkage

Financial Statement Audit Versus Fraud Examination

A financial statement audit offers assurances that financial statements are materially correct. The auditor is not required to search for fraud. The majority of testing is performed utilizing statistical sampling—not every transaction is examined. An audit is generally most beneficial to outside parties with a financial interest in the organization being audited. A fraud examination may be operational or financial in nature. It is not looking for material correctness but is instead looking for the unusual. There is typically no set pattern when conducting a fraud examination—the review follows where the evidence leads. A fraud examination will not necessarily produce a "smoking gun," but every fraud examination should be conducted as if it will end in litigation.

A strong control environment with effective internal controls creates a "perception of detection" which is considered the greatest deterrent of fraud.

Evaluating and Communicating Identified Deficiencies

Evaluators can conclude that they have sufficient, suitable information when they can conclude either that the risk of a control failure material to the organization's objectives is below the level of a reasonable possibility or that a control weakness exists.

Findings of internal control deficiencies should be communicated to the individual who owns the process and related controls and is in position to take corrective actions, and to at least one level of management above the process owner. Significant deficiencies should be communicated to top management and the governing board or audit committee. Management should develop a list of control deficiencies that seriously threaten the reliability of financial reporting that, if they occur, are required to be reported to senior management and the governing board. Types of deficiencies fitting these criteria include deficiencies relating to illegal or otherwise improper acts, significant loss of assets, and improper external financial reporting. Deficiencies reported from internal and external sources should be considered, with timely corrective actions taken.

Upon completion of the review of internal control effectiveness, a report on process controls should be prepared for senior management and the governing board covering: the scope of work, including identification of the controls evaluated; description of major risks and appropriateness of the controls; and identified deficiencies and management's response and proposed remediation.

Guidance for Regulators and Elected Officials

In representing that the financial statements are fairly presented in accordance with generally accepted accounting principles, management implicitly or explicitly makes assertions regarding the recognition, measurement, and disclosure of information in the financial statements and related disclosures. In order to consider management's performance in presenting reliable financial information, regulators and elected officials should consider the assertions made by management.

What Assertions Auditors Examine

Assertions by management used by the auditor fall into the following categories:

- Occurrence/Existence
  - —Transactions and events recorded have occurred and pertain to the utility.
  - —Assets and liabilities exist.
  - —Disclosed events and transactions have occurred.
- Rights and Obligations
  - —The utility holds or controls the rights to assets.
  - —Liabilities are the obligations of the utility.
  - —Disclosed transactions pertain to the utility.
- Completeness
  - —All transactions and events that should have been recorded have been recorded.
  - —All assets and liabilities that should have been recorded have been recorded.
  - —All disclosures that should have been included in the financial statements have been included.
- Accuracy/Valuation and Allocation
  - —Amounts and other data relating to recorded transactions and events have been recorded appropriately.
  - —Assets and liabilities are included in the financial statement at appropriate amounts and any resulting valuation or allocation adjustments are recorded appropriately.
  - —Financial and other information is disclosed fairly and at appropriate amounts.
- Cut-Off
  - —Transactions and events have been recorded in the correct accounting period.
- Classification and Understandability
  - —Transactions and events have been recorded in the proper accounts.
  - —Financial information is appropriately presented and described, and information in disclosures is expressed clearly.

What Questions Should Regulators and Public Officials Ask?

The control environment is shaped by the expectations set by the regulators and the tone at the top established by the utility director and senior management. The utility should have a written code of business conduct and ethics and be responsible for monitoring and reporting compliance with this code. Regulators and elected officials can ask these types of questions of management to ensure that appropriate controls are in place:

- What accounting and financial reporting "surprises" occurred during the past year?
- What were the most significant financial reporting risks that were identified?
- How did you assess the effectiveness of the control environment?
- What process level controls were assessed?
- Were there any management overrides of significant controls?
- Do you believe that your understanding of the automated controls is sufficient?
- What are your conclusions about the internal control design effectiveness?
- How did you decide which issues to bring to the attention of the governing body?
- Have the financial statements been corrected or restated?
- What has been the involvement of the external auditor in the review of controls?

Board members have a fiduciary responsibility for internal control and for ensuring the integrity of senior management and the independence of the internal auditor. These are basic level questions to engage management and staff in introductory discussions on internal controls and can be supplemented with relevant follow-up questions.

The Prudent Official Test

When evaluating the significance of a deficiency, the final step in the evaluation is to conclude whether a prudent official (having knowledge of the same facts and circumstances, the likelihood and magnitude of the potential misstatement, and other controls that were tested) would agree with the classification of the deficiency.

Summary

Utilities continually change and evolve. The system of internal controls must change and evolve with the utility. The design of internal controls for one utility may not be effective for another. Understanding the financial reporting risks facing the utility will help management design appropriate controls. The internal control environment is shaped by the management and the governing board of the utility. A written code of business conduct and ethics is an important feature of the control environment. Weaknesses in the code or in monitoring compliance with the code would create the likelihood of a material weakness. The utility management must assess whether entity-wide controls are designed to adequately support the control objectives. Key entity-level controls that should be assessed are internal audit, management information systems and performance measures, human resource policies and practices, organization structure, and communication of material information.

Acknowledgments

Several organizations were authoritative sources of information on internal controls, and this chapter development relied upon materials especially from the following:

- American Institute of Certified Public Accountants
  —AICPA Audit and Accounting Guide—State and Local Governments
  —American Water Works Association
  —Policy on Finance, Accounting, and Rates
- The Committee of Sponsoring Organizations of the Treadway Commission (COSO)
  —Internal Control—Integrated Framework
  —Enterprise Risk Management—Integrated Framework
  —Internal Control Over Financial Reporting—Guidance for Smaller Public Companies
  —Guidance on Monitoring Internal Control Systems
- The Canadian Institute of Chartered Accountants
  —Understanding Disclosure Controls and Procedures: Helping CEOs and CFOs Respond to the Need for Better Disclosure
  —Internal Control 2006: The Next Wave of Certification Guidance for Management
- The IT Governance Institute
  —COBIT: Control Objectives, Management Guidelines, and Maturity Models
  —COBIT Mapping: Overview of International IT Guidance
  —IT Control Objectives for Sarbanes Oxley
  —The Importance of IT in the Design, Implementation, and Sustainability of Internal Control over Disclosure and Financial Reporting
- The Institute of Internal Auditors
  —Sarbanes-Oxley Section 404: A Guide for Management by Internal Controls Practitioners
  —Tone at the Top: Paying Attention
  —Tone at the Top: Controls Are Everybody's Business
- International Federation of Accountants
  —Internal Controls—A Review of Current Developments
- Public Company Accounting Oversight Board
  —Auditing Standard No. 5—An Audit of Internal Control Over Financial Reporting That Is Integrated With an Audit of Financial Statements

These materials are recommended for further research when developing a program of internal controls for utilities.

This page intentionally blank.

References

American Institute of Certified Public Accountants (AICPA). 2009. *Understanding Internal Control and Internal Control Services.* New York: AICPA, Committee on Auditing Procedure.

American Water Works Association (AWWA). 2012. AWWA Manual M1, *Principles of Water Rates, Fees, and Charges.* Denver, Colo.: AWWA.

———. 1992. *Organization and Management of Publicly Owned Water Utilities.* Statements of Policy on Public Water Supply Matters. Denver, Colo.: AWWA.

———. 19XX. AWWA Manual M29, *Fundamentals of Water Utility Capital Financing.* 3rd ed. Denver, Colo.: AWWA.

National Association of Regulatory Utility Commissioners, Committee on Accounts and Statistics. 1962. *List of Retirement Units for Property for Water Utilities 1962.* Washington, D.C.: National Association of Regulatory Utility Commissioners.

National Association of Regulatory Utility Commissioners, Subcommittee on Valuation and Plant Costs of the Committee on Engineering. 1975. *Model Valuation. Plant Costs and Continuing Property Records Manual.* Washington, D.C.: National Association of Regulatory Utility Commissioners.

National Association of Regulatory Utility Commissioners (NARUC). 1996. *Uniform System of Accounts for Class A Water Utilities 1996.* Washington, D.C.: National Association of Regulatory Utility Commissioners.

National Association of Regulatory Utility Commissioners, Committee on Accounts. 1988. *Interpretations of Uniform System of Accounts for Electric, Gas and Water Utilities, January 1988.* Washington, D.C.: National Association of Regulatory Utility Commissioners.

National Committee on Government Accounting (NCGA). 2005. *Governmental Accounting, Auditing, and Financial Reporting.* Chicago, Ill: Government Finance Officers Association.

This page intentionally blank.

Index

Note: *f.* indicates figure; *t.* indicates table; *n.* indicates (foot)note.

www.ingramcontent.com/pod-product-compliance
Lightning Source LLC
LaVergne TN
LVHW080026210926
848481LV00011B/3116